AF364605

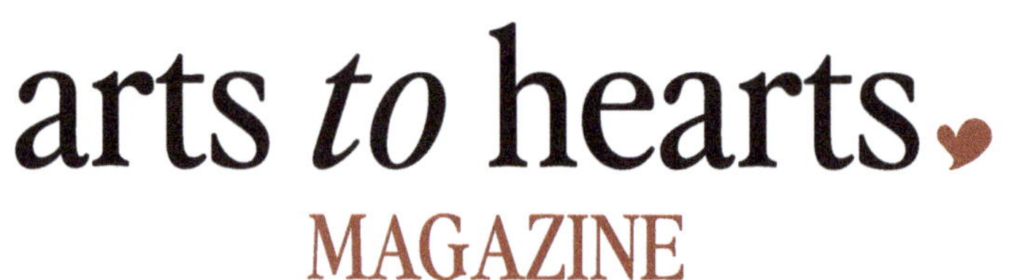

Arts to Hearts Magazine is a contemporary art publication with a mission to discover, connect, and engage with contemporary & emerging women artists from around the world.

A Product of

ARTS TO HEARTS PROJECT

We are a global creative community uniting contemporary & emerging women Artists to build successful, fulfilling, and money-making careers via collaboration, learning, community, networking, and peer-to-peer learning.

SUBMIT YOUR WORK

We have several opportunities throughout the year for people interested in the global arts. From open calls to grants to exhibits, you can stay on top of all our upcoming and ongoing opportunities by subscribing to our newsletter on our website.

COVER ART

Rebecca Brodskis | Si seulement, 2020
24 × 21 3/10 in | 61 × 54 cm
Oil on linen

JOIN ARTS TO HEARTS CLUB

http://www.artstoheartsproject.com/athclub/

VISIT OUR WEBSITE

www.artstoheartsproject.com

FOLLOW US ON INSTAGRAM

@artstoheartsproject

EMAIL

info@artstoheartsproject.com

"Artists have the superpower to turn terrible things into something beautiful"

and that is what I am going to do.
I will use my artist's superpower
to express my feelings.

ARTS TO HEARTS PODCAST

Season 3 Episode 2

Overcoming moments of self-doubt
w/ Danielle Krysa aka The Jealous Curator

Scan to listen

Available on spotify,
apple podcasts or
anywhere you listen
to your podcasts.

E D I T O R:
Charuka Arora

C O N T R I B U T O R S   W R I T E R S:
Charuka Arora
Sonam Bindra
Rabia Khan

L E A D   D E S I G N E R:
Neha Garg Dwivedi

F I N D   U S   O N:
www.artstoheartsproject.com
https://www.facebook.com/groups/womenartistsworldwideath/
instagram.com/artstoheartsproject

G E N E R A L   E N Q U I R I E S:
info@artstoheartsproject.com

**R E A D   O U R   D I G I T A L
E D I T O R I A L S   A N D
R E S O U R C E S   O N:**
www.artstoheartsproject.com

J O I N   A R T S   T O   H E A R T S   C L U B
http://www.artstoheartsproject.com/athclub/

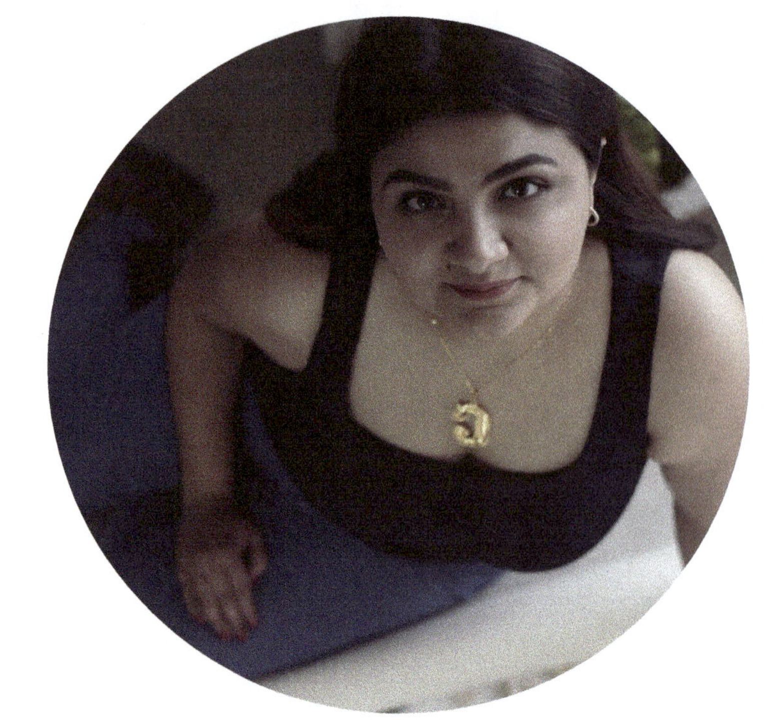

Editor's Note

Dear Reader,

It's time to raise the roof and celebrate! Women boldly claim their rightful place in the art world, creating a vibrant collective voice of strength and power. Here at ATH Magazine, we are proud to present our second issue, which dives deep into everything about how to be a successful artist.

From Rebecca Brodskis's breathtaking cover art to a candid conversation with Sarah and Jason from Paradigm Gallery about their vision and work in art, this issue is packed with stories of success and motivation. Our writers discuss how to make your artist portfolio, How to believe in your creative powers, strategies for thriving in the art world, and interviews with artists worldwide.

We invite you to join us as we explore the world of women artists and their unique perspectives. Get ready to be moved as they share their deepest fears, their zones of genius, and their creative masterpieces. We are so grateful to our team of writers, designers, and artists for making this issue possible and paving the way for a brighter future.

So here's to our *INCREDIBLE WOMEN ARTISTS!* We are here, and we are here to stay.

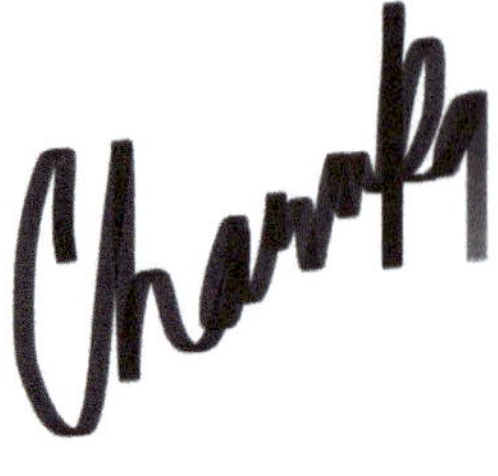

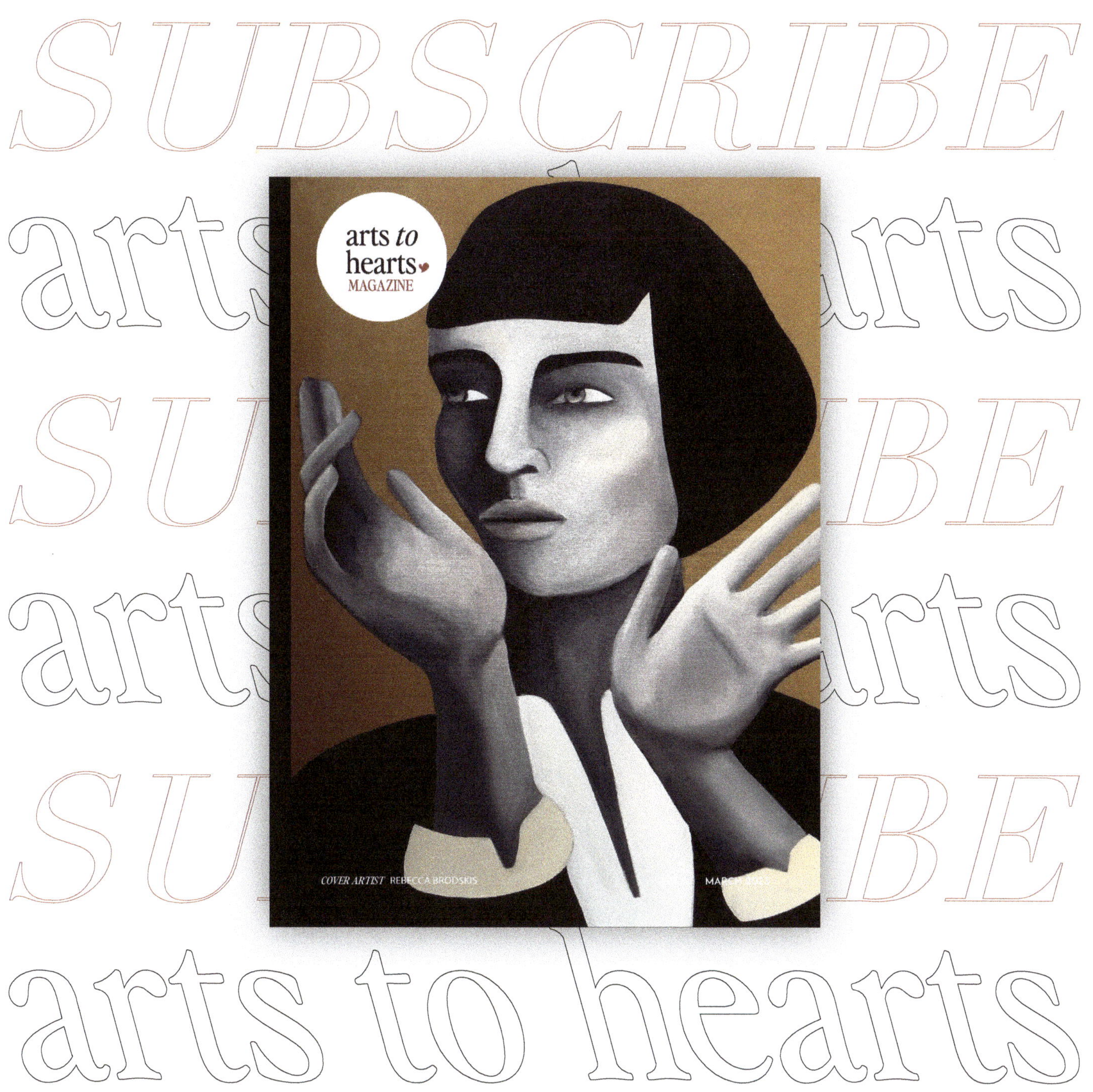

arts *to* hearts♥

MAGAZINE

Subscribe to our Digital and Print Issue from our website

WWW.ARTSTOHEARTSPROJECT.COM

WWW.ARTSTOHEARTSMAGAZINE.COM

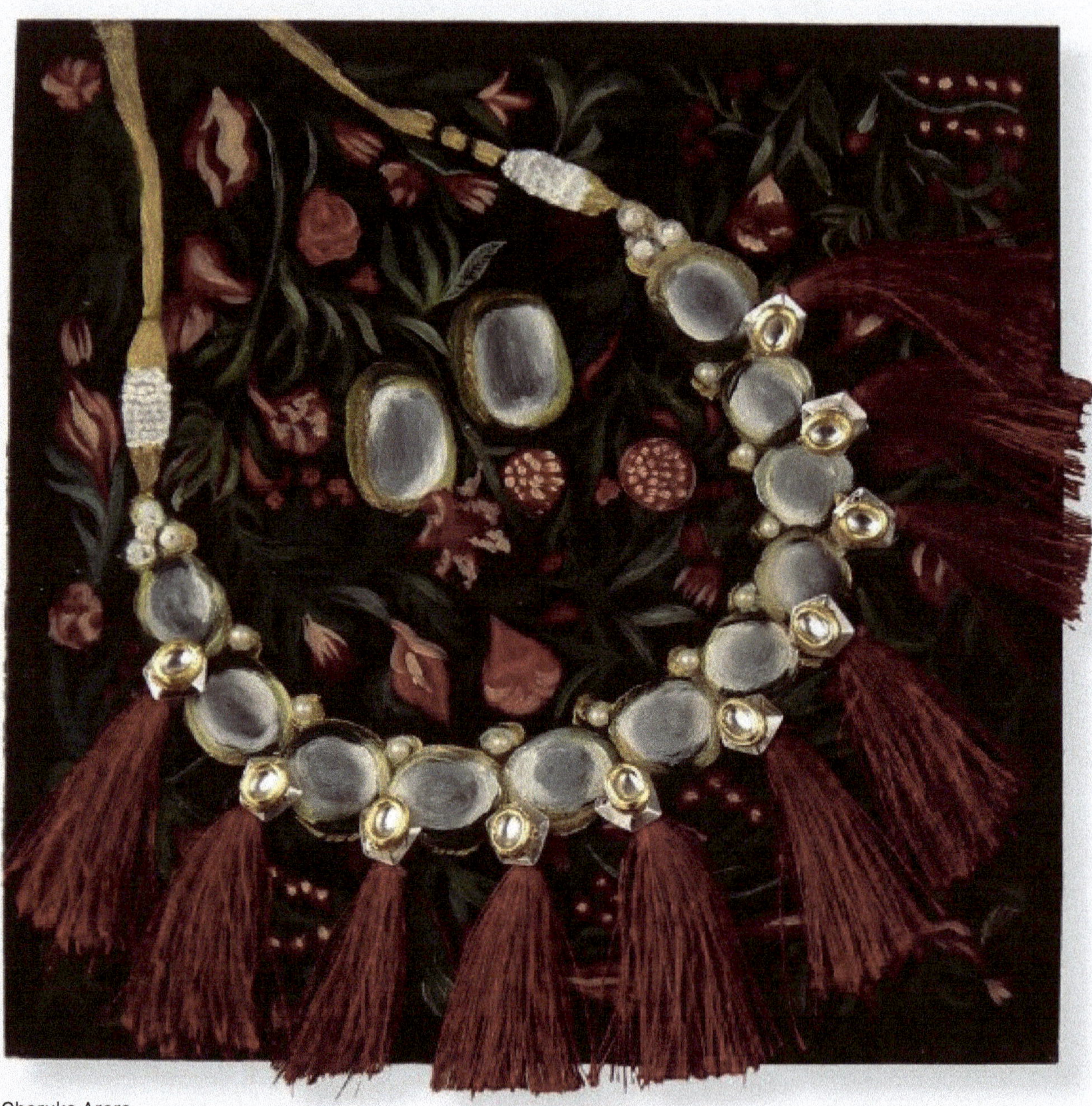

Charuka Arora
RANI
2022
8 x8x 0.8 inches
Oil painting,embroideries on cradled panel.
Sealed with Archival varnish.

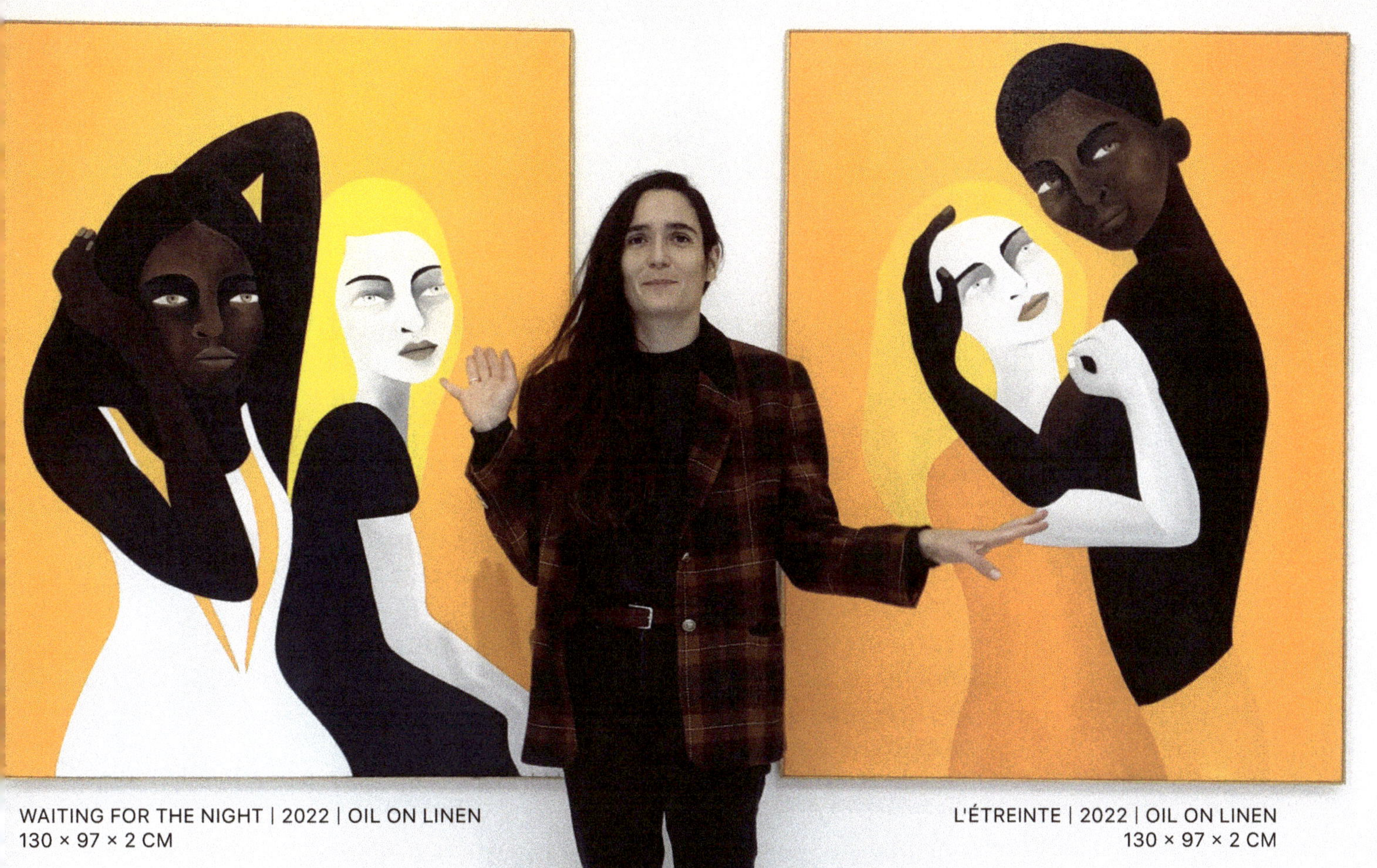

WAITING FOR THE NIGHT | 2022 | OIL ON LINEN
130 × 97 × 2 CM

L'ÉTREINTE | 2022 | OIL ON LINEN
130 × 97 × 2 CM

Meet
Rebecca Brodskis

Our Cover Artist

Interview by *Charuka Arora*

Rebecca Brodskis (b. 1988 in France) lives and works in Paris. She spent most of her childhood travelling and living between France and Morocco. Brodskis studied painting at the Ateliers des Beaux-Arts de la Ville de Paris and Central St. Martins in London, graduating in 2010. In 2015, she also completed a Master's degree in Sociology, focusing her research on vulnerabilities and social crisis themes. Exploring the borders of the sensible world, Brodskis' work evolves between conscious and unconscious spaces, leading to a reflection on existence, the self and the otherness. A central idea throughout Brodski's work is that of being in-between: intermediate space at the crossroads of empirical reality and imagination, order and disorder, materialism and spirituality, determinism and freedom.

Rebecca Brodskis has been widely acclaimed for her work in the art industry, with multiple solo and group exhibitions featured in well-known galleries around the world, including Kristin Hjellegjerde Gallery in London, Cuturi Gallery in Singapore, Fabienne Levy Gallery in Lausanne, Septieme Gallery in Paris, Koenig zwei gallery in Vienna and Galeria Anna Marra in Rome. Her work has been featured in prominent private and public collections such as the Huma Kabaki collection, Alan Lo Collection (Hong Kong), Museum Azman Collection (Malaysia), Pamela and David Hornik Collection (USA), Selebe Yoon Collection (Senegal), The Bunker Artspace Museum (USA), Tiroche DeLeon Collection (Israel), Zeifang Collection (Germany), Xiao Hui Wang Art Museum, Suzhou (China), W Art Foundation (China), SUSU Collection (China), Arndt Collection (Germany/Australia) and AMMA Collection (Mexico). Upcoming exhibitions include Kristin Hjellegjerde Gallery, Palm Beach (2023) and Cuturi Gallery, Singapore (2022).

> 66
>
> *The only advice I can give is to work and work and work. Creativity is a matter of discipline. People often think that artists are barely working, but it's the opposite!*
>
> 99

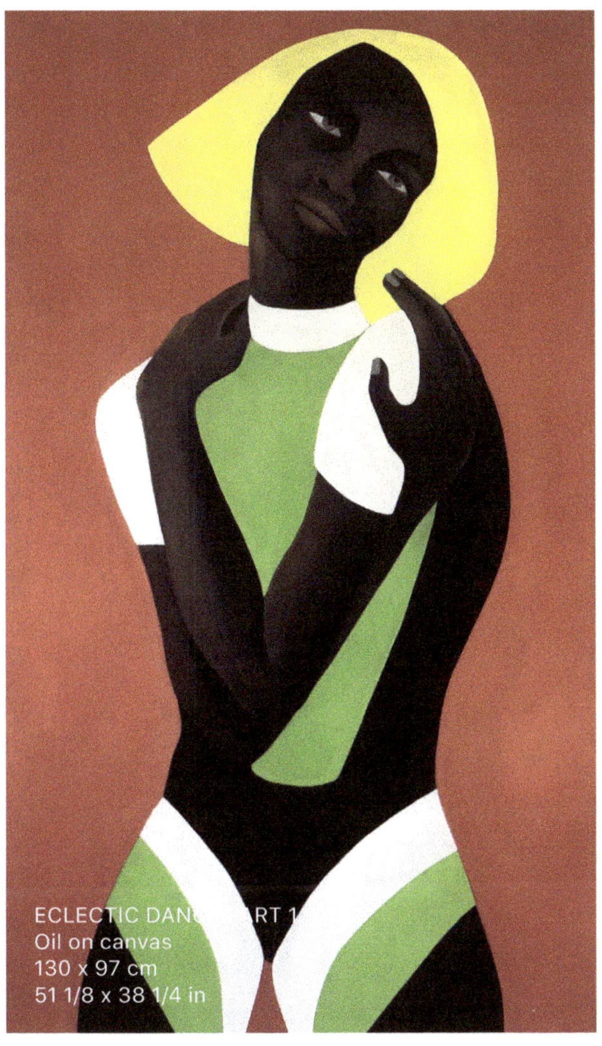

ECLECTIC DAN... ART 1
Oil on canvas
130 x 97 cm
51 1/8 x 38 1/4 in

Rebecca, Let's start with understanding your creative affair with painting? How did it start?
As a kid I was not allowed to watch television, only films from time to time, which would be a Chaplain, a Ketone, or even some Cocteau at age five. So in my free time, I would be very creative. I was always drawing a lot, painting and reading. We would spend most winters in the house of my grandmother in Morocco. She was a painter, and there was a place in her home that turned into an atelier.I would spend a lot of time there painting. Art has always been a form of expression in my life. I was always drawn towards creativity. I also love to write. I have kept a diary every day since I was eight years old! Painting for me is like meditation, a time of self-introspection that allows me to function. Basically, art allows me to digest life. And, that's how this has always been for me.

How does travel influence your creative process - what aspects do you draw from different cultures when creating new pieces?
To be confronted with different cultures as a Kid is something that shapes your existence and brings you to an understanding at an early age that there are many ways of existing. It did have a significant impact on my creative journey since I traveled often between Morocco and France . The diversity of humankind is something very present in my paintings. We only know the world we live in. It's a fact. When we travel, however, we can connect, empathize and then live cultures, thoughts and habits different from ours. I don't think about the aspects I want to draw the people I paint. My work is very spontaneous. Things just appear very naturally, I guess, mainly guided by emotions.

Could you tell us a bit more about your personal journey to becoming an artist, from studying painting at Ateliers des Beaux-Arts de la Ville de Paris and Central St.Martins in London?
Honestly, art schools have never been a place of accomplishment for me. I quit painting almost two years after art school. I started painting again after being attacked in Paris. I got my feet broken and couldn't move for a while. A friend of mine went to get me oil paints and canvases and that's how the obsession started again.

What advice would you give to those just starting on their creative journey?
The only advice I can give is to work and work and work. Creativity is a matter of discipline. People often think that artists are barely working, but it's the opposite!
We work all the time.

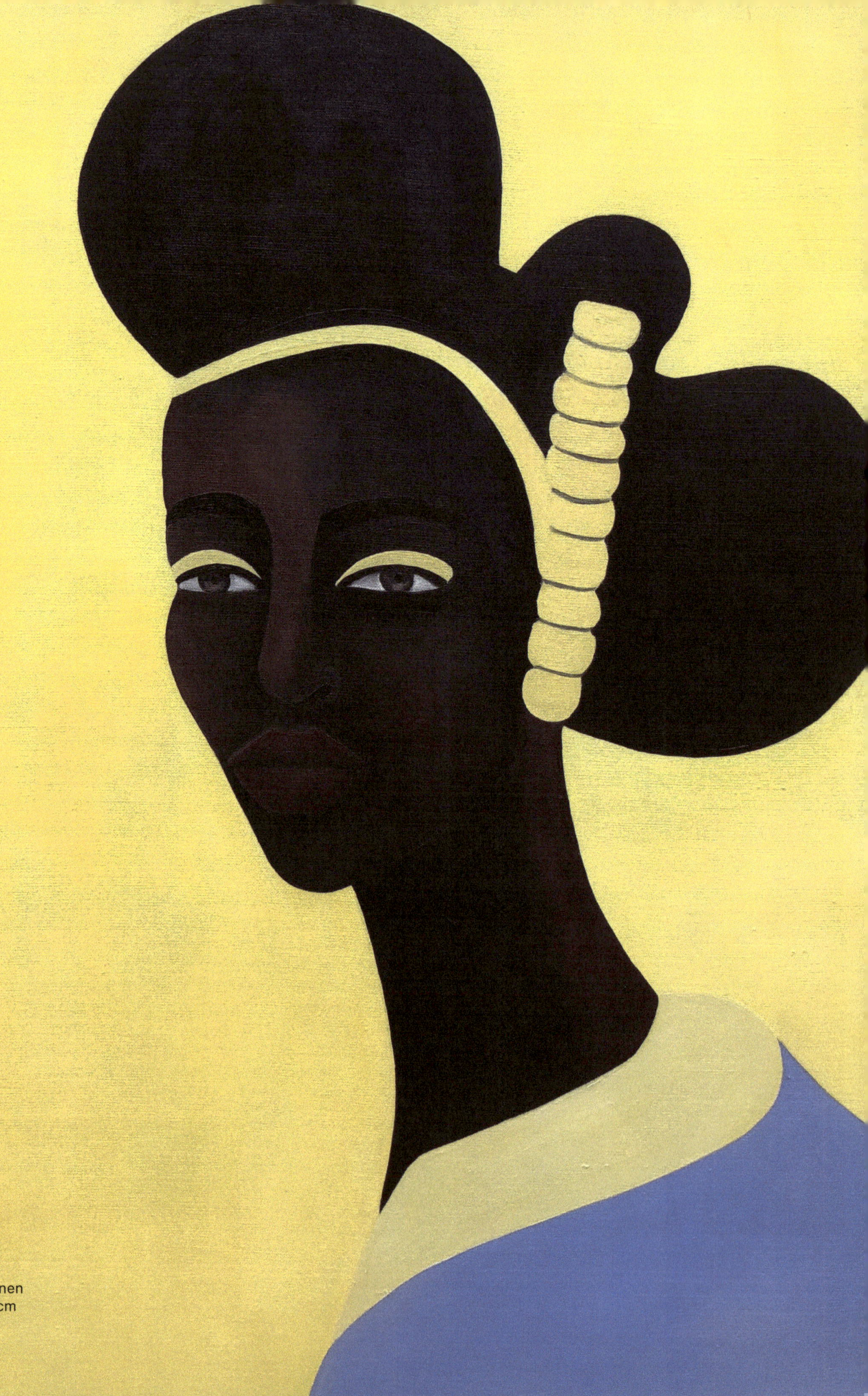

ASSIA
2021
Oil on linen
100x81cm

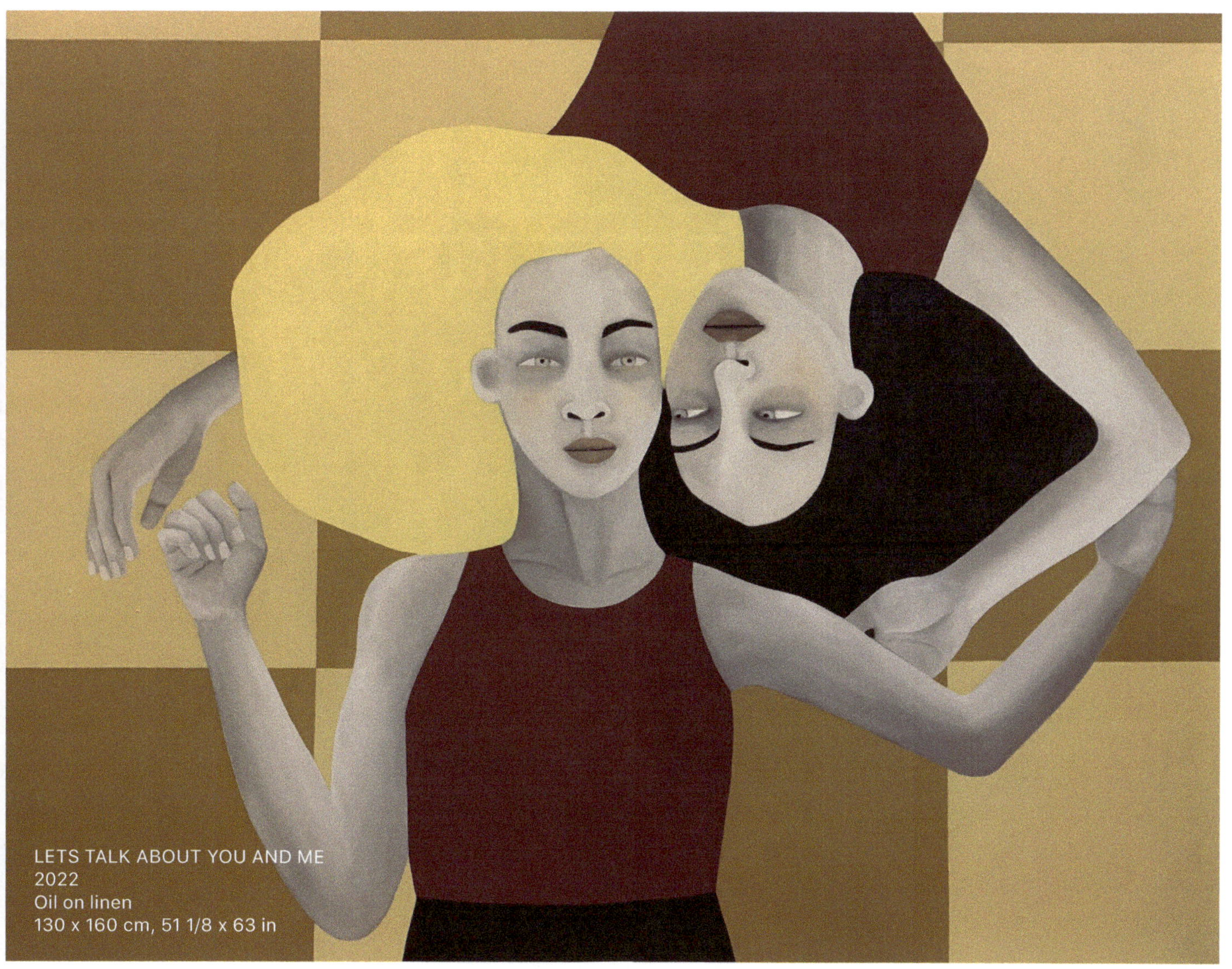

I also noticed that your artwork often explores the idea of being in between - could you tell us more about this concept and how it is reflected in your work?

My work is a form of exploration through the painting of the relationship between the being and matter and the impact of the social on the individual. Captivated by moments of life that surround me, by discussions, images or characters, I question those fleeting moments of everyday life that we do not remember, but that shape existence. Analyzing the foundation of human relationships while questioning the social context in which we live, a world in perpetual change, interwoven with ties that we do not understand. I use this complex richness, the social diversity surrounding me, and the confrontation of cultures and individuals. In between is, for me, this unknown space where everything is happening.

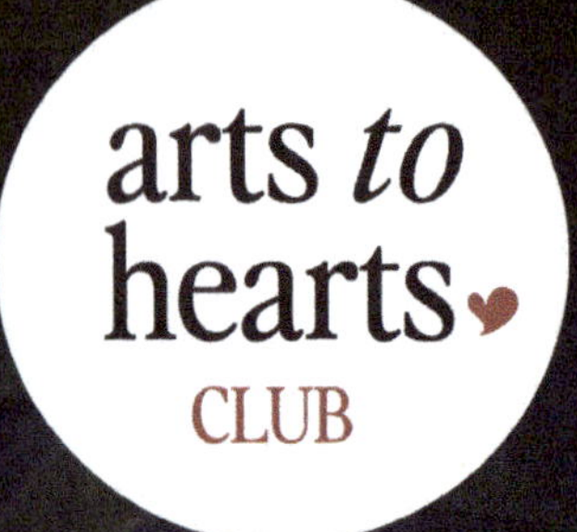

arts to hearts
CLUB

Unlock the magic of
Your creative soul

WITH A GLOBAL COMMUNITY OF
WOMEN ARTISTS.

Join now only for 6$ for each session

WWW.ARTSTOHEARTSPROJECT.COM/ATHCLUB

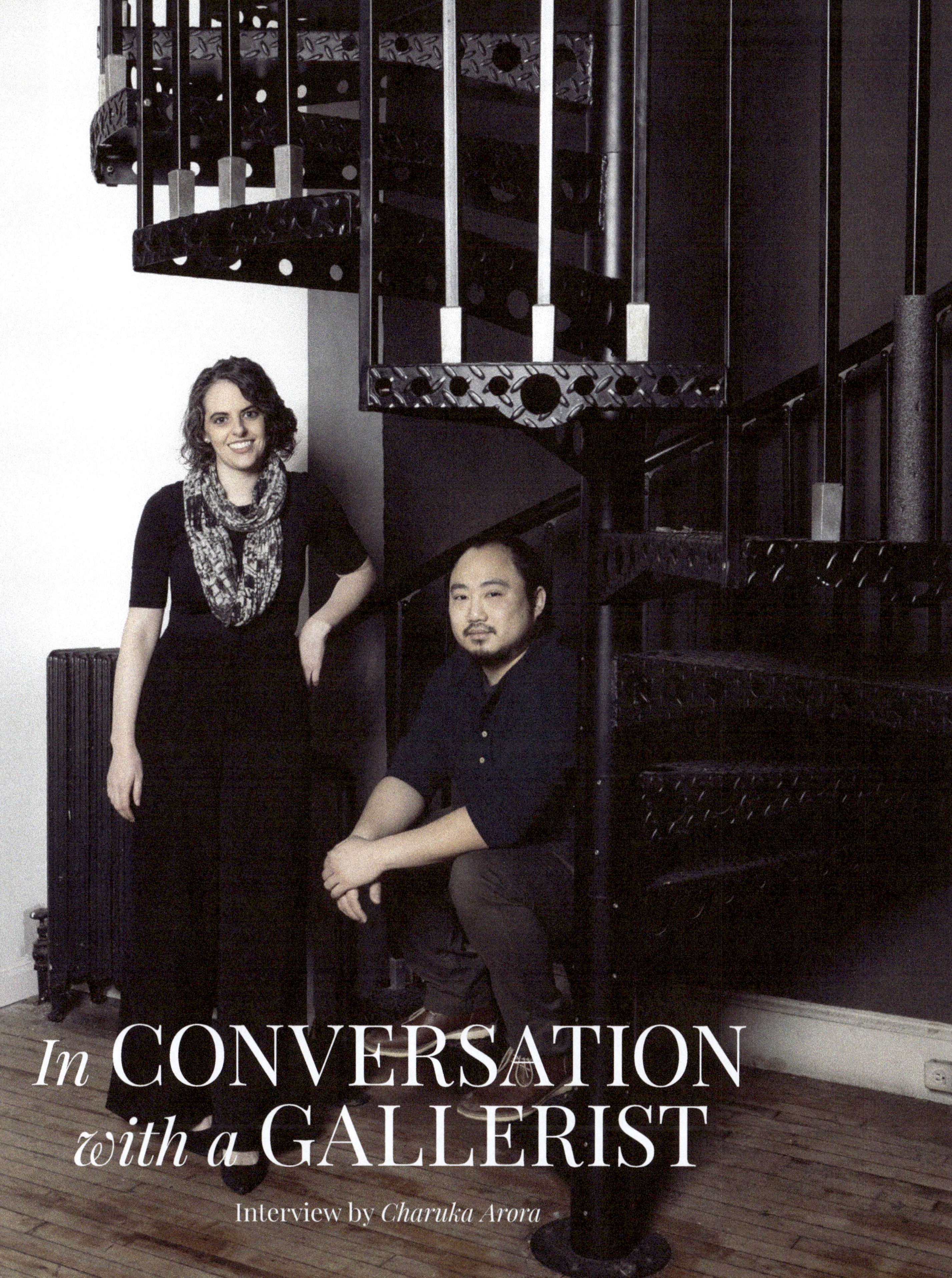

In CONVERSATION with a GALLERIST

Interview by *Charuka Arora*

Sara & Jason

Paradigm Gallery + Studio® was established in 2010 by co-founders and curators Jason Chen and Sara McCorriston. The gallery exhibits meaningful, process-intense contemporary artwork from around the world. Now open for 13 years, Paradigm Gallery is globally recognized and known as a tastemaker within the greater Philadelphia arts community. As the gallery grows, it maintains its original mission to keep art accessible. Through monthly donations, free public art installations, and initiatives like Insider Picks, Paradigm Gallery, continues to be a champion of small businesses and emerging and mid-career artists.

What prompted you (Jason and Sara) to establish Paradigm Gallery?

We had known each other since college when we started collaborating artistically! We started to look for a space to continue making art together and happened upon a tiny storefront that we could fix up for very cheap. Jason suggested that we show some work by our friends in the space, and before we knew it, we had the beginnings of a business. While our path to being business owners and running a gallery came about organically, our growth has been much more intentional since those early days. The constant driving force along the way has been our enthusiasm for the remarkable talent and passion of the artists with whom we work.

And, as we all know, you are relocating Paradigm to a new home. Can you tell me about your latest crowdfunding campaign and what prompted you to make this decision?
This exciting new chapter for Paradigm has unfolded, in part, due to a significant setback; when we tried to purchase our current building and sadly lost the bid, the outpouring of support and encouragement we received gave us the courage to hold onto our dream of property ownership. The experience reminded us that it is not a physical location that determines our success or failure but rather the strength of the community we have built over the years. With our community rallied behind us, we could take a leap of faith and embark upon this bold, new journey.

Can you describe how you've felt since initiating the campaign? Are there any success stories or significant achievements that have made it particularly important for you and the Paradigm team?
Beyond the immense gratitude we have felt towards everyone who has contributed, the concrete commitment we have made to our supporters to actualise our long-held dreams for Paradigm has been one of the campaign's greatest gifts. Outlining our plan for Paradigm's relocation and expansion has helped us to solidify our vision for the future and challenged us to make our most ambitious goals a reality. The accountability we now have to our crowd funders to ensure that we follow through on our plans has been just as rewarding as their generous support.

Could you offer any unique ideas or approaches that have helped you to make this goal a financial and logistical reality?
Being successful as a small business, and especially as a gallery, is a combination of tough work and, sometimes, pure luck. It is not easy, and neither one of us could honestly recommend this life to anyone who wants to feel comfortable – but for us, we thrive on the challenge of owning a business, constantly learning, figuring out the math, and somehow making it all work. Our community keeps us going, as does our shared mission of making art accessible to everyone.
The trials and tribulations we have faced over the years have laid bare the fault lines in the system that prevent so many successful businesses from having a stable and secure future. Seeing and personally experiencing these barriers has been eye-opening and puts a fire under us to be involved in making the change we wish to see. Through hardship, we have been buoyed by the camaraderie of the greater Philadelphia community of business owners, who have so freely shared advice, resources, and a wealth of knowledge gleaned from their collective failures and hard-won successes. We would not be in the position we are today without their guidance in navigating this confusing and exclusionary system and their validation of the pain and sacrifice required to persevere.

Aside from this adjustment, you completely rebranded Paradigm; can you tell us a little about that?
When we started in our early 20s, we didn't know who we were or where we were going. As we find ourselves at a significant turning point in our business, preparing for a big move and even more significant changes, it seemed like the perfect moment to refresh our brand to reflect what Paradigm is becoming. Twelve years into the business, which has become so much more than we could have ever imagined, it was the ideal time to work with Smith & Diction – a team we have known and admired for years – to visually define our brand with a bolder aesthetic and greater adaptability. Smith & Diction nailed it, and we are proud to unveil a new brand identity that conveys who we are at this pivotal stage, with plenty of room to grow.

> **"**
> *Being successful as a small business, and especially as a gallery, is a combination of tough work and, sometimes, pure luck.*
> **"**

How has the community reacted to the news that Paradigm is relocating to a new, permanent location?

———— 💔 ————

Our community has reacted much the same as we have ourselves – bittersweet about leaving our beloved South Philly neighborhood but thrilled for what's ahead in Old City. We feel lucky to have found a new home for Paradigm within walking distance of our current location so our local community can grow alongside us. It's always hard to see our streetscapes amid change and the fabric of small businesses in flux. Still, the opportunity to revive the storied legacy of art and design in Old City is a privilege we are fortunate to have as property owners and stakeholders in the district.

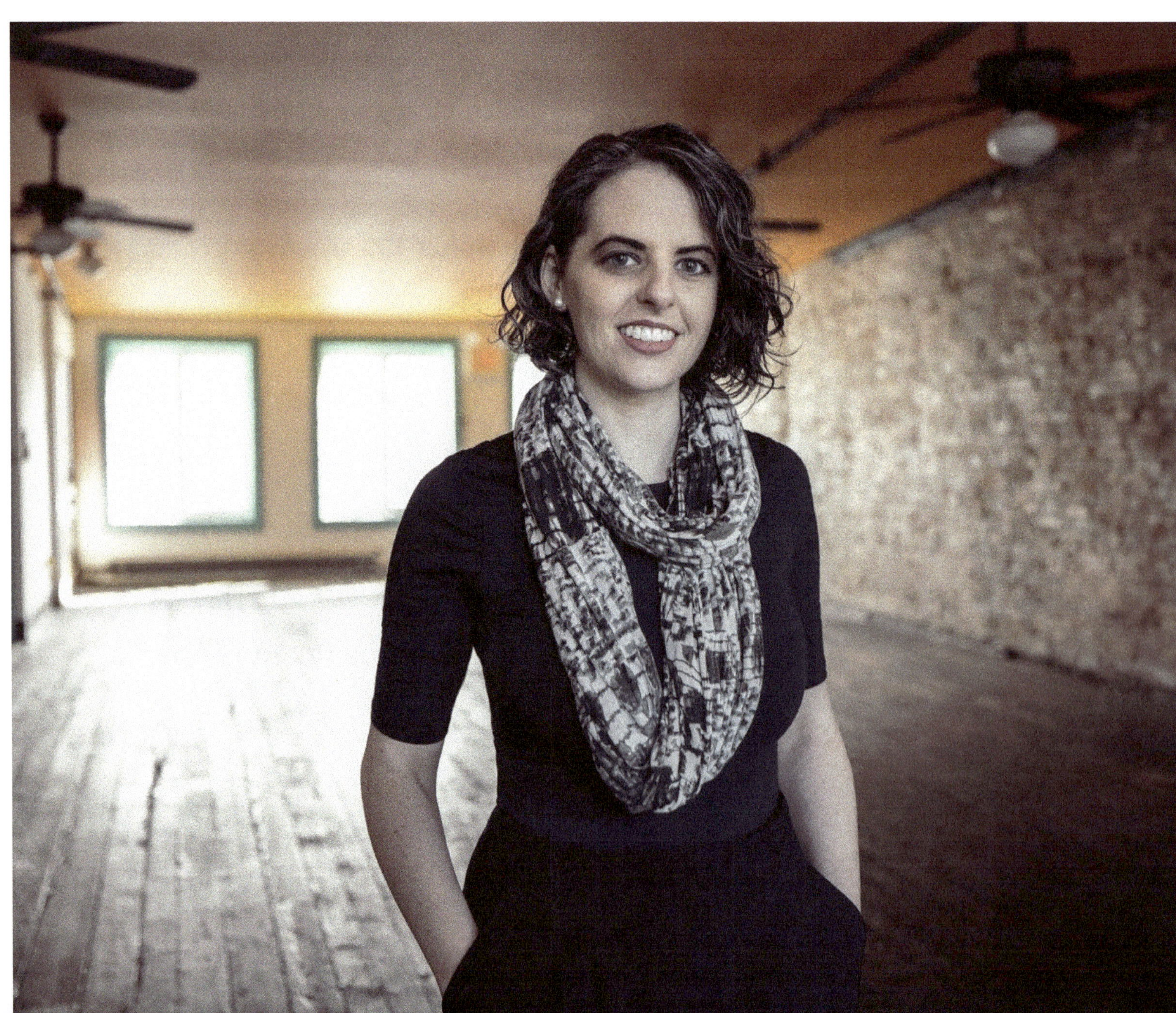

The gallery has been here for nearly 13 years, and you have directly worked with and built an uplifting arts community in Philadelphia. How would you sum up your overall experience?
Being an inviting, welcoming gateway to the art world is not always financially rewarded. Nevertheless, this approach has brought together an incredible community of people who believe in what we're doing and the sustainable future we are building for artists; this community is worth its weight in gold and is what makes Paradigm so much greater than just the two of us. Since we quit our backup jobs and transitioned to focusing full-time on Paradigm, we are just as dependent on our artists as they are on us. This shared hunger has made us better art dealers and strengthened our relationships with artists because they know we are committed to their success. As we have advanced the careers of our artists – developing their markets, cultivating amazing collectors, presenting their work to new audiences, and connecting with prominent cultural institutions and the public art sector – we have managed to feed ourselves, too. We've never taken the safe route, nor have we adopted any exploitative yet lucrative practices of our industry, but we have the buy-in of our artists every step of the way.

What changes will occur once you relocate to the new building this spring?

For years we have been doing 3+ floors worth of programming in a one-floor gallery, constantly shifting and pushing the limits of our physical space. Not only will our new building afford us enough space to handle everything we do and plan to accomplish comfortably, but also the chance to invest in its maintenance and renovation as owners rather than tenants. The security of having a permanent location has allowed us to dive into all sorts of projects and plans that we had always dreamed of but never were able to realize in our current location. In addition, having two floors of gallery space with different programming will allow us to curatorially engage with everything from art to design to the crossover. We will also have dedicated space for classes and in-house printmaking, which has been our longtime dream. The vertical structure of the building has helped us envision a new model for Paradigm as a place where the whole creative process can take place and be nurtured under one roof – learning, making, collaboration, display, and dialogue.

Could you kindly tell us how Paradigm Gallery collaborates with small enterprises and emerging/mid-career artists?

Our new space will allow us to take our collaborations with other small businesses to the next level – literally! We're so excited to welcome BYO Print to our 5th floor and Butterfield Editions to our 4th floor. We love working alongside our fellow small businesses and believe in growing together.
The opportunities for our artists will also increase tenfold in the new building. Aside from the space's creative potential, enabling larger-scale exhibitions and more daring installations, the expansion of Paradigm's offerings beyond the gallery will provide additional income streams for our artists and introduce new audiences to their diverse practices. For example, artists can teach classes and workshops in our 3rd-floor studio spaces or sell reproducible items in our gift shop for collectors with smaller budgets.

In the end, we would like to ask if you have any recommendations for emerging artists looking for gallery representation.

Don't overlook potential opportunities to show your work outside a gallery setting. An exhibition space can be anything you decide, and many public spaces, coffee shops, and other small businesses are eager to open up their walls to artists. Invest in relationships with fellow artists, and develop your network by consistently putting yourself out there. Membership programs and artist collectives can be excellent resources. Submitting your work to juried shows and open calls gets your work in front of curators and other art professionals, even if you're not selected. While it's great to shoot for the moon and never lose sight of your loftier career goals, it's critical to demonstrate an exhibition history and a fully-developed portfolio when presenting your work to galleries.

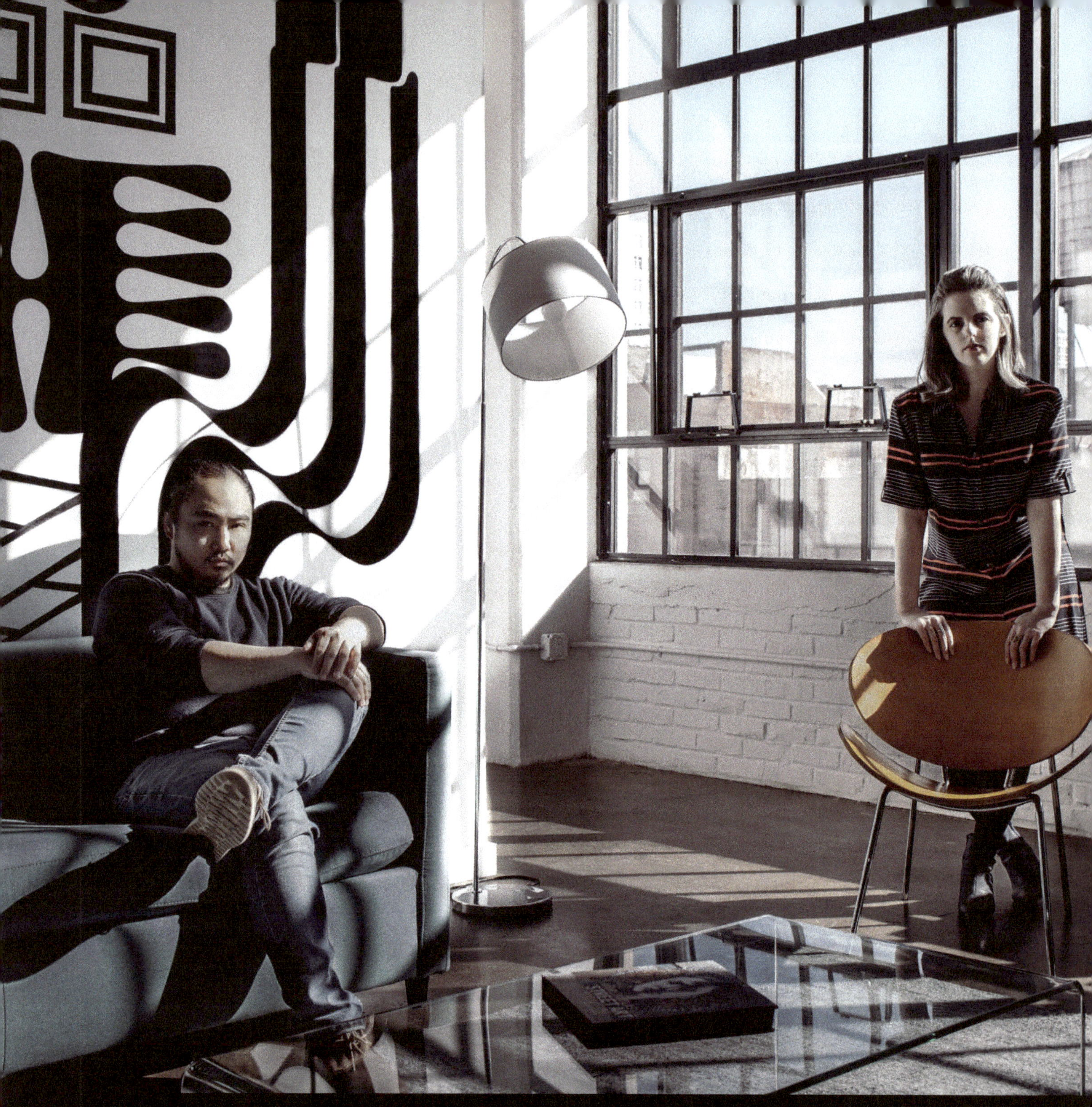

> 66
>
> *While it's great to shoot for the moon and never lose sight of your loftier career goals, it's critical to demonstrate an exhibition history and a fully-developed portfolio when presenting your work to galleries.*
>
> 99

Winning a
Creative War

Article by *Charuka Arora*

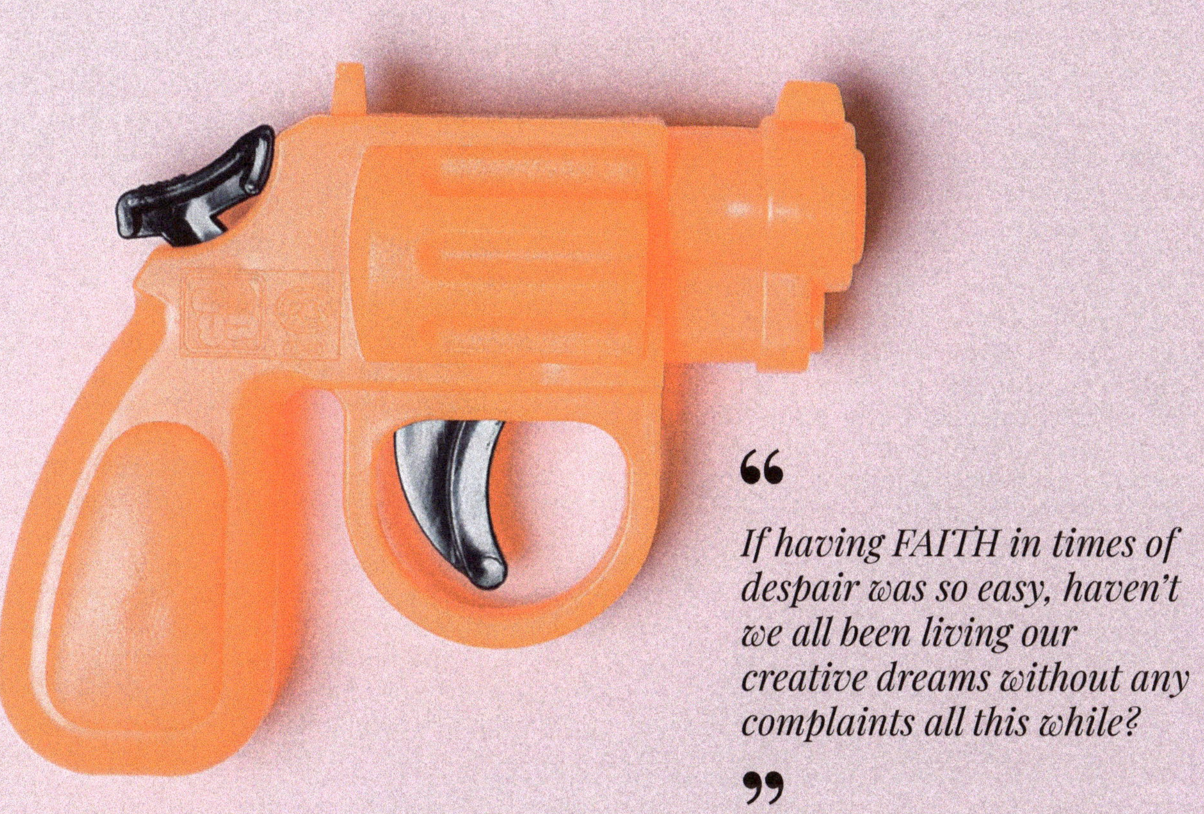

At the beginning of my career, I spent hours on YouTube, Instagram, Facebook, books, and podcasts anywhere. Looking for answers on, 'How can I find creative success?' Of Course I found tons of resources that have tremendously helped me learn new skills, fine-tune my perspective, and help me navigate this whole structure of how to become an artist. But, I knew I was missing something, Something I then couldn't put my finger to. Just like when we are in the midst of war, we always look for the next step in trying to survive.
I didn't know then, but I know now.

Now you would say building a creative career isn't like a war, but isn't it?
When you step into a career as an artist, you are a dedicated soldier, focused on winning this war with so much passion and love for something you worship, aka your creativity. You don't know the path it would take for you to survive, but you know you will have to figure it out; you have to fight it out. That you know that the stakes are high. And that the probability of winning isn't very clear. Where the world and your peers are walking on chalked-out paths and safer bets. And, you are here walking on an uncharted path.

Worshiping your creative thoughts. So knee-deep in this commitment, you have to go down this road no matter how bizarre the outcome. All set to fight this war. As you pack your bags and go down this road.

In this creative war, you find collaborators, mentors, and guides to help you win. Like any soldier, we creative soldiers get up every morning knowing we'll have to fight another day to find our unchartered paths. We, creative soldiers, know that we have something worth fighting for, so every day, we get up, pick up the tools, aka our intuition, thinking, imagination, and some sort of unwavering belief on what's possible, and dress for the day to go out in the field.

In this war, we have not one but many enemies, but the one we are running this war against is the INNER CRITIC! Ah! Haven't we all met this one? Often the one that tells you that you aren't enough. That how miserable you have made your life. Oh! How terrible this thing you have made. Yeah yeah, we all got this one. Your inner critic knows you, your weakness, and your thoughts, but most of all, it knows how to fight this war. The inner critic has been doing this for far too long to so many other creative soldiers who have succumbed to its tactics and its torture. The inner critic has a Set of its bagful of tricks. The same tricks that go on for years and years and bully us all. Now, do you want to hear the good news? There have been many, many successful wars led against the inner critic. A lot of creative soldiers have won. And what do they all have in common?

Their relentless FAITH. This unwavering FAITH in themselves is what weakens this inner critic to its bones. That none of its cheap tricks any longer work. So, if you are reading this and feel deep in this strife, not Knowing what your enemy is the most afraid of? Well, it's your FAITH. Know that it's your strongest weapon. And your guide to your destination. The inner critic will try all its tricks to make you believe otherwise. It will tell you things and show you ways that will make more sense.
After all, how can the answer be so plain and simple?
Well, you are right and not. But you know that already, don't you? If having FAITH in times of despair was so easy, haven't we all been living our creative dreams without any complaints all this while?
There wouldn't be any silently killed thoughts and heartbroken creatives now, never taking this path.

So, my dear creative soldier, no matter where you are in your journey. Know that the only way to keep moving forward AND WIN THIS war is by your unwavering faith in your craft and creativity. That things may not make sense just now, but if you keep fighting this for long enough and soon enough the noise of the inner critic will diminish. All of it is going to work out. And, by then, you may have already won this war and paved your path.

That's it, my Brave Army! You got this! We got this.

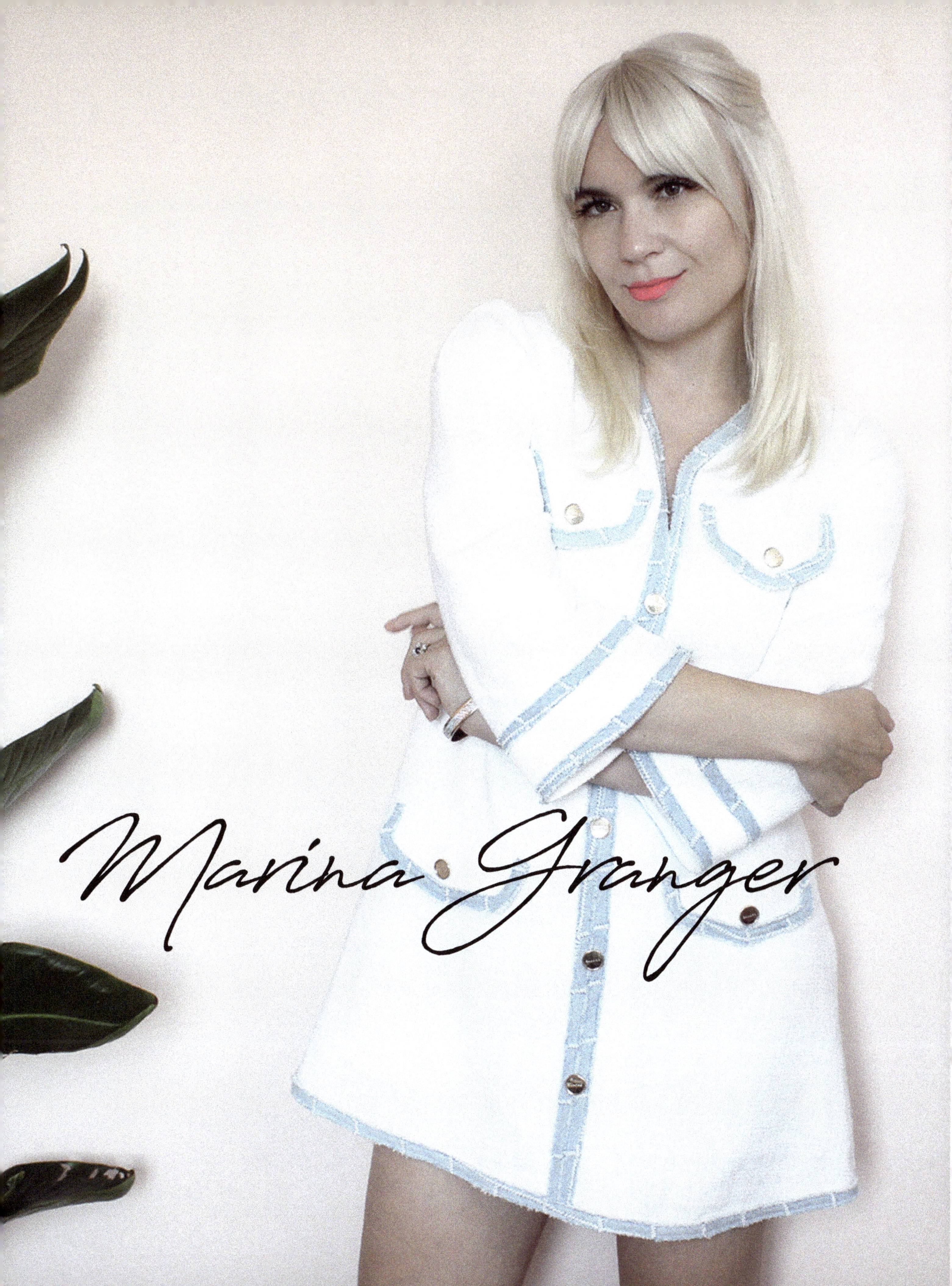
Marina Granger

How to craft a unique
ARTIST BRAND
for yourself

Interview by *Rabia Khan*

Marina Press Granger has nearly 15 years of experience working in the museums and galleries in New York City. She holds a master's degree in Art History and a special place in her heart for artists.

Her work has brought her in close contact with a plethora of players in the art world; artists, collectors, curators, dealers, and consultants. Granger has also curated independently and contributed to gallery exhibition catalogues. It is her advice and experience that she wishes to share with you.

Since starting The Artist Advisory in 2018, Granger earned a Certification in Classical Chinese San Yuan Feng Shui and Reiki. In addition to her practical experience and analytical skills, Granger has been using these spiritual tools to guide artists and businesses towards success.

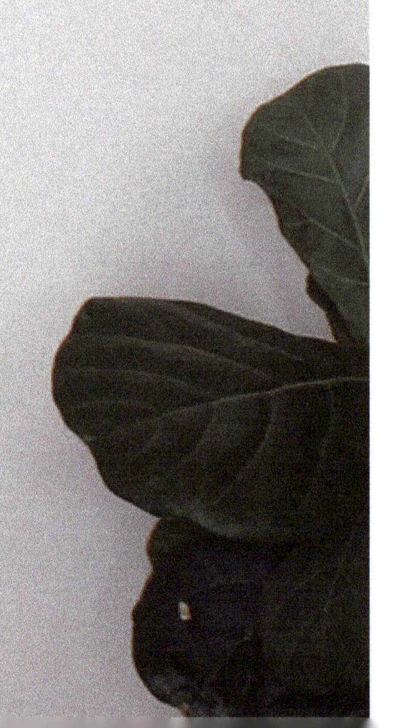

Marina, What kind of marketing strategies have you found to be most effective in helping artists reach their desired audiences?

First of all, the answer is really in the question. You have to identify your desired audience and then communicate your story to them, so they resonate with your work. This is a very organic marketing approach that will withstand the test of time as technology evolves. The key here is to find where your desired audience hangs out. Then, you want to find others with an authoritative voice in those communities to amplify your work to their audience.

Now, as of 2023, it's safe to say that many people are on social media platforms like Instagram and TikTok so those are great spaces to start to form connections. Within these massive networks, some audiences focus on the themes in your work.

For example, if you are a painter of puppies, you want to find a podcast or magazine that is devoted to dogs and share your work on those platforms. You can begin to connect by sharing screenshots of you listening to the podcast and tagging their account in your Instagram stories. Once they see your account, they should see a good overview of your portfolio and a clear idea of your work. Then, they'll see you're aligned and probably invite you onto their show. You can always ask how to apply to their podcast over social media if they do not. After that, many "puppy people" are going to know about you and your work and you'll get more opportunities.

How do you advise artists to balance showcasing their work with marketing it?

Well, in a way, it's the same. Whenever you increase your visibility by showing your work, you are marketing your work. Just be mindful of three things: A. Include your story every time you showcase your work. Either in the wall text in an exhibition, a printed card, your social media caption or description, or just verbally when you greet people in your studio.

> **"**
> *Always aim to get the attention of amplifiers – those with a voice of authority for your desired audience*
> **"**

I want to share with you a quick note on sharing your story. I have worked in the NYC Art World since 2004.... that's nearly 20 years now. The majority of that time I had spent working in galleries. This took me to art fairs where I truly learned the importance of the "story" in the marketing strategy. There were many times that I only had a few moments to capture a potential collector's attention and get them inspired to purchase the work. So, I developed what I call an "elevator pitch" which is a quick and easy way to communicate the story behind an artist's work. What sets you apart is your motivation and perspective. So, the formula for this pitch is "Why you do what you do + How Your Perspective Informs Your Work + What you do" Once you craft this in just a few quick sentences, you will win over your desired audience.

B. Display your work in a similar way that the galleries you want to be in eventually display the artwork they exhibit. You want to mimic the vibe - at an exhibition or in photos.

C. Always aim to get the attention of amplifiers - those with a voice of authority for your desired audience.

What is your opinion on the power of social media and other digital platforms in promoting an artist's work?

Before the internet, artists had to go through a lot of gatekeepers to get their work out there. They'd have to go to art school, get a gallery's attention, and hope that they could connect with the right people. But now, with the internet and social media, artists have a whole new set of tools at their disposal. They can reach people all over the world, without needing anyone's permission. That's why I started The Artist Advisory - to help artists take advantage of these new tools and make the most of their careers. My goal is to show them how to use the internet and social media to build an audience, connect with collectors and curators, and achieve their goals as artists. It's all about empowering them to take control of their own careers.

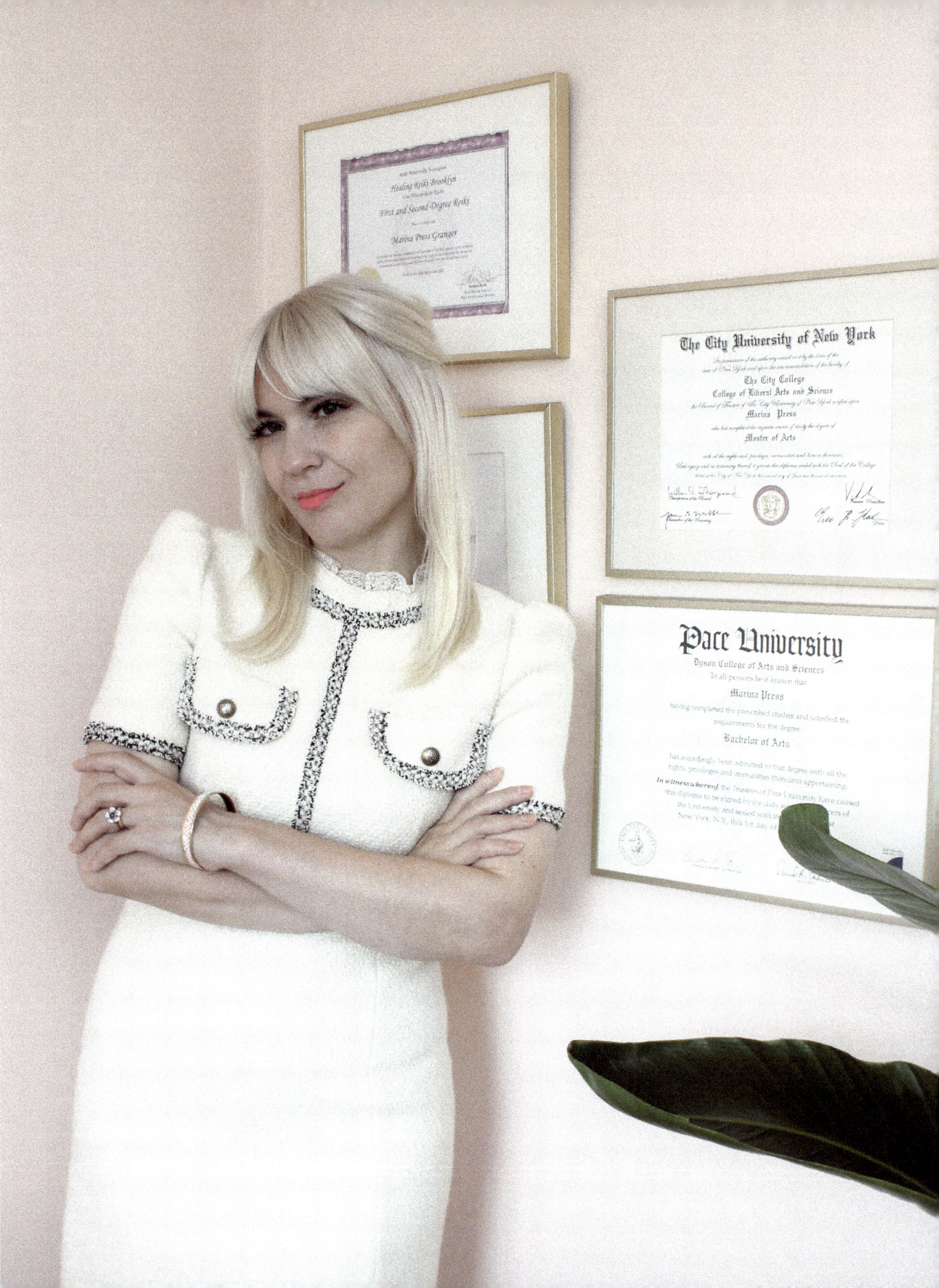

In your experience, what are some of the common mistakes that artists make when it comes to marketing themselves or their artworks?

There are four common mistakes that I tend to see when artists market themselves. When posting to social media as an artist, it's important to remember a few key things to make the most of the platform. Firstly, don't just post a single image of your work. Provide context by showing the wall it is hanging on, or the space it is in. This helps communicate the vibe of the piece and is crucial for building an audience. Additionally, don't just post one photo - keep your followers engaged by providing alternative views, and close-up details of your work.

On your website, which is an important platform for collectors, curators, and gallerists to visit, you need to have a clear and comprehensive view of your work. Make sure to have a grid view of your work where the thumbnails are uncropped and there's a full description underneath (Title, Date, Medium, and Size), and whether or not it's available. If it is sold, make sure to follow the description with the words "Private Collection," and if it is available, you can leave it off or follow the description with "Available."

When it comes to describing your work, be specific and clear. If you create sculptures, paintings, drawings, photographs, installations, performances, etc. don't just refer to them as "pieces." Being specific and clear about what you make helps people retain that information and elevates your work.

When you write anything about yourself, it's important to avoid using your first name in subsequent mentions of your name. Instead, use your last name when referring to yourself throughout the text. Using your first name can be diminutive, and it is important to be consistent with the way you refer to yourself. It's also worth noting that throughout history, historians have always referred to men by their last name only and women by their first name, so it is important to use your full name first and then your last name when you repeat your name throughout.

Are there any particular tools or services that you suggest for artists who want to maximize the impact of their marketing efforts?

Sure, I have an online group program that I am currently doing for the 11th time. It's called The Artist Academy and it teaches artists how to get in front of the right people by teaching them how to navigate the art world and use the internet and social media as a starting point. Some who have completed this program were recently on my podcast and shared what they have learned. So, similarly, I'd love to recommend my podcast The Artist Advisory Hotline as a resource for artists. On the podcast, I also interview art world experts to demystify the industry and provide a wide range of perspectives. In addition to the podcast, artists can also check out my YouTube channel where I post informative videos and upload all of my podcast episodes with closed captions, making them accessible to those who are hearing impaired.

It is crucial, regardless of the industry, to seek out a variety of guidance and perspectives, especially in the art world. As one of the artists I have worked with explained, even Beyonce has a coach! That's why I would also like to give a shoutout to some of the best guides and coaches for artists, such as Victoria Fry of Visionary Arts Collective, Dina Brodsky who teaches a workshop on Instagram for Artists, Ekaterina Popova who runs an amazing community called The Art Queens, and Paddy Johnson who started a community called Network. There are many more out there, so if you find someone who resonates with you, don't hesitate to work with them.

What advice would you give to aspiring artists who are just getting started with developing and executing a successful marketing plan?

Creating a successful marketing plan for your art is akin to constructing a towering skyscraper. It all starts with a solid foundation, upon which you can build and soar to new heights. Your foundation consists of your unique story, your compelling presentation, and a mindset that is unshakable. Don't let the stereotype of the "starving artist" discourage you. You don't have to be as famous as Jeff Koons to make a living as an artist. There are countless successful artists out there, but we often only hear about the ones who didn't achieve fame during their lifetime, like Van Gogh. It's no wonder that many of us were taught to pursue careers other than art, but as a former gallery director, I can assure you that I wrote some substantial checks to artists who were just like you.

> 66
>
> *Creating a successful marketing plan for your art is akin to constructing a towering skyscraper.*
>
> **–Marina Granger**
>
> 99

Start Selling Your Art Like a Pro!

With these easily customizable plug.

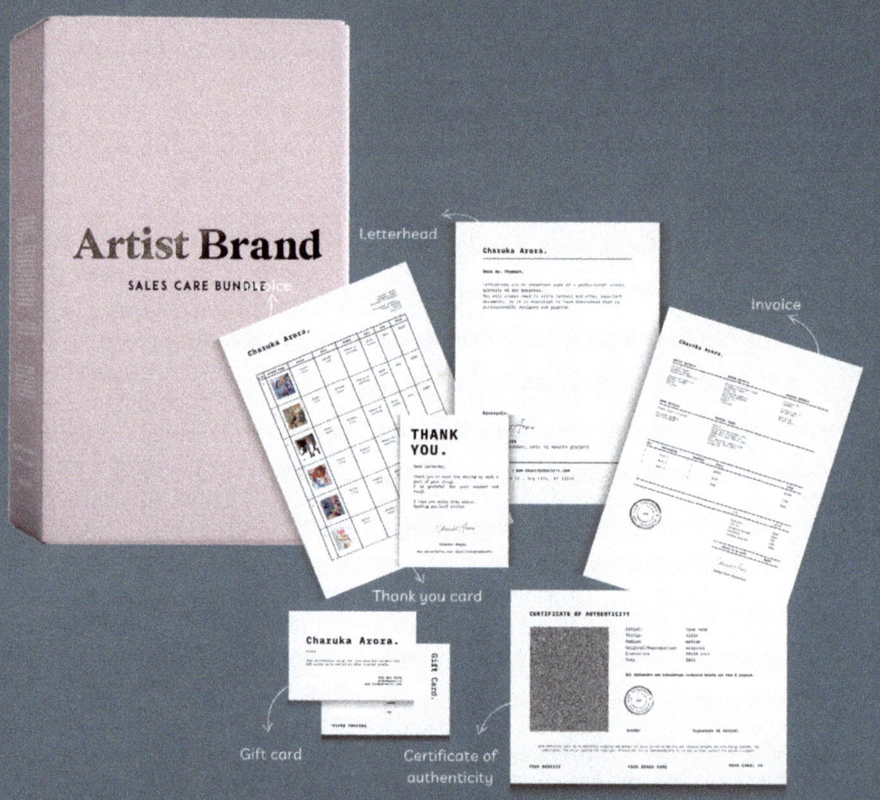

The Artist Brand Pack is a great way to get started in the world of art sales. It includes everything you need to get started. It Includes a gift card, thank you card, invoice template, image list, authenticity certificate, and letterhead. Plus, a bonus brand card is included for good measure.

Shop Your Artist Brand Pack Now on,

shop.artstoheartsproject.com

Meet
Elisabeth Pardoe

Interview by *Sonam Bindra*

She was collected by the:

**- Springville Museum of Art (2022, "Tell Me About Your Day"),
- Won an Exhibition Award in the 15th International ARC Salon (2021), and
- Exhibited at noteworthy institutions such as the Utah Museum of Contemporary Art (2020).
Meyer Gallery currently represents her (Park City, UT).**

Lis Pardoe is a contemporary U.S. American artist whose oil paintings narrate a return to a quieter environment. In response to the dissonance she feels from existing in our current world, her work is anti-anxiety, inherently domestic, and soft. Ultimately a commentary on human ecology, she illustrates meditative themes of introspection that portray a world she believes exists within us. Working from observation, photography, and imagination, Pardoe's paintings offer bold colours, intricate detail, and multidimensional light. From self-portraits and figures to still-life and interiors, Pardoe's intimate scenes serve as a catalogue that documents her inner world and daily life. Often described as mundane, uniquely human experiences inspire and root her to the core of what feels essential. She feels at ease by portraying these stories as it helps document her observations and emotions. She paints in layers to deepen the spectrum of light and colour, which is her most successful tool for capturing sentiment. As someone who deals with generalized anxiety, this medium gifts her an element of control while encouraging her to loosen up. Pardoe was born in Sandy, UT, USA, and grew up along the Wasatch Front. Shortly after graduating from Viewmont High School in 2010, Pardoe began a five-year apprenticeship at the Hein Atelier of Traditional Art, from which she graduated in 2015. In early 2022, she moved from Salt Lake City to Mazatlán, Sin., Mexico, and as of 2023 Pardoe currently lives and works in Portland, OR, USA.

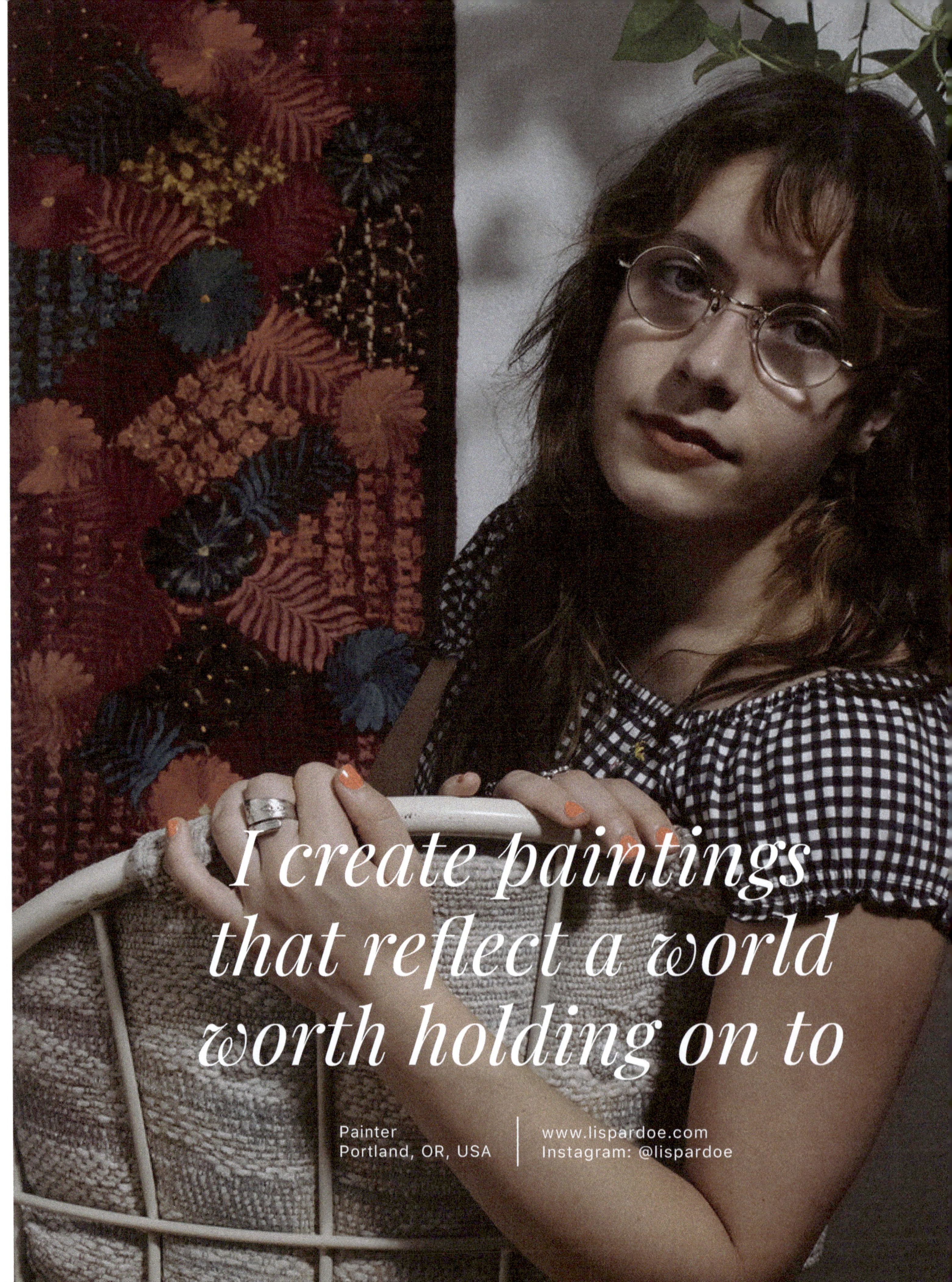

I create paintings that reflect a world worth holding on to
Painter
Portland, OR, USA
www.lispardoe.com
Instagram: @lispardoe

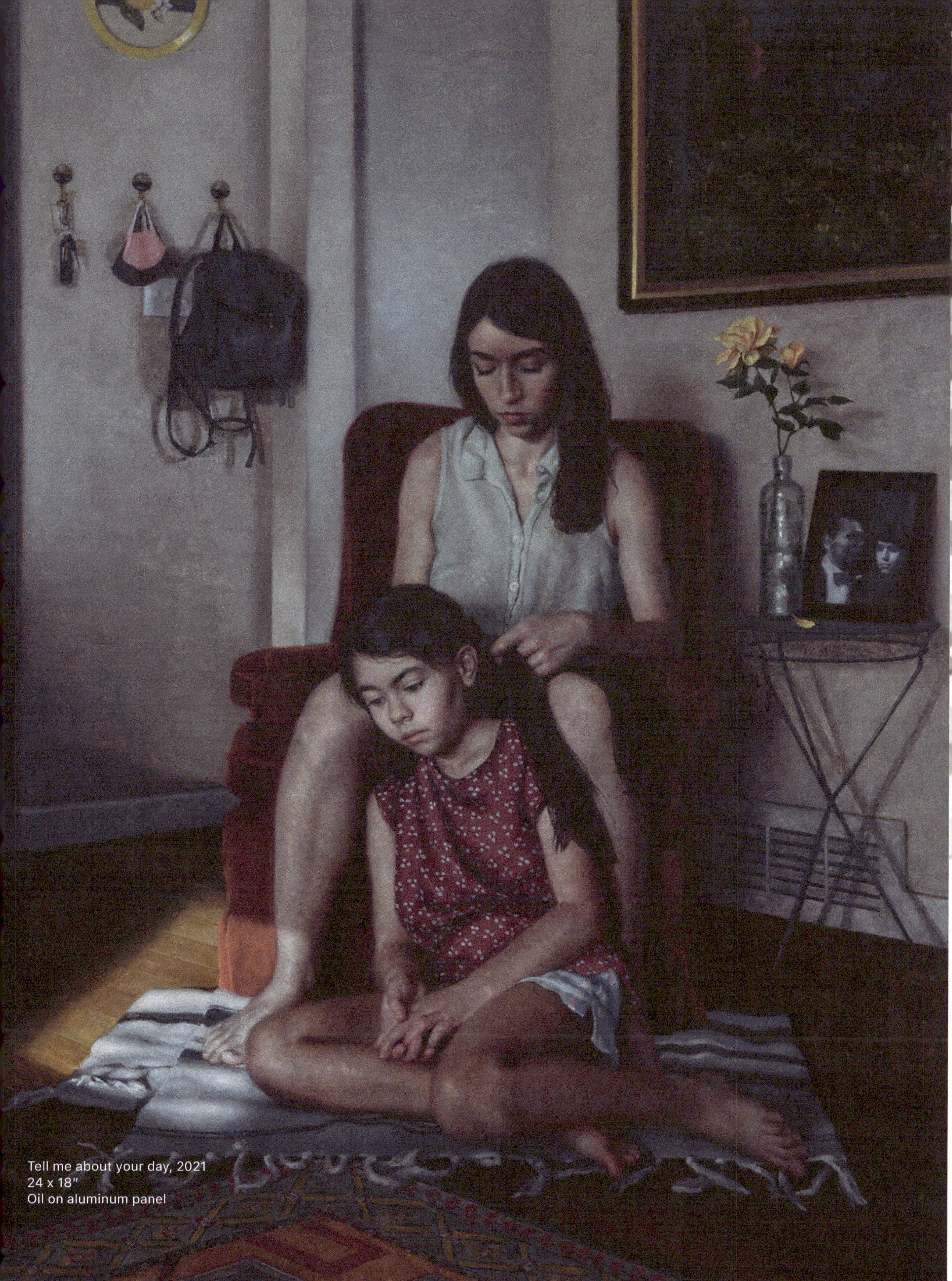
Tell me about your day, 2021
24 x 18"
Oil on aluminum panel

> ❝ It's a reminder of what it means to *be alive*, *to feel the breeze on my skin* and the sweat on my neck, which *lifts* me out of my *anxieties.* ❞

Your artwork "Breathing Out" gives me nostalgia. I can feel the breeze while in the sun. What inspired you to create such a QUIET painting?
Thank you! Breathing Out was an idea I've had for a long time, but I only had the right scenery once I lived in Mexico. There's something so human about laundry blowing in the wind. I'd be drying my clothing on the roof of my apartment, looking around at my neighbours' homes that attracted the same summer sun, feeling a relaxation and bodily process that I don't want to forget — sunglasses protecting my eyes, the cool dampness of fabric in my arms before hanging, and the crunch of the sun-dried jeans. "It's a reminder of what it means to be alive, to feel the breeze on my skin and the sweat on my neck, which lifts me out of my anxieties." Painting "Breathing Out" is my attempt not to let that memory go. I wanted to portray the brief meditations that can find us no matter our location.

Lis, your paintings make me feel present in the moment. Each portrait tells a story. What inspires you to capture such unique moments in your artwork?
I appreciate that. I want my portraits and figurative work to be interactive yet reflect my experience. I still want them to fit under my theme of existing in the present moment, free from societal pressures. When are we allowed just to be and reflect? To take care of our emotions, relish in good company, and eat luscious fruit? I've painted simple portraits that look posed in the past, but in my more recent work, the narrative is the most important. If I'm going to take up space, I hope it's dazzling.

Lis, I am absolutely stunned by the warmth and 'at-home' your work makes me feel. Where do you find inspiration for such unique artwork?
My ideas usually come when I'm quiet and alone: on a walk, lying in bed, or washing the dishes. I reflect a lot when solo. I like to write a line about the feeling or jot a quick drawing in my sketchbook to remember it. When the idea is persistent, I'll start by setting up my easel on location, photographing, or filming. My finished paintings are always on aluminium composite panels. Still, if the scene is complex, I'll draw on paper first and transfer it vs. going straight into the paint. My process is indirect, so I paint multiple layers. I have a "look" that I want to achieve. This look differs in what scene or object I'm painting, but I typically know what I'm after.

What is most striking about your work is how vivid and life-like it is. Lis, what techniques do you use to achieve such details in your artwork?
I think about three main concepts: value, colour balance, and depth. Each of these impact chroma and dictate if I use a transparent or opaque pigment and how dark or light I will push it. While I may paint certain things alla prima (in one layer), I generally paint indirectly (in layers). I glaze (transparent pigment suspended in medium) large areas every so often and regularly use (what I call) "micro glazes" when painting skin to mimic the translucency. When paired with opaque highlights worked into a glaze, it's luminous. It gets pretty techy, but that's what I love about oil paint.

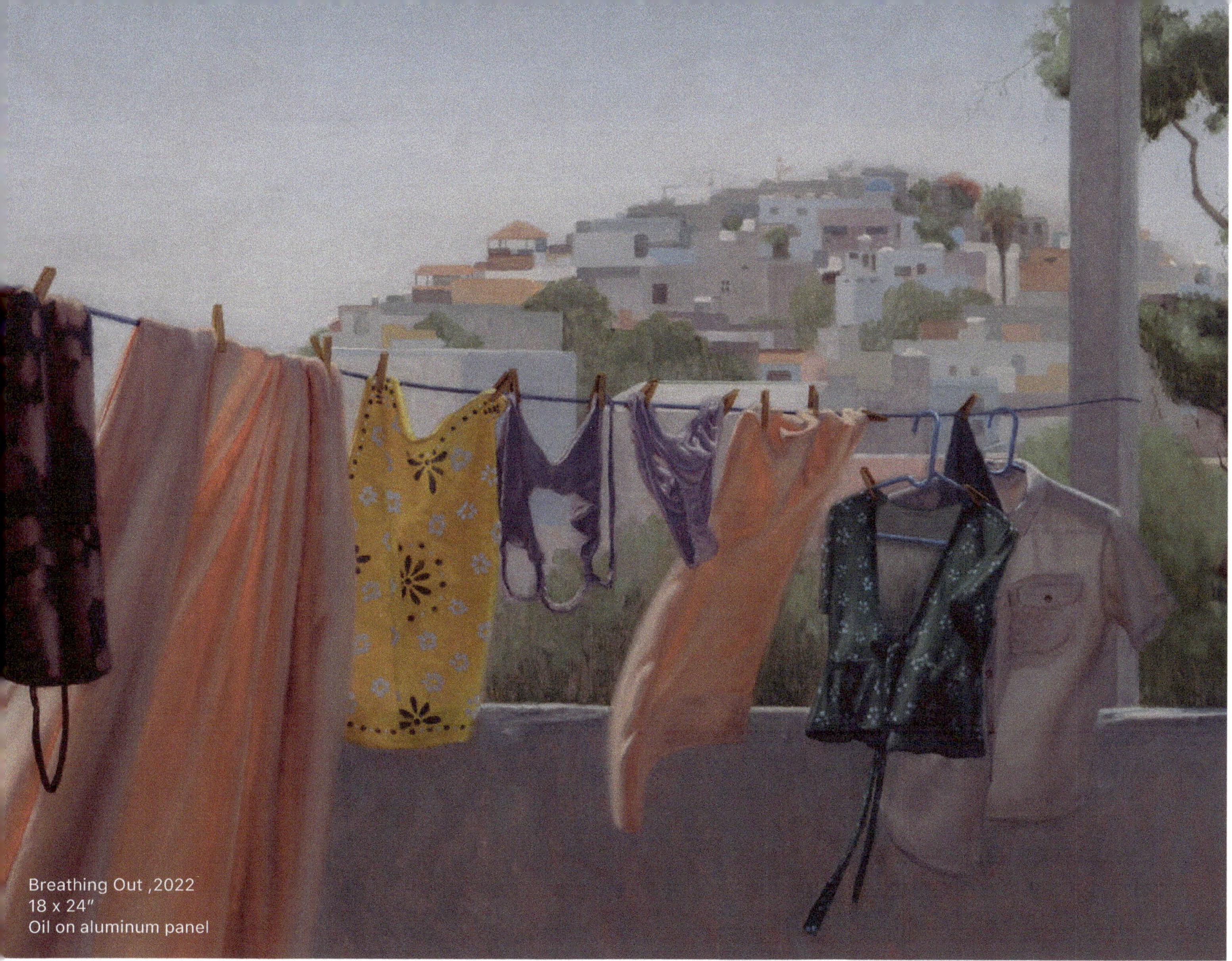

Your artwork takes me to a serene state, almost like meditating. I feel myself being lost in them. How do you feel the painting is for you?

Painting is like meditation; you have to quit everything else and focus on what's in front of you, effectively calming the nervous system. Pair it with music, and you've got a golden gem, at least during your painting session! I may be more anxious on a lousy painting day, but learning to ride the wave and trust that you'll find your way through the artwork and come out on top is a valuable tool. While I often wish I didn't have anxiety, my experience interacting with it propels my inspiration and subject matter. Rather than fighting it so hard, I can thank my sensitivity for allowing me to view life through a delicate perspective. It's why I'm the painter I am.

Lis, we have already witnessed some mundane yet unique moments through your artwork. Is there anything new you are working on?

I just moved from Mazatlán to Portland, so I'm in between projects. I'm looking forward to starting on an idea that has been persistently knocking! It will be a figurative painting that I hope will capture the transitory feeling of "when you've moved, but your home doesn't feel like home yet," specifically commemorating my love for Mazatlán. Right before the move, I finished up some portrait commissions, which I do have more openings for at the moment ;)

Lis Pardoe is an American oil painter, whose artwork will take you to a serene state. Her mundane yet unique paintings will remind you of that quiet corner in your house or being with that favorite persown. It sure will give you nostalgia.

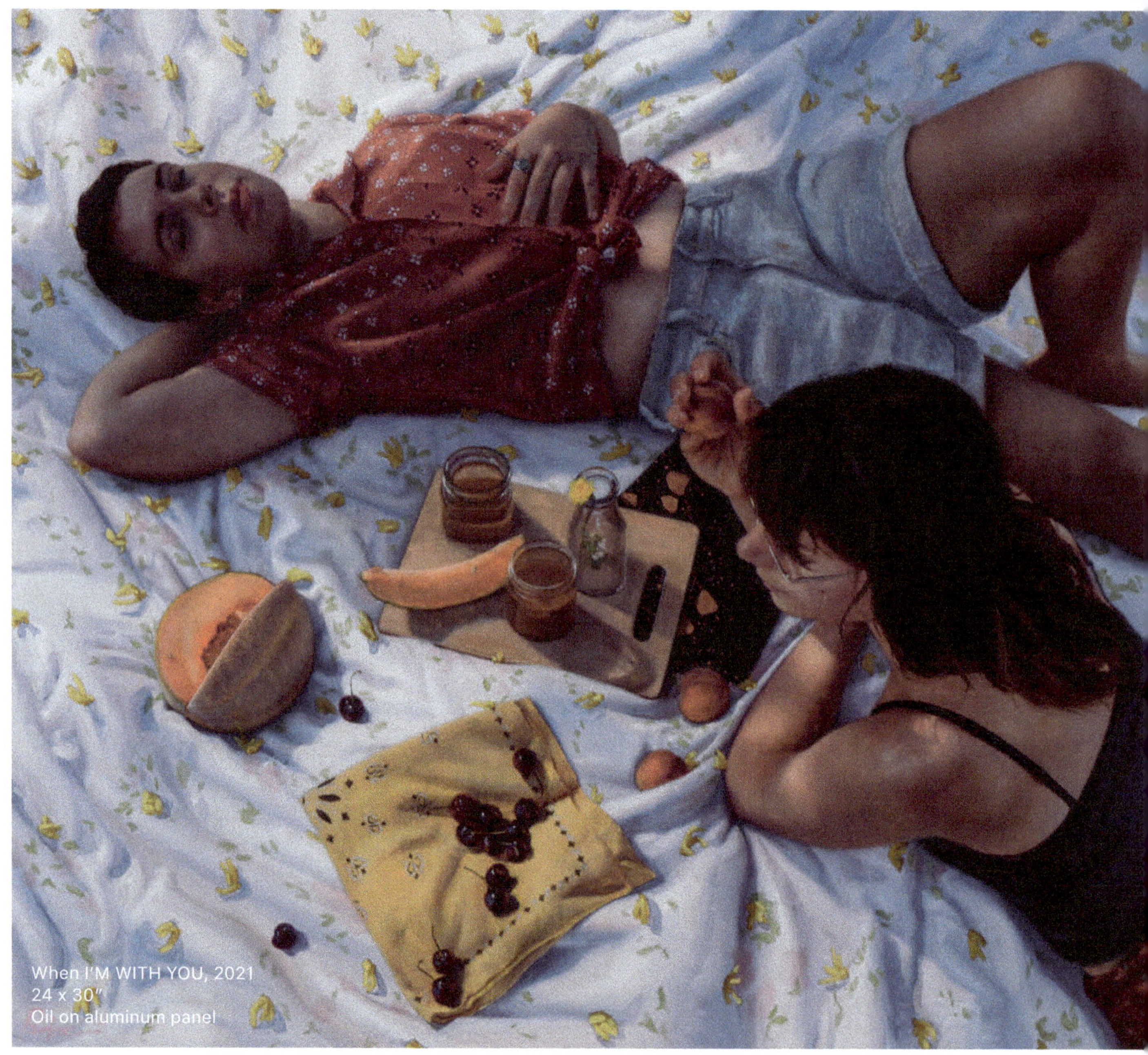

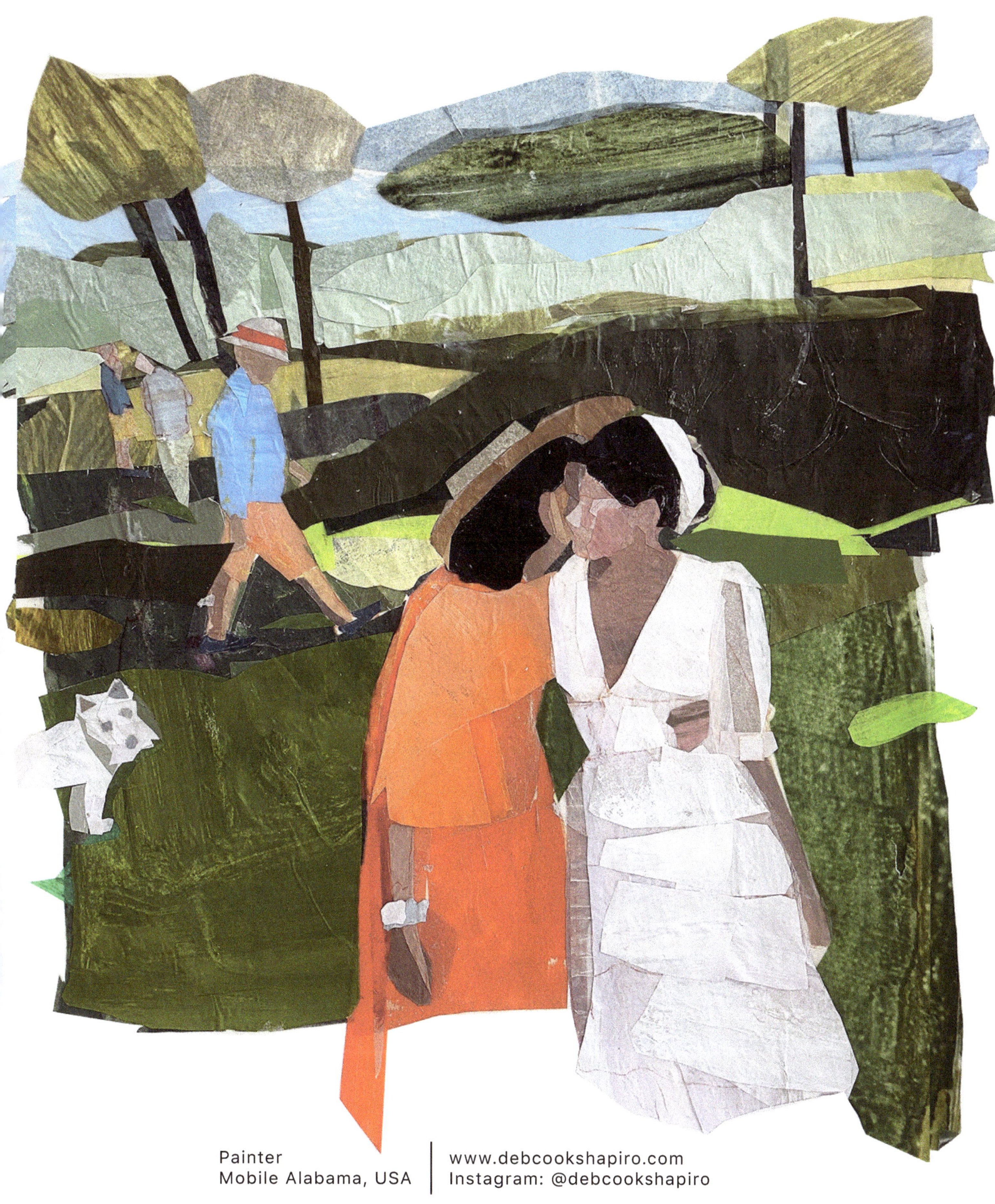

Painter
Mobile Alabama, USA

www.debcookshapiro.com
Instagram: @debcookshapiro

Meet Debra Cook Shapiro

Interview by *Sonam Bindra*

Deb studied painting at the *Istituto Lorenzo di Medici* (Florence, Italy), *Istituto per l'Arte e il Ristauro* (Florence, Italy), the *University of California, Berkeley Post-Baccalaureate* in Painting (San Francisco, CA), and studied painting at *San Francisco Art Institute and Academy of Art College*. Shapiro had solo exhibitions at the *French Consul Residence*, (San Francisco, CA), *Ice House Gallery*, (Petaluma, CA), and *Summerhouse*, (Mill Valley, CA). Her group shows have been at the *Palette gallery, The Office of the California State Senator, Scott Weiner, and 111 Minna Gallery.* Her work is in domestic and international collections.

Deb Cook Shapiro is an American artist, who lives and works in San Francisco, CA. Her paintings explore fleeting emotions and memories. They aim to awaken feelings of joy, love, fear, insecurity, and heartache that define the human condition. In many paintings, her teen and young adult subjects act out their dramas against familiar backdrops such as beaches, parks, and backyards. The timeframe of their settings and implied narrative is hard to pin down, like memory itself. A sense of longing is a strong theme in the paintings, as though the artist is remembering scenes from her own youth that are infused into the present-day creation of work that addresses modern people. Her process begins by reviewing photographs, movie clips, or her own staged photoshoots. She then uses these references as a springboard for the memories and feelings she will paint. The work is repeatedly painted, scraped, and radically revised as the thoughts and memories take shape and change.

Deb, I love how your artwork tells a story. What inspired you to create such life-expressing portraits?
I loved to draw and colour as a child but painting was particularly exciting for me. In my home painting was usually off-limits due to the mess-making potential, which may have been the initial attraction it held. Expressing my life experiences and emotions through art was a way to process big feelings that weren't always welcome in my family or my school life. I didn't have the courage or the encouragement to pursue art at the beginning of my professional life.

As I developed my tastes, worked on my skill set, travelled, and studied in San Francisco and in Italy, I started appreciating contemporary paintings, while keeping my love of classical and historic masterworks. From the Bay Area figuration to the East Coast painters like Erik Fischl, I broadened my artistic horizons. My painting practice was invigorated by the deep appreciation of both historic and contemporary artworks.

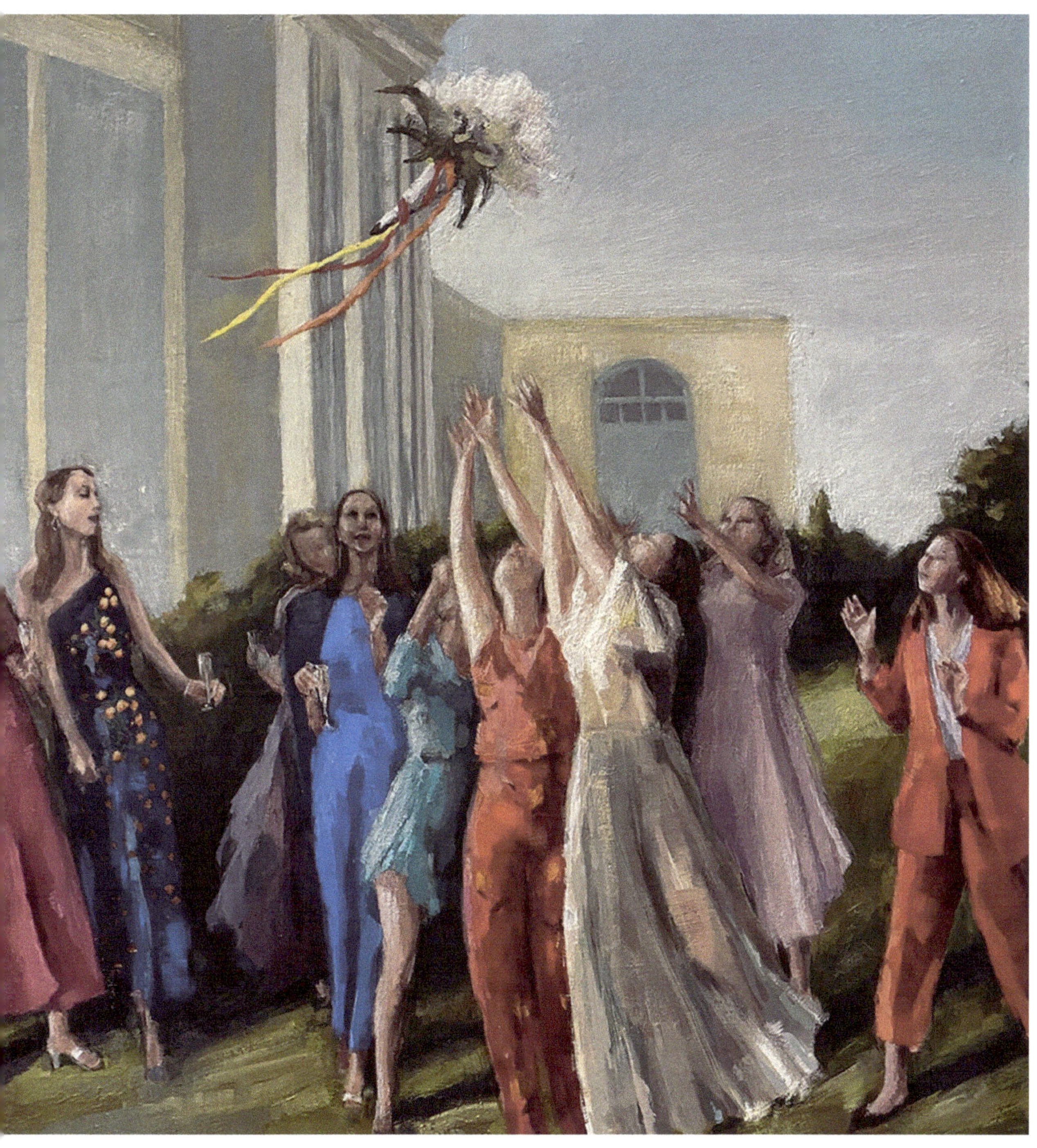

So your artwork 'Mother & Daughter' is a collage of emotions. I am curious to know how you were able to capture the bond in your painting.

The photos from this wedding in France were complex, having many people, colourful fashions, and beautiful scenery. In an effort to pace myself before painting on canvas, I started making collages of papers I had painted with oil in the colours I would be using in a painting. Collaging for the first time was labour-intensive but I fell in love with the process of layering pieces of paper into a composition. This phase seemed more forgiving as an exploratory phase because I could correct the design by cutting and glueing another piece of paper. The bittersweet emotions between the mother and the bride were such a compelling subject to approach with subtlety and delicacy. The layers of paper seemed to be the perfect medium to convey the beautiful costumes and tender emotional state between joy and sadness for the passing of a phase of life between a mother and daughter.

❝ It is a never-ending challenge but such important work to continue discovering who I am and what I believe so I can determine what is meaningful for me to express in my work. ❞

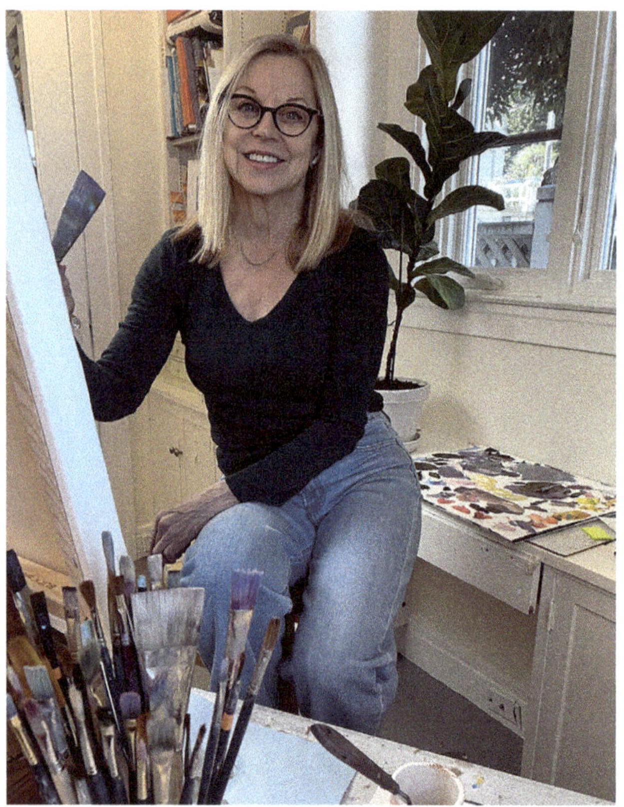

Debra Cook Shapiro is an American artist. Her artwork brings back so many memories of our own. They aim to take you on a roller coaster of emotions, from enjoying on a beach to a nuptial in Paris. Through her artwork, she wishes for her viewers to understand the importance of being with our loved ones and sharing happiness on their special occasions as it helps us build stronger relations and happy memories.

Debra, what I love most about your paintings is how expressive they are. They keep me hooked. What is your motivation behind such mesmerizing artworks?

Life is always a journey of reflection and self-discovery. I set out to paint scenes from my life with authenticity and truthfulness. I could never have imagined that becoming a painter would lead me into such a deep inner journey. The courage and grit required to shine a light upon me and then work to overcome some negative beliefs that block my progress. Through meditation, reading, listening to inspirational speakers, and taking long daily walks I have gotten closer to knowing myself which becomes evident in my work. "It is a never-ending challenge but such important work to continue discovering who I am and what I believe so I can determine what is meaningful for me to express in my work."

Working on "Fêtes & Celebrations" must have been uplifting. Can you share how it felt while you were in the process of making it?

The vivid colours and joyful subject matter in "Fetes and Celebrations" seem appropriate to convey my reactions to the beauty and excitement of these delightful and lavish celebrations. The colours not only lifted my spirits while attending the events but working with vibrantly saturated and high-key colours in my studio have had a positive impact on my mood and energy level while I am making the work.

Deb, your artwork brings back so many memories of my own. What message do you wish to convey through the artwork?

I hope to convey the importance that feeling connected to others and sharing their joy in social settings holds in our lives. The vibrance of the colours, costumes, and compositions of my paintings will give pleasure to the viewer while serving as an invitation for them to smile and relate to their own memories and experiences in festive events. "Fetes and Celebrations" embodies the importance of being present physically and spiritually for our loved ones when they celebrate special occasions. Connecting with our friends and family during their moments of joy, memory-making, and a chance to transform ourselves as we witness rites of passage.

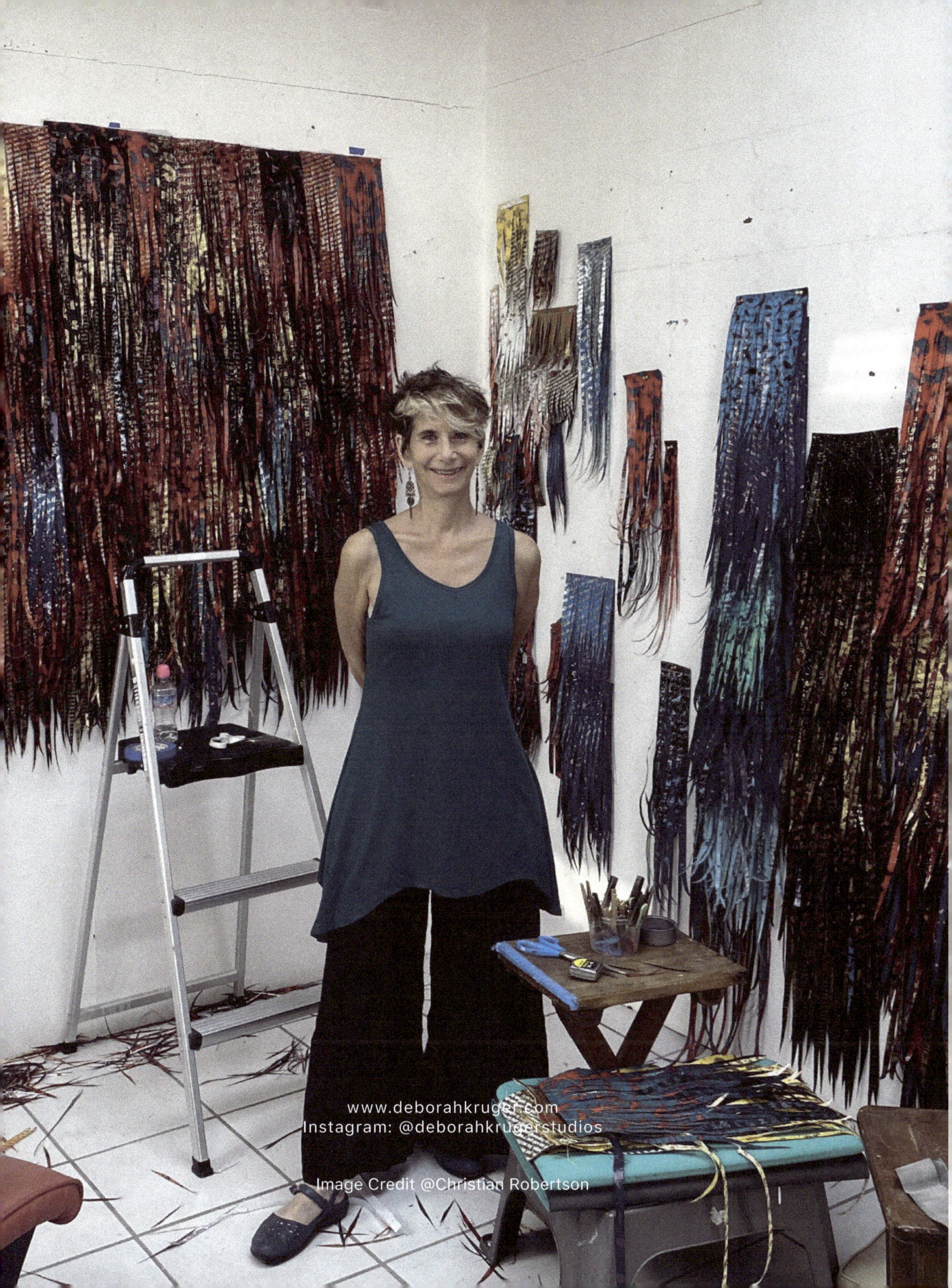

www.deborahkruger.com
Instagram: @deborahkrugerstudios

Image Credit @Christian Robertson

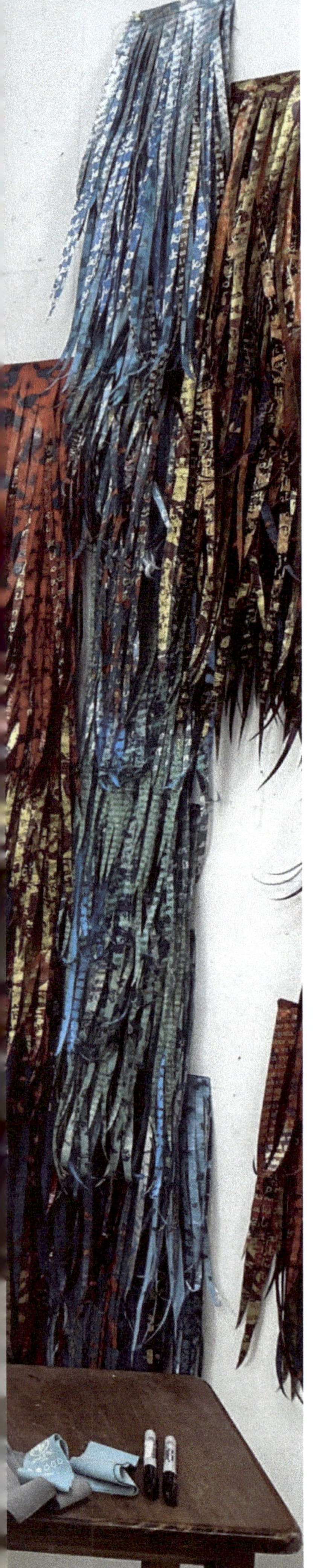

Meet
Deborah Kruger

Interview by *Sonam Bindra*

Her artwork focuses on conveying the impacts of climate change and habitat fragmentation on bird extinction, with recycled plastic bags screen printed with images of her drawings of endangered birds and languages. Her feathers are overprinted with text in endangered indigenous languages such as Yiddish, Ladino, Tzotzil, Zoque, and Cho'lol, whose last living speakers are in steep decline.

Deborah Kruger is a highly respected Environmental Artist whose work has been exhibited across the world since the 1980s. Deborah's recent career highlights include being a finalist for the 2023 Arte Laguna Prize in sculpture and installation with an upcoming exhibition at the Arsenale Nord in Venice, Italy. She has also exhibited her work in solo shows such as "Plumas" in Mexico City and in two international Biennials. The Museum of Art and Design (MAD) in New York City has recently acquired two of her large-format environmental works which will be exhibited in 2024. Deborah has attended residencies at prestigious art institutions such as the Millay Colony for the Arts, Austerlitz, NY, La Porte Peinte Centre, Noyers-sur-Serein, France, and Hypatia-in-the-Woods, Shelton, WA. Her artwork invites a dialogue about preserving wild spaces and animals, especially vulnerable birds, and protecting the habitat for all species, including humans.

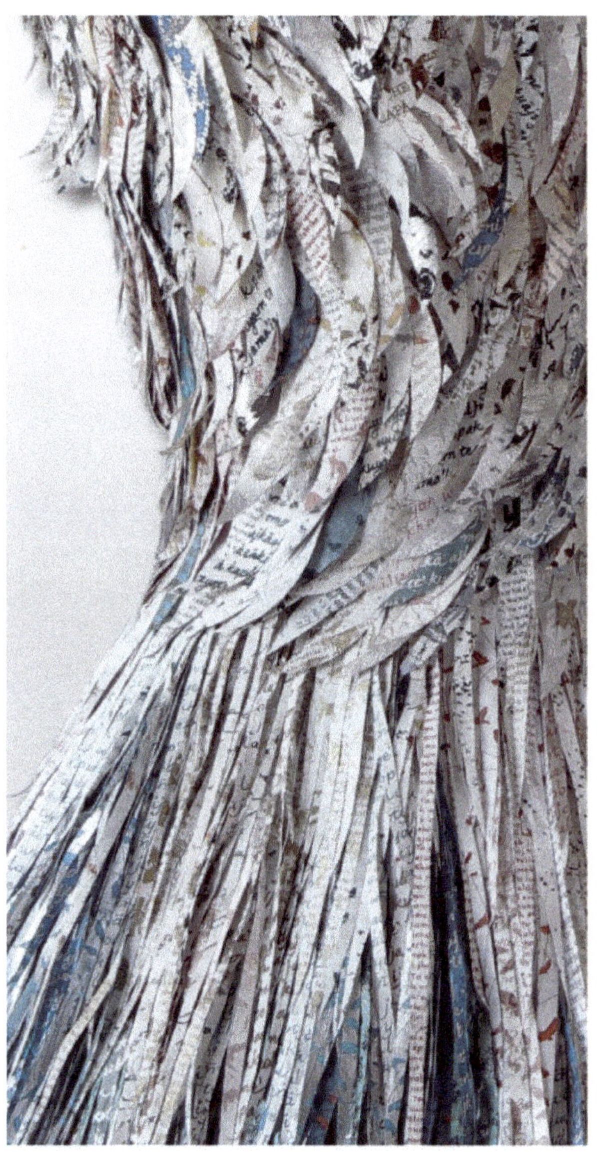

Deborah, What I love most about your artworks are that they are so distinctive and imaginative. What is your inspiration behind such unique work?

The photos from this wedding in France were complex, My artwork has gradually evolved over many years. What makes it unique is the confluence of content about endangered birds and languages and the form and construction of the artwork using recycled materials and incorporating my background in wallpaper and surface design. "I have always worked best collaboratively and within a community of women." I believe that the more authentic our artwork is, the more universal it becomes. "I am driven by the desire to make and show artwork that amplifies the challenges to our natural world."

Deborah your work is on such unique themes about protecting endangered bird species and languagues. How do you think your work enriches our society and creates meaningful connections?

Rachel Carson, whose environmentalism inspired me as a young woman, wrote: "The more clearly we can focus on...the wonders...of the universe...the less taste we shall have for destruction." Protecting birds and other species by addressing habitat fragmentation and climate change will ensure that future generations will have the opportunity to be awed and renewed by nature. Losing indigenous languages and cultures means that we are losing histories, memories, and wisdom that can never be retrieved. If we adopted the First Nation's habit of thinking ten generations ahead, our planet and its species, including us humans, would have a better chance of survival. "I hope that my artwork generates dialogue and inspires action. Remember, there is no planet B!"

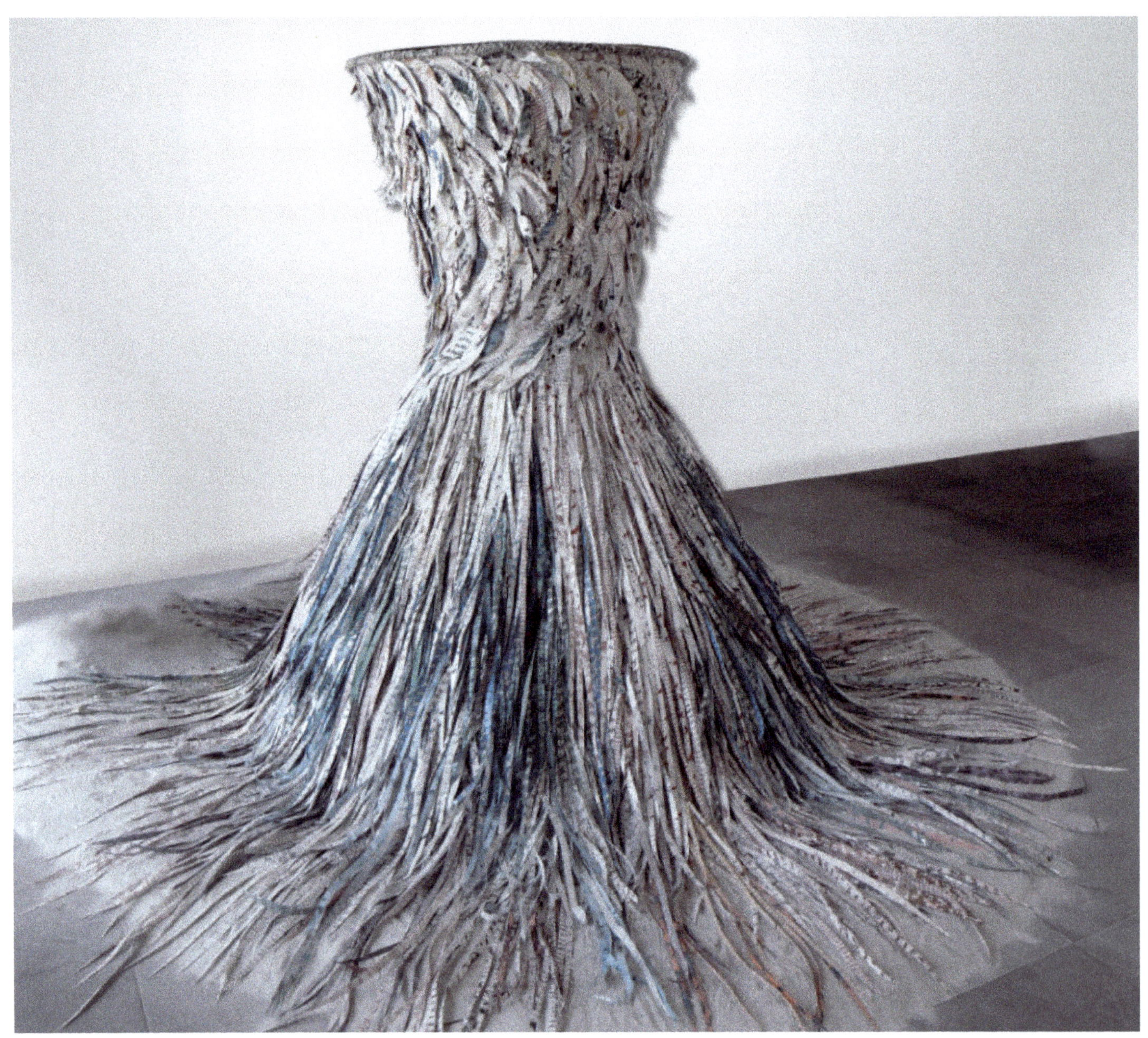

So, Museum of Art & Design (MAD), New York acquired your artworks 'Accidentals' and 'Ropa Pintada'. Congratulations for the win. Could you tell us a little more about these artworks and what they mean to you?

There is nothing more affirming than a major museum acquiring my artwork. 'Accidentals' is a large environmental mural (7.5 feet high by 14 feet wide) that combines the best of my pattern and decoration aesthetic with my passionate call to action on behalf of our vulnerable birds. The title Accidentals refers to birds that are found outside of their natural habitat due to the impacts of habitat fragmentation and climate change. 'Ropa Pintada' is inspired by the hand-woven huipils woven and worn by the indigenous women in Chiapas, Mexico, and Guatemala. Both pieces are constructed using feathers made from recycled plastic bags and printed with images of endangered birds and endangered languages such as Yiddish, Yakme, and Zoque.

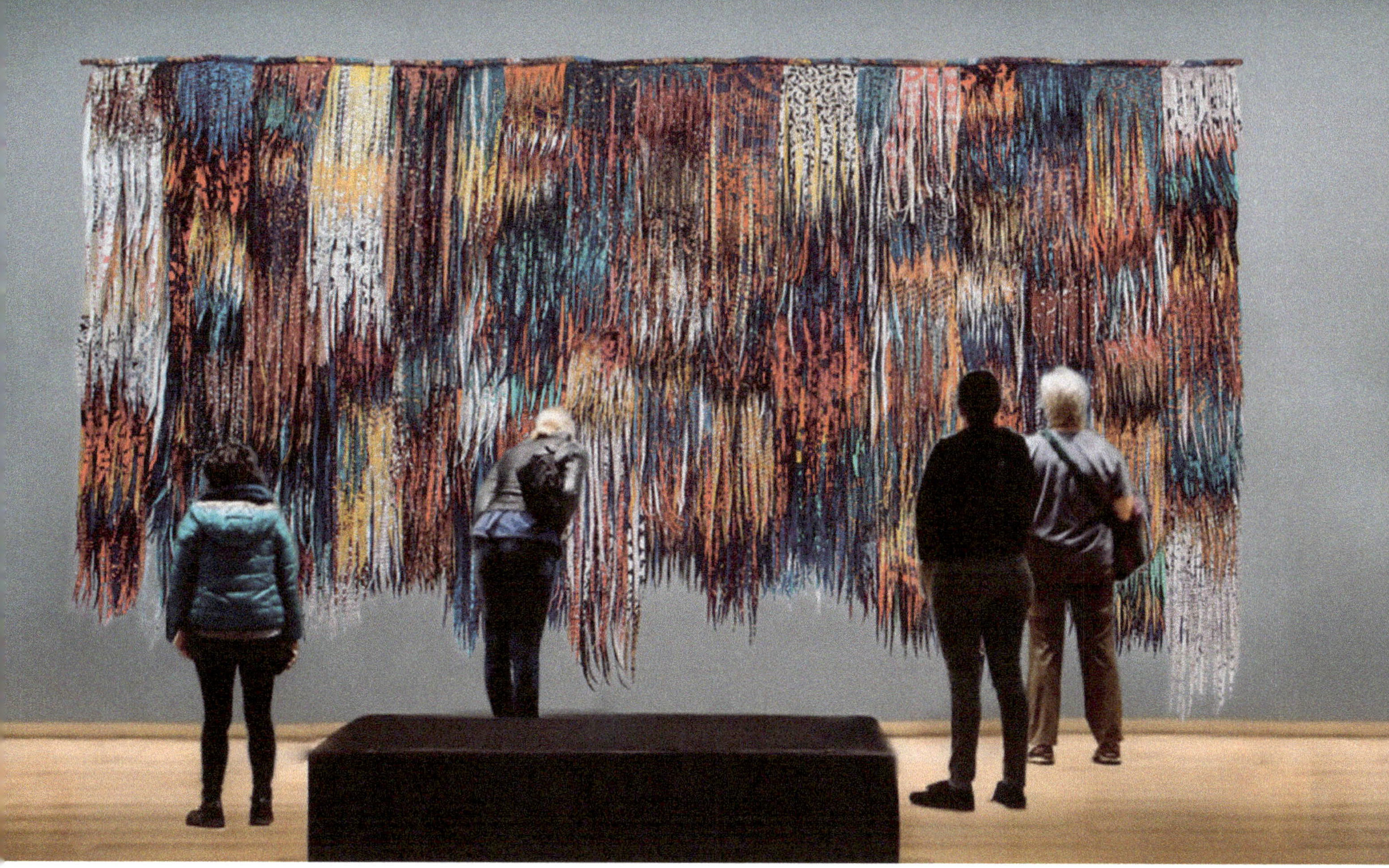

Your work seems to be of large-scale productions involving recycling plastic bags, silk-screening then sewing. It seems such an intricate process. What will be your team strength and where is your studio located?

There is really no way that I could produce these large-scale works or prepare for international exhibitions without a lot of help. My primary production studio is located on Lake Chapala, Mexico where I have assembled a team of dedicated Mexican women who help me with the preparation of the recycled bags, silk-screening, sewing, and cutting required for making the feathers that I use in all my artwork. Creating reliable and empowering jobs for these women is very important to me. Together we mutually benefit from our collaboration. I also have a studio in the vibrant arts community in Durham, North Carolina.

Deborah we have seen your artwork in series Red and White and all of them are fascinating. What other projects do you have in pipeline?

As usual, I have a lot of balls in the air! In the studio, after working on a series of white pieces for many years, I am now meditating on blackness by creating a series of primarily black artwork. I am a finalist in Sculpture and Installation for the Arte Laguna Prize and I am attending an exhibition for the finalists at the Arsenale Nord in Venice, Italy. This is my first trip to Italy and I am very excited to see my artwork in this historic city! I just got back from teaching classes in Making Art with Recycled Materials at the San Diego College of Continuing Education department of Clothing and Textiles. I have more upcoming teaching gigs at colleges and universities and it feels great to share these techniques with students who are considering sustainability as part of their art practices. In May 2024, I will be at the opening of the exhibit at MAD in New York City and welcome anyone in the Metro New York area to join me to see 'Accidentals' and 'Ropa Pintada' installed in their new home.

Do you want to get the most out of your creative practice?

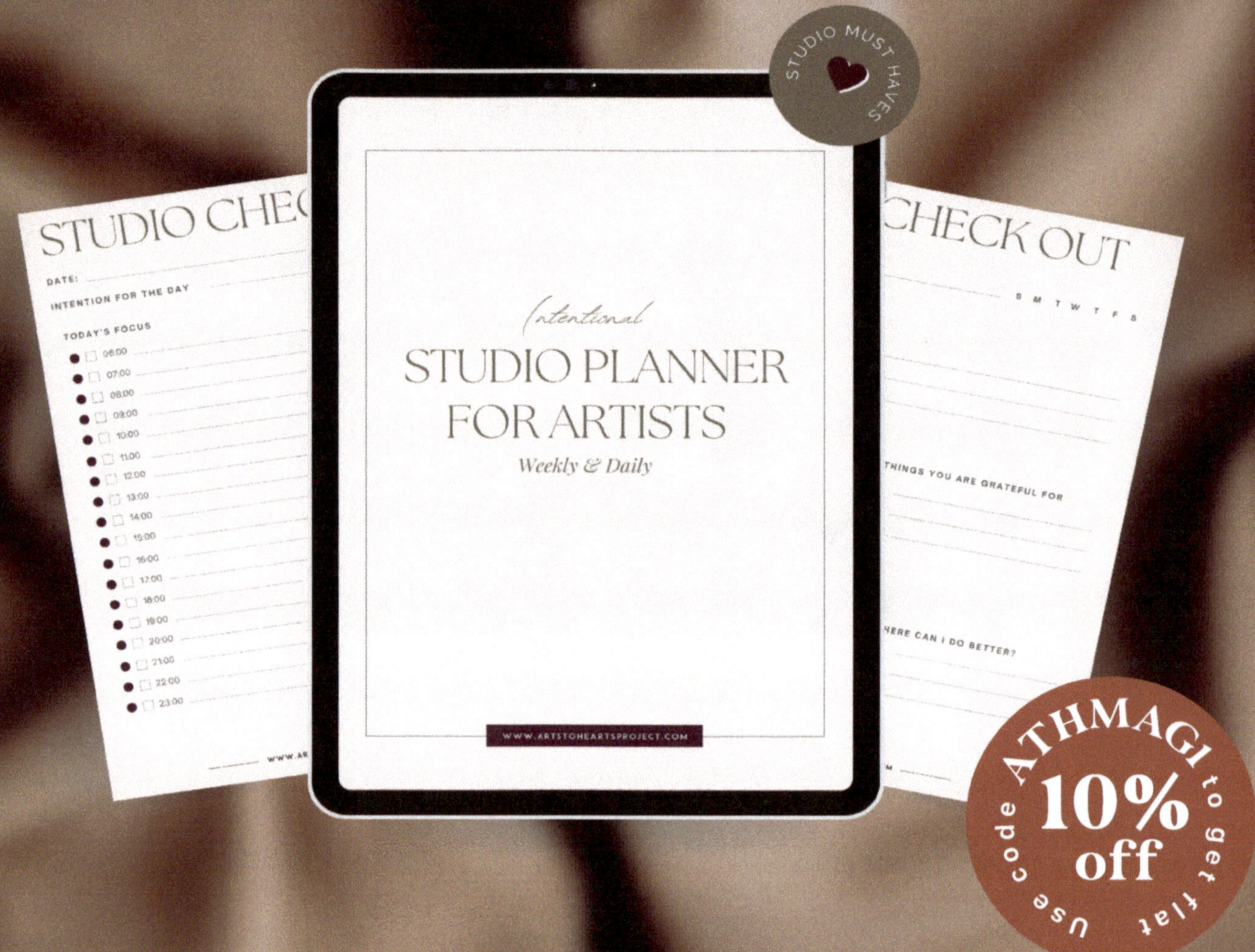

The Studio Planner for Artists is the perfect way to plan your week. This planner includes everything you need to create your to do list, Track your things to get done, and track your progress with studio check in and check out and a space to dump your creative ideas. It is undated so you can start using it at any time, and it has plenty of space for you to write down your thoughts and ideas.

Get your own Studio Planner for Artists today!

shop.artstoheartsproject.com

How to create an

ARTIST PORTFOLIO

that brings more attention

Written by *Rabia Khan*

Have you ever wondered what it takes to create an artist portfolio that stands out and attracts the attention of collectors, galleries, art lovers and other people who can help you showcase your work? If so, then you know how important it is to create a portfolio that reflects your unique style and talent. However, making an artist portfolio that gains attention goes beyond having a body of work – you need to find ways to present this work in the best light possible.

However, the process of creating a portfolio is often daunting to many artists. Your portfolio should be more than just images; it should also include descriptions of each piece, information about your background and experience as an artist, and any awards or recognition you've received for your artwork.

So, we've done the research for you and put together all the tips and tricks you need to create a portfolio that will turn heads. Read on to find out how you can make your portfolio stand out and attract more attention.

But, before that let me share with you some of the common questions that artists have in their minds when creating an artist portfolio.an artist portfolio.

How do I make my portfolio stand out?

What should I include in my portfolio?

How often should I update my portfolio?

What are some common mistakes artists make with their portfolios

What are some portfolio tips for artists just starting?

How many pieces of art should I include in my portfolio?

What type of art should I include in my portfolio?

List your professional experiences &/or a resume

The first thing to place in your artist portfolio is a list of your professional experiences. If you are a beginner these experiences can be listed in a way that can reflect your interest and work in the field in a form of a CV or resume.Making a CV or resume helps you outline your professional accomplishments and any relevant education or experience in the art world; this helps people interested in your artwork understand your level of expertise and know what they can expect from you. We see a common hesitation from Artists when it comes to building a CV or resume. But, our advice is to start from wherever you are and know that building a quality resume is a task of time. So, keep going.

List your creative work

Okay, so the most common question we see when it comes to listing your work in an Artist portfolio is how many and what to list. But, first let's address that when it comes to selecting your Artwork for inclusion in your artist portfolio, it's important to choose pieces that demonstrate your skill level and unique style. It may be hard to narrow down which works to include, but remember: quality is more important than quantity. Keep that Faith. You may also want to consider including images of installation shots or documentation of past exhibitions; this will show potential viewers that you can professionally handle large projects and have experience exhibiting artwork in public spaces. And if you are someone that has not yet exhibited their artwork then no need to worry. Turn any wall or corner of your house/studio into your gallery and hang/display your artworks in a way a gallery would hang/display and take pictures of it. This way it will give anyone seeing your portfolio a clear idea of how your artwork would look in a public space. Along with that, If you have any press coverage (e.g., articles written about you or interviews conducted), adding those materials can also be beneficial since they provide further evidence of accomplishment and recognition within the art community.

Now, Let's address the question of how many pieces and what type of art should be included in the portfolio.

When it comes to creating a balanced portfolio, determining how many pieces of art to include can be tricky. But with the right strategy and some careful consideration, you can determine the ideal number for your portfolio. The first thing to consider when deciding how many pieces of art to include in your portfolio is what type of medium or media you will use. If you are purely a painter or sculptor, then focusing on quality over quantity is key. Aim for only including 5-10 pieces that show off your range of skills and abilities as an artist - more will just clutter up your portfolio and distract you from showcasing the very best work.

On the other hand, if you dabble in different forms such as photography or printmaking then showing a greater variety may be advantageous –so aim for 10-15 works with this route being taken as having too few might suggest limited creativity while too many could overwhelm anyone seeing the portfolio.

So there is no one size fits all answer when it comes to deciding exactly how much artwork should go into any artist's portfolio so taking time out to carefully consider what you wish it says about yourself (both technically & conceptually) alongside ensuring quality stands high above quantity overall remains paramount here regardless of whichever media form used along the way! And So, select only your finest pieces to include in your portfolio.

Now to answer what type of art to include in your portfolio

We would suggest that when you are selecting art for your portfolio select it in a way that should reflect your unique style and interests while also showing off your technical skill set. Not only will this help people interested in your art identify with your work, but it can also help you in demonstrating yourself more professionally.

So, choose just a few pieces that truly demonstrate what you can do rather than throwing everything under the sun. Consider each piece carefully and ask yourself if it truly reflects the best of your work in terms of style and skill level before including it in your portfolio.

After that Consider the types of media you are interested in being known for or want to attract more opportunities —whether it's sketching with graphite pencils, painting with watercolours or acrylics, photographing landscapes or still life shots—and make sure to feature these artistic mediums prominently throughout your portfolio.

And If possible, invest in professional photography which showcases the artwork clearly without any background distractions detracting from its beauty; this will go a long way towards giving anyone viewing your portfolio the best possible look at what you have created.

Artist Bio & Statement

Okay, so now let us get the cat out of the bag. The most pressing question for artists is how to make an Artist Bio & statement. So, let's talk about this now. An important component to include in your artist portfolio is to include your artist bio and artist statement. So when it comes to writing your artist bio our advice is to try to create engaging content about yourself as an artist as well as listing any awards or exhibitions you may have won as part of creating credibility for yourself as a professional creator within the industry. Don't worry about how big or small these accomplishments are. Remember it's a building block. And, you can always update your Bio with each accomplishment you add to your kitty.

In general, It's good to showcase any relevant experience such as internships at galleries or residencies, or museums volunteering; these accomplishments should be proudly featured along with insights into who you are as a person behind the canvas. While doing so make sure not only to list any past experiences but also mention any current projects too so that anyone viewing your portfolio knows exactly what you're working on right now. And if you are wondering why to include your artist statement then it should also be included so that people viewing your portfolio can understand the context in which your work was created and what motivates you to continue creating artwork. This statement gives the viewers a window into your creative process and can help them better appreciate what they see in your portfolio. One last piece of advice on this is to remember that you can have different statements for different bodies of work.

Be approachable

One of the other common mistakes we often see in portfolios is artists often miss adding their details to get in touch. You definitely should include contact information such as email addresses or social media handles in your portfolio. So when your portfolio is being shared or floats around then this makes it easier for anyone to reach out with questions or commission requests if they are interested in viewing more of your work online or offline.

Now the question comes:

How often should you update your portfolio?

It completely depends on you but it's suggested that try to keep updating your artist portfolio with new work so it remains fresh and relevant. So try to keep adding ne projects periodically even if they're small accomplishments or works in progress.

Size & Medium matters

So, this is a crucial step for you so pay attention. No matter how good a portfolio you make but if it's harder to access, there is absolutely very little chance of any success.

We at Arts to Hearts Project, receive several artists portfolio's every month. And, guess what? A majority of these portfolios aren't even looked at by us. Don't get me wrong. We love looking at your work. But, the most common mistake artists make while sharing a pdf is not checking how heavy the file may be. Is it easily attachable to the email or is it too heavy for someone to download? Making it easy and accessible is a very important key to this.

Double & Triple Check everything

Finally, once all of the components have been assembled, make sure to proofread everything so that there are no grammatical errors or typos present in the documents. With all these elements combined into one comprehensive portfolio, you will be well on your way to achieving success as an artist.

I hope these tips will help you in making a stellar portfolio for yourself but If you still need some assistance with your portfolio then we offer expert assistance. Here at Arts to Hearts Project, we are dedicated to helping women creatives build their careers. We offer regular workshops on artist portfolios and art business, giving you the resources and advice necessary for long-term success.

> *"Here at Arts to Hearts Project, we are dedicated to helping women creatives build their careers."*

You can find out more about our services by visiting our website www.arstoheartsproject.com or or drop us an email at info@artstoheartsproject.com. On our website, you will see information on upcoming workshops and events relevant to artist portfolios and art business that can help take your career in the right direction.

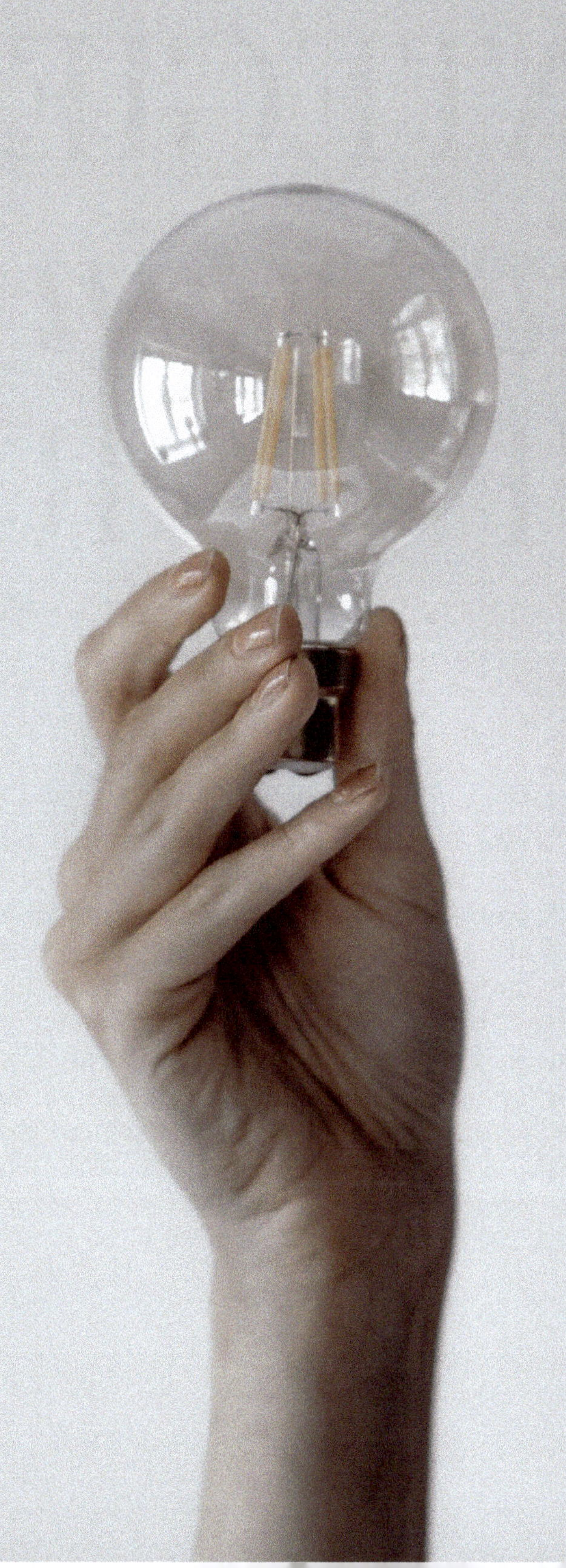

STRATEGIES *for* *thriving in the* ART WORLD

Written by *Rabia Khan*

Women have played an essential role as role models for artists throughout history. We all Know *Frida Kahlo,* who defied traditional gender roles and cultural expectations in her art. Using vivid colours and expressive brushstrokes, she painted classic works like self-portraits that encouraged other women artists to push the boundaries of artistic expression. And who can forget *Georgia O'Keeffe*, who captured the beauty of the American Southwest, besides them, there are many artists who have left a lasting impression in the world of art. These women artists are an inspiration to anyone trying to make their mark in the modern world. Their boldness in a male-dominated artistic field is a powerful reminder that *we can all realize our potential if we believe in ourselves and never give up on our dreams.*

And as 2023 begins, our international community of women artists are eager to take on the obstacles that stand in their way. To gain insight into what our members view as the most significant challenges, we asked, *"What is the biggest obstacle you want to overcome in 2023?"* on Arts to Hearts Project Instagram. The answers we received from them were inspiring and gave us a glimpse into the determination of our wonderful community. From *improving communication skills* and *finding strength* in vulnerability to making their mark *professionally,* our members are ready to *face their fears* and *push their boundaries.*

We can feel the commitment to self-improvement and growth in our community, and it's a fantastic source of inspiration for anyone looking for guidance in the new year. Whether facing fears head-on or achieving career goals, we wish each person the best in overcoming these obstacles in 2023!

So, let's give you an insight into all the responses from our *Arts To Hearts Project Community Members.*

So, these are all the responses we have got, and the resilience and courage demonstrated by the women artists in our community at Arts to Hearts Project are genuinely inspiring.

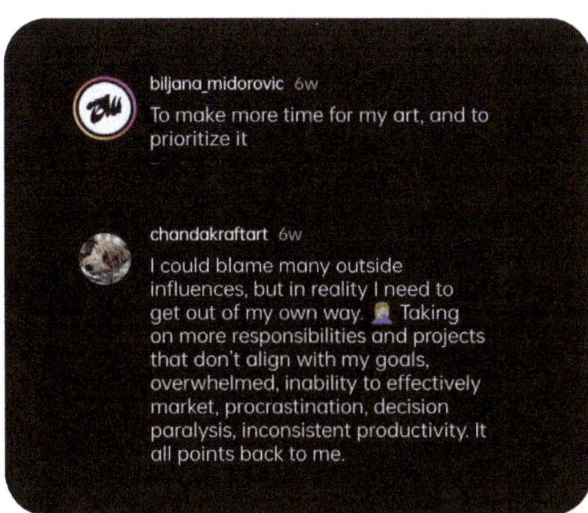

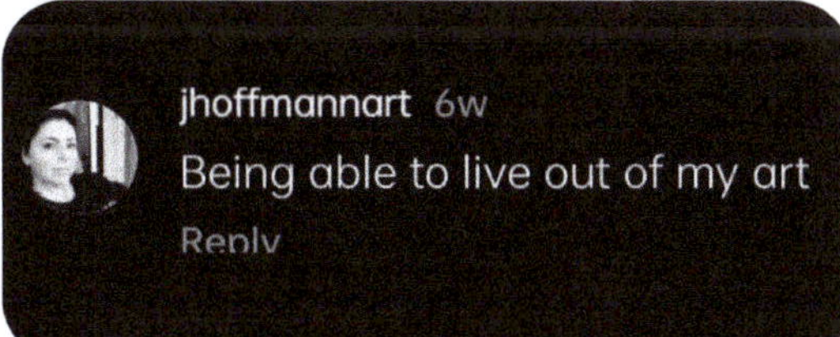

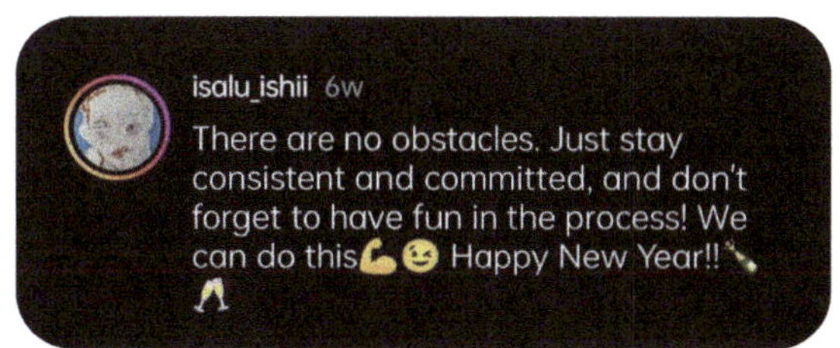

No matter where you are in your life and no matter where you want to be, to make the most out of a situation, **it is important always to remember these three points.**

1 Belief in Yourself

No matter how tricky or challenging the situation gets. Always remember to believe in yourself. Believing in yourself and your abilities is key to achieving success. Take advantage of any positive feedback or praise you receive from your peers, instructors, and mentors to help build your self-esteem.

2 Take Risks

Always remember to take risks and do what your heart desire. Because taking risks is essential if you want to stand out from the crowd as an artist. Don't be afraid of trying something new – it could pay off greatly down the line. Taking risks also shows you're not afraid of taking on challenges and pushing yourself creatively.

3 Listen to Your Voice

Every artist has a unique voice which sets them apart from others – listening to this voice will help ensure your work stands out among other artists' creations, thus increasing its value both commercially and personally. Always listen to your voice, and don't let any pressure lead you away from what feels natural. Trust your instincts when approaching projects or creating artwork - this will help keep things exciting and engaging for viewers who are looking for something special among all the images they see each day.

And no matter where you are in your journey as an artist, Arts to Hearts Project will be there every step of the way by providing resources, support networks, and professional guidance so that you can bring your exceptional works of art into reality. With this, I will take your leave and I wish you all the best in your future endeavours.

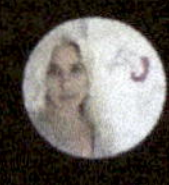
susanjamison 6w
I would like to overcome the invisibility that seems to happen to women artists over 50!

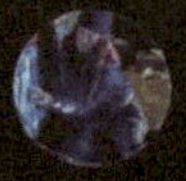
faristland 4w
Being recognized by art collectors, curators, art dealers.May they see my art and me as an asset to their world and welcome my work into their galleries. I want to make a generous living from my art practice.

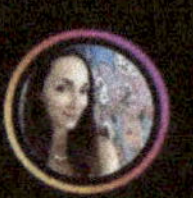
simonavojteskova_art 5w
Paint and take care of 2 kids under 4. I am due with second one in a few weeks.

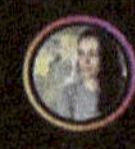
veredbrett 5w
To not have any conversations about art and gender anymore.

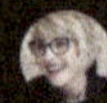
cgcollage 6w
Would love to eradicate the word female from in front of the title artist.

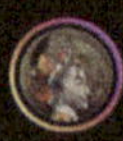
mental.paint 6w
Expanding my audience outside of Instagram 👊

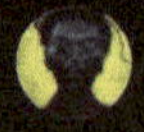
thescarvinartist 6w
Working effectively without it affecting my mental health

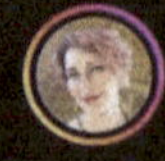
tamisatrommer 5w
Sell my art in Europe. I just moved in to italy so nobody knows me here yet.

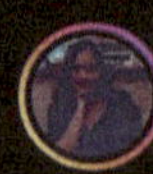
drooling.rainbowz 6w
Being recognised as a competent artist whose work is worth buying and not done just as a hobby.

Curated Artists

Learn all about the work, process, and inspiration of the curated artists from all around the world by digging into their creative careers.

Joanne Steinhardt
NEW YORK

Finnley J Kirkman
LOS ANGELES

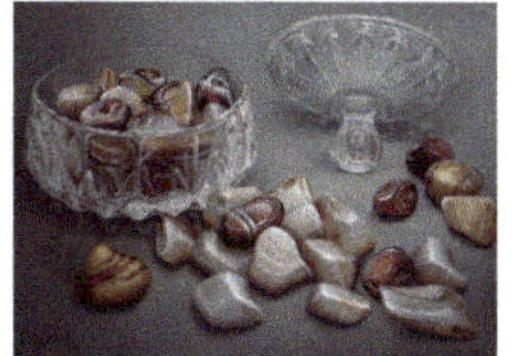

Sioban Scanlon
CALIFORNIA

Rebecca Youssef
LOS ANGELES

Lara Restelli
MIAMI

Ellen Holleman
NETHERLANDS

Erin ONeill
CHICAGO

Sarah Verardo
PROVIDENCE

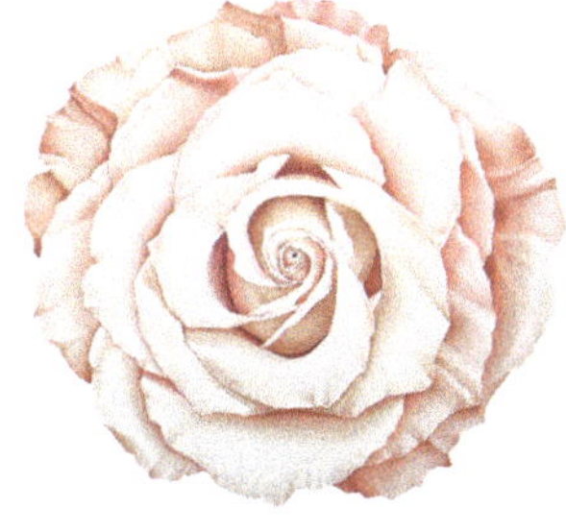

Marie-Jose Njoku-Obi
LOS ANGELES

Shuoran Zhou
BROOKLYN

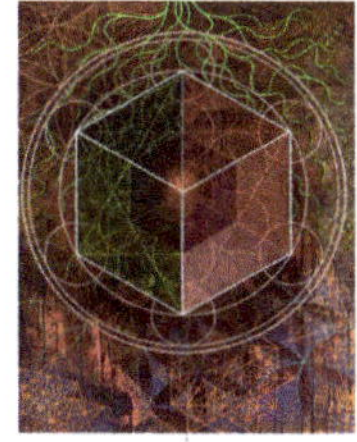

Katherine Mason
HOUSTON

Nancy Andruk Olson
LOS ANGELES

Debi Slowey-Raguso
LOS ANGELES

Kristin Reed
BROOKLYN

Lexa Walsh
OAKLAND, CA

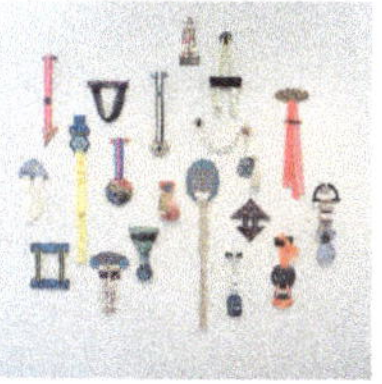

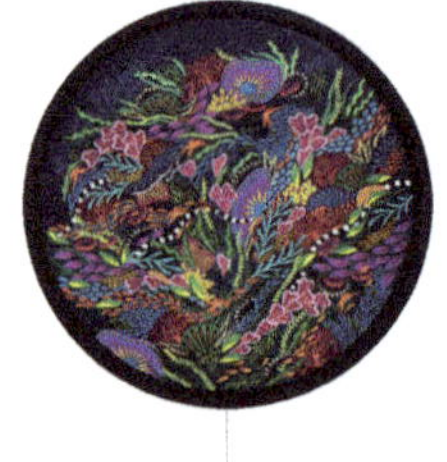

Taylor Bamgbose
INDIANAPOLIS

Lauren Lewchuk
TEXAS

Sarrah Zadeh
USA

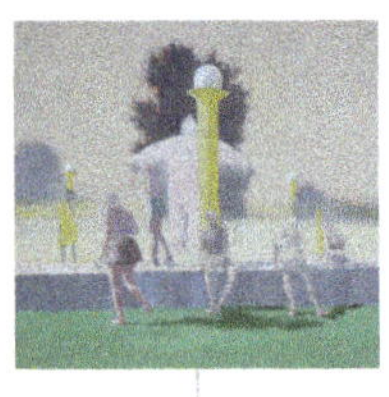

Jena Thomas
SOUTH CAROLINA

Sharon Moody
WASHINGTON

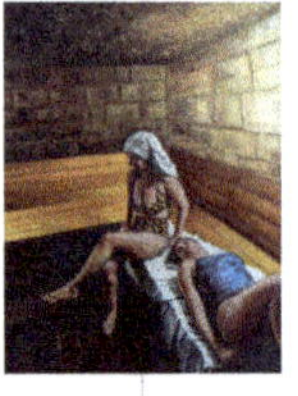

Frances Melhop
USA

Tanya Levina
NEW YORK

Ellen Burgin
SAN FRANCISCO

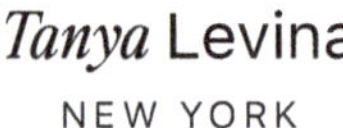

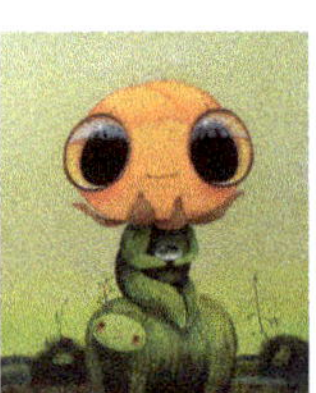

Shelly Pamensky
NORTH LONDON

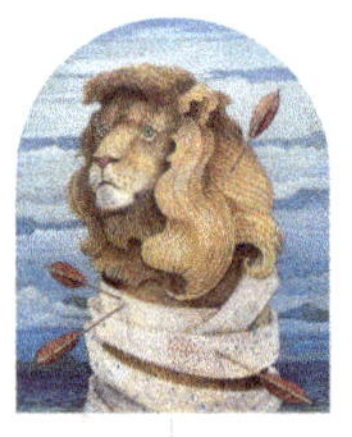

Aleksandra Paranchenko
UKRAINE

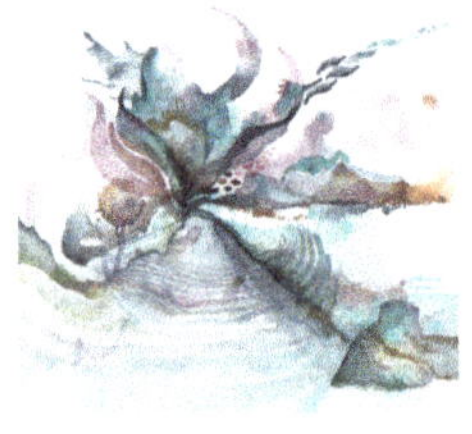

E.E. Kono
LOS ANGELES

Gale Rothstein
NEW YORK

Juliana Alonso
HOUSTON

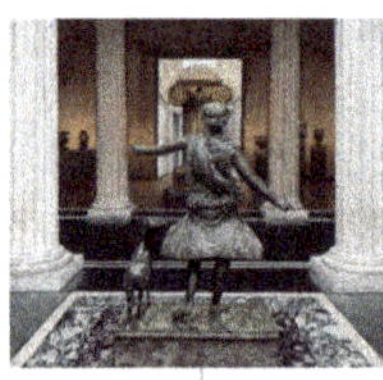

Linda Mann
WASHINGTON

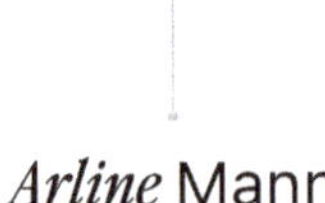

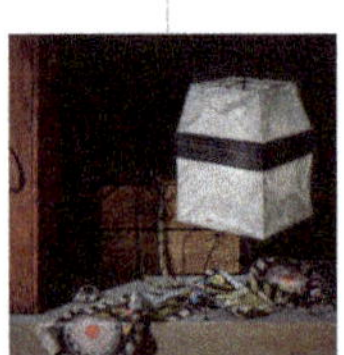

Tricia Townes
TENNESSEE

Arline Mann
TENNESSEE

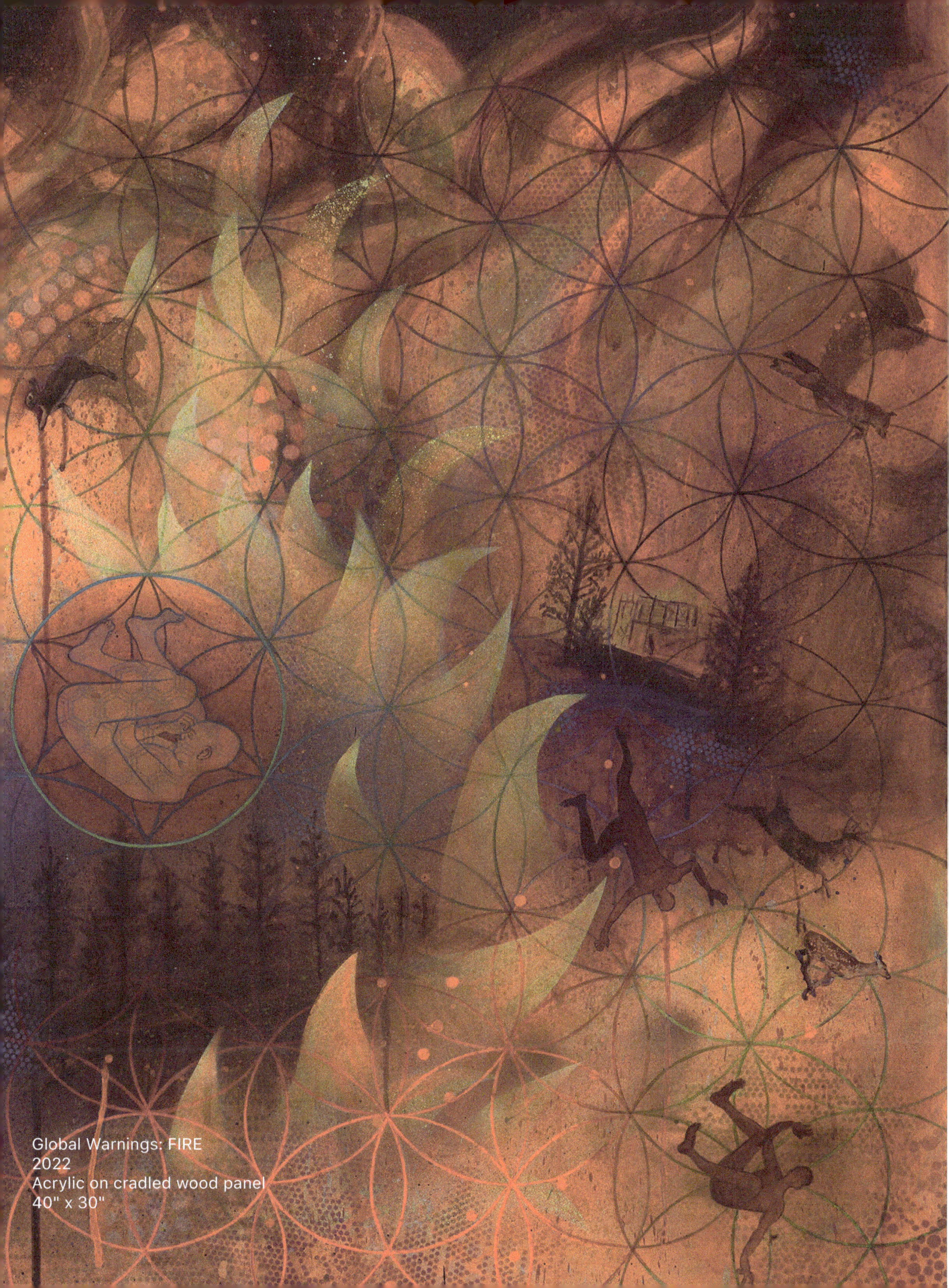
Global Warnings: FIRE
2022
Acrylic on cradled wood panel
40" x 30"

Kristin Reed

My work is an exploration of *human consciousness* and learning to see an *inner reality* within a very *large cosmic reality.*

Born in Morristown, NJ Reed has a BFA from Massachusetts College of Art in Boston and an MFA from Pratt Institute in Brooklyn. In the 1980s she participated in the community mural movement in NY, painting several large public murals in NYC and elsewhere. She has worked as a photojournalist, a graphic designer and a designer of projected images for theater. Currently she lives in Brooklyn where she has a studio residency award with chashama.org at the Brooklyn Army Terminal.

In addition to her artistic career, Reed practices and teaches hands-on energy healing work, frequently traveling to Central and South America with the humanitarian group, Healer2Healer.org. The group exchanges knowledge with indigenous Maya and Amazonian populations, training them in running acupuncture and Reiki clinics. Her work as a healer has greatly effected her work as a painter.

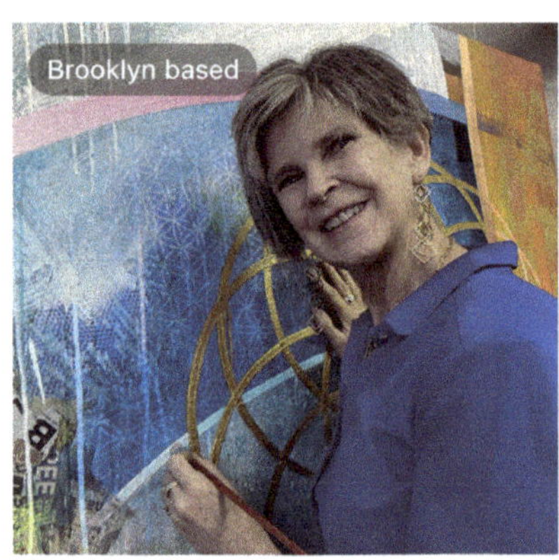

http://www.kristinreed.com
@ kristinreed@mac.com
@luminousgeometry

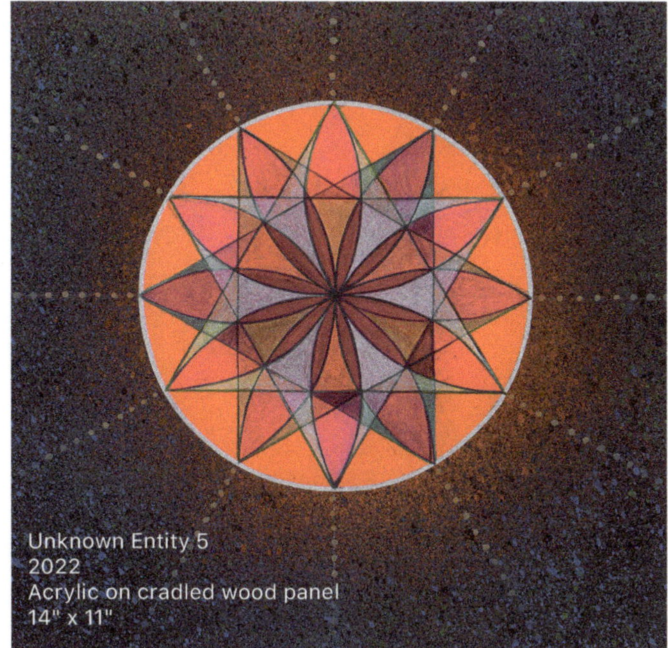

Unknown Entity 5
2022
Acrylic on cradled wood panel
14" x 11"

My work is an exploration of human consciousness and learning to see an inner reality within a very large cosmic reality. What is the structure of this inner/outer space and time? I am becoming much more aware of the cosmos, our planet, and our connection to and reflection in both.

I look back to the most ancient human geometrical symbols and find that quantum physics is now rediscovering this very geometry as the 2-D representation of how space/time is constructed. I like to contrast the chaos and balance in our lives. The chaos is represented by expressionistic marks, drips, color/light, random patterns, and found-objects. The symmetry and order of sacred symbols found in Earth's most ancient civilizations represent perfection, unity, wholeness and infinity.

In this current series I am telling a story of how humans and all sentient beings on our planet are falling out of alignment with the natural elements of earth, air, water, fire and ether. This is a series of environmental warnings based on the 5 Platonic Solids and their corresponding elements: Earth (Hexahedron), Air (Octahedron), Fire (Tetrahedron), Water Icosahedron) and Ether (Dodecahedron). For thousands of years it was believed that these 5 geometric regular polygons were the building blocks that everything on earth and in the universe were made of. They were named for Plato who hypothesized that these classical elements were what everything in the universe was made of. To live in harmony on earth is to live in balance with what these polygons represent.

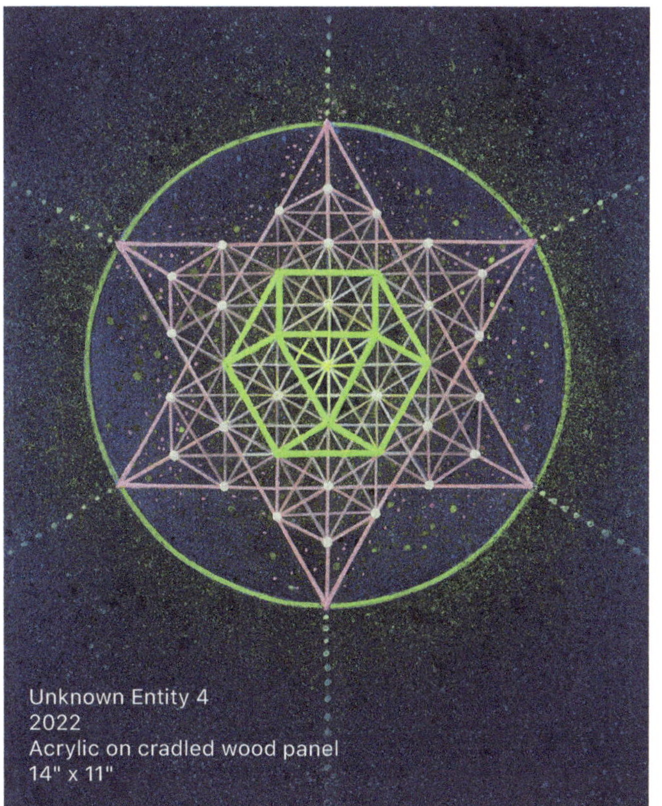

Unknown Entity 4
2022
Acrylic on cradled wood panel
14" x 11"

What drives you to be an artist?
Art helps me keep my sanity and enables me to explore the things that interest me.

How would you describe the art that you create and what inspires you?
I've become very interested in our earthly connections to the universe and the math that makes us human. I'm interested in doing that through the sacred geometry of circles which to me represent cycles of human consciousness—birth, life, death and infinity.

If you could overcome all of your fears, what would you do with your art?
I would probably show my work more if I overcame all fear.

When it comes to art making, how important is experimenting vs. sticking to a routine or set of rules?
I both like to experiment and stick with certain rules that provide cohesion.

What are some of the challenges or experiences that have shaped your artistic journey so far?
The biggest challenge was finding the right place to work which took many years and some serious visualization.

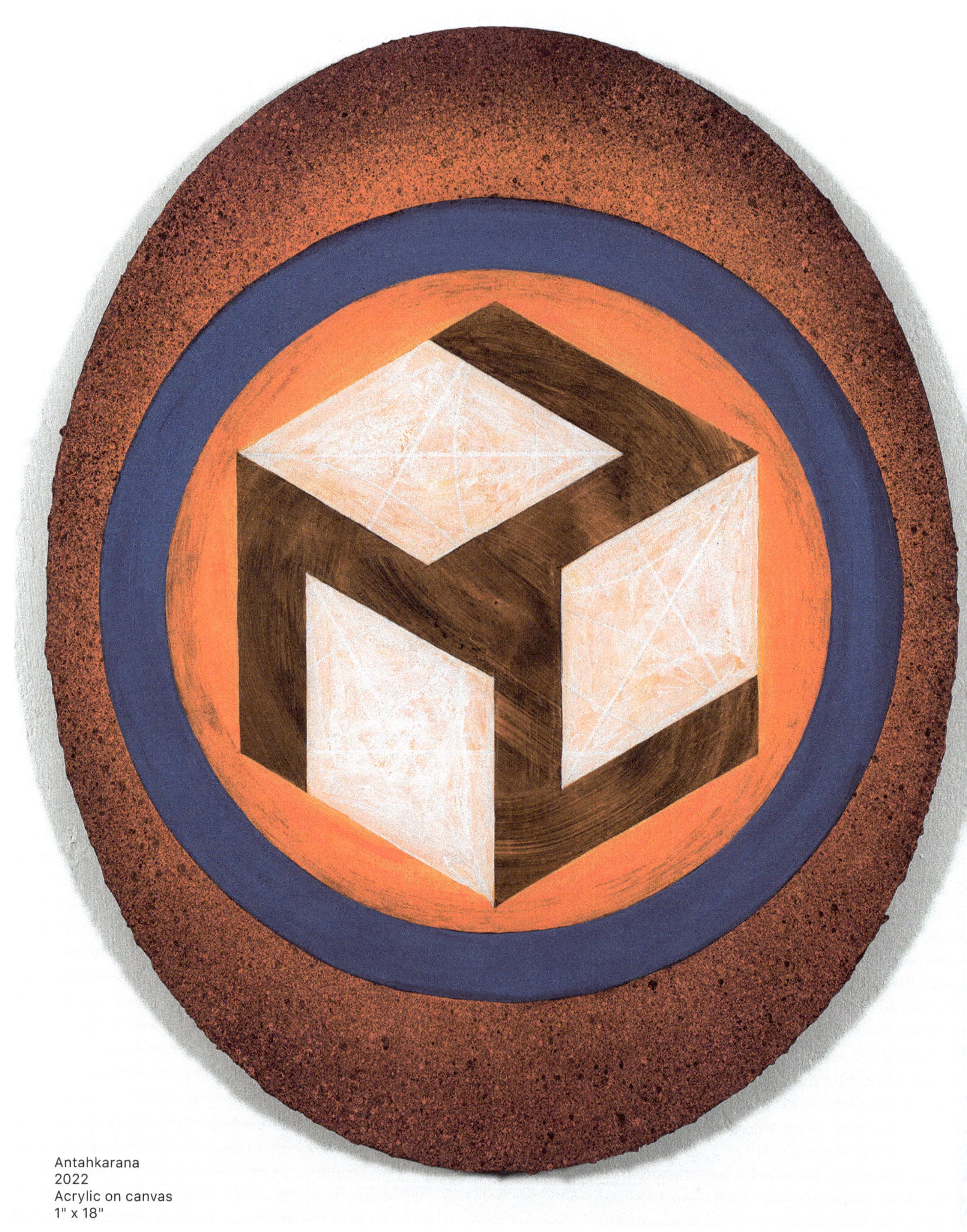

Antahkarana
2022
Acrylic on canvas
1" x 18"

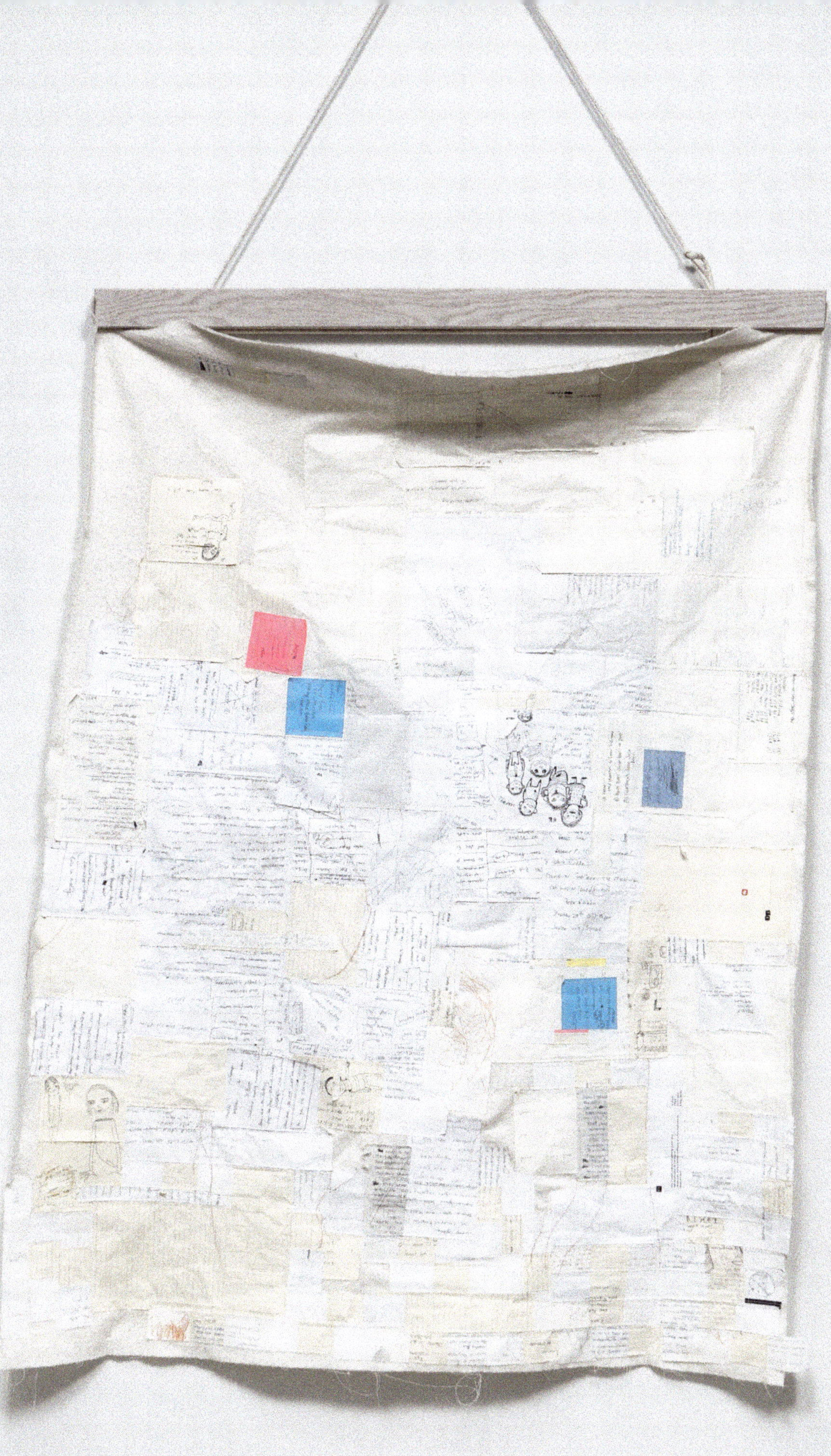

CRAZY
2020
Paper, pen, ink, crayon, cotton batting, thread
46inches x 40inches

Finnley J. Kirkman

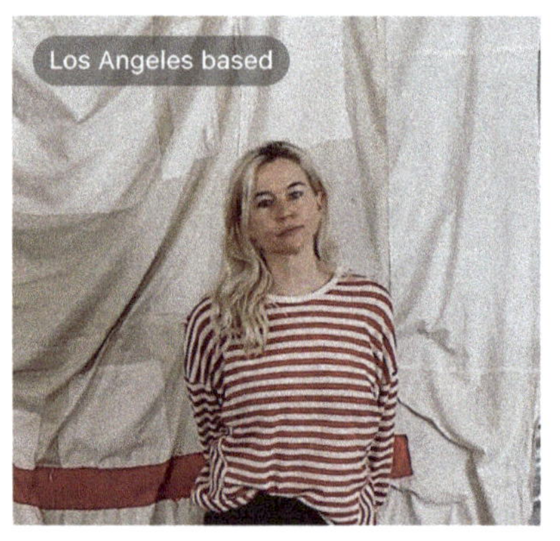

https://finnleyjkirkman.com
@ yknotstudiola@gmail.com
@finnjk

My Practice Incorporates *Photography, Textiles, Painting, And Sculpture.*

I am currently exploring relationships and the power differentials inherent in them. The dynamic tension between the empowered and disempowered – this undergirds my work across media. My most recent show explores the labor imposed on women that often goes unnoticed. The work is informed by the way women have historically taken on service roles and have not received equal pay or treatment in the labor force. I use anecdotes from my ledger as an entry point for viewers to reflect on dynamics of power, control, and relationship structures. I am a Los Angeles-based multidisciplinary artist. I received my B.A. in Education with a Minor in Photography from Washington State University, Pullman, WA and studied Contemporary Theatre for Performing Arts at the Lost Studio, Los Angeles, CA. My last solo exhibition was in DTLA arts district, I have also been featured in various group exhibitions, all in Los Angeles, CA.

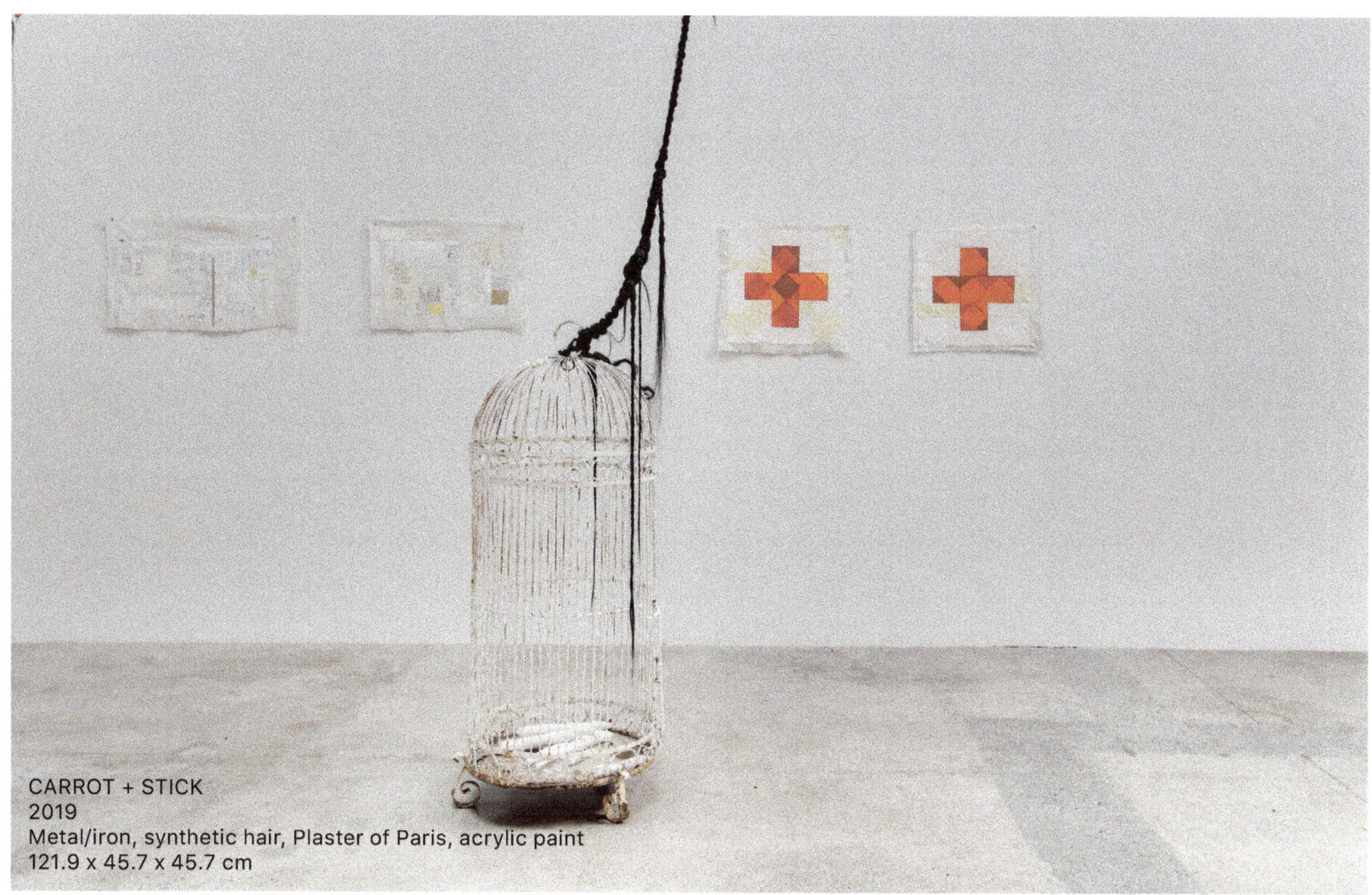

CARROT + STICK
2019
Metal/iron, synthetic hair, Plaster of Paris, acrylic paint
121.9 x 45.7 x 45.7 cm

What drives you to be an artist?

Life...drives me to be an artist.
I process, connect, and ground myself through my work.

How would you describe the art that you create and what inspires you?

The art I'm currently creating is an exploration of thought, that is expressed through the work.
It's the persistent 'why' moments I find myself working through as an artist. The ones that don't leave me alone. I'm not necessarily in search of an answer, but a deeper understanding of the moment leading to the question. In this process I find the work that I want to create.

If you could overcome all of your fears, what would you do with your art?

"My last show "Living, Assisted" was in many ways about overcoming some of those fears that held me hostage. I was scared sh*tless about showing this body of work. This fear came from a place of being vulnerable. Open. Fear will always be present, so it's about leaning into that discomfort. If I can make work that consistently rest in this space, I'll be pushing my comfort zone as artist.That's what I wish for, growth through that fear."

When it comes to art making, how important is experimenting vs. sticking to a routine or set of rules?

I think it's sticking to a routine that allows me the freedom to experiment. With a consistant studio routine I know I can count on myself to show up every day. That gives me the opportunity to not only fail but the opportunity to try again until I get it right. If I know there's tomorrow, I can be present in today...

What are some of the challenges or experiences that have shaped your artistic journey so far?

"Past and continuous challenges: Doubt. Fear. Money. Space. Time. Support. To name a few.
A recent experience that has shaped my journey as an artist, sprouts from a place of of mis-alignment with myself that affected my metal and physical health. Getting to such a low place took away some of the power these 'challenges' had over me. What mattered most in this moment was making the work. That's when I noticed a different and was able to really committed to my practice. There was no longer a plan B, only a plan A. Making that commitment to myself, showing up for myself, made it much easier to become aligned with my priorities again as an artist.

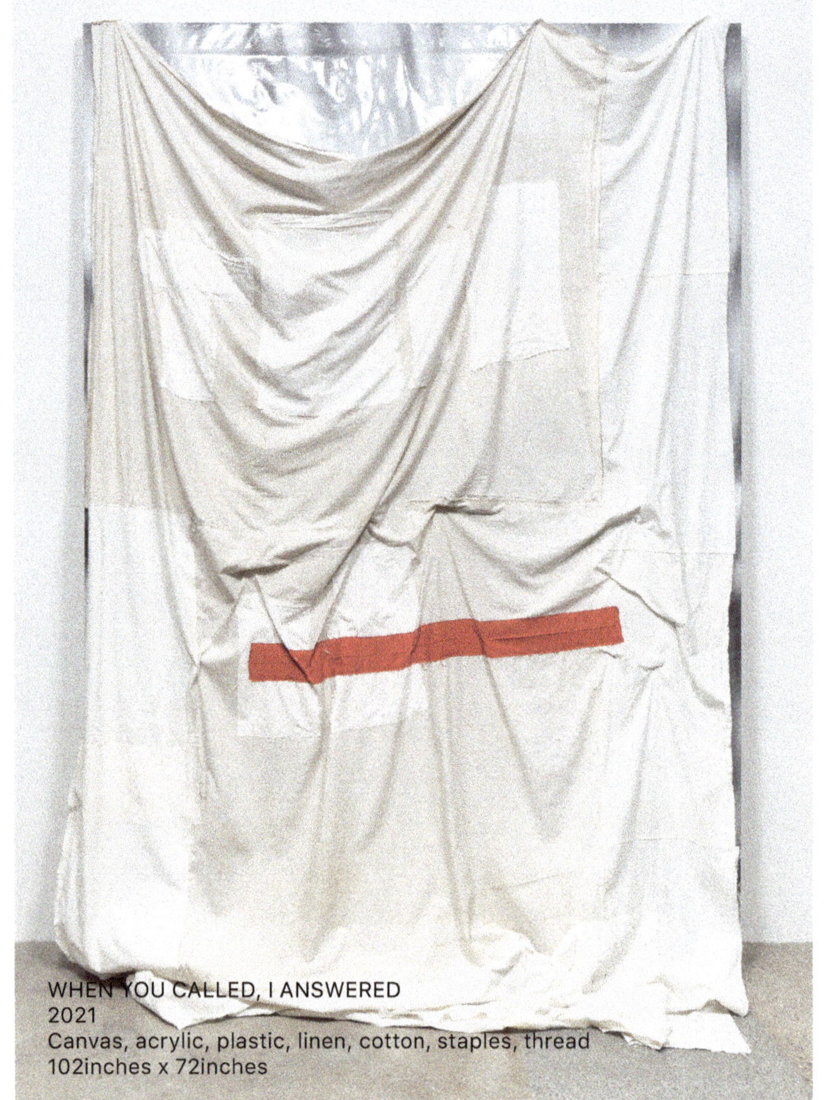

WHEN YOU CALLED, I ANSWERED
2021
Canvas, acrylic, plastic, linen, cotton, staples, thread
102inches x 72inches

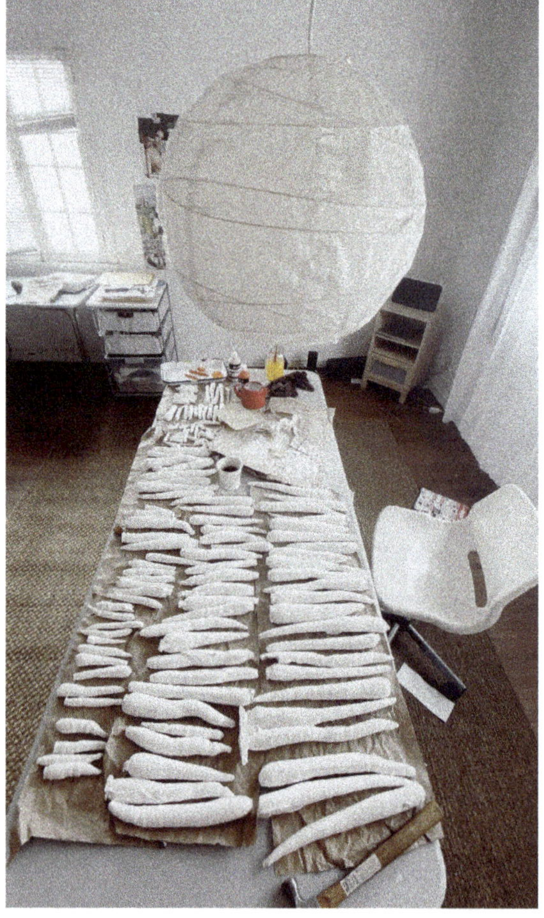

*"It's the persistent 'why' moments
I find myself working through
as an artist. The ones that don't
leave me alone."*

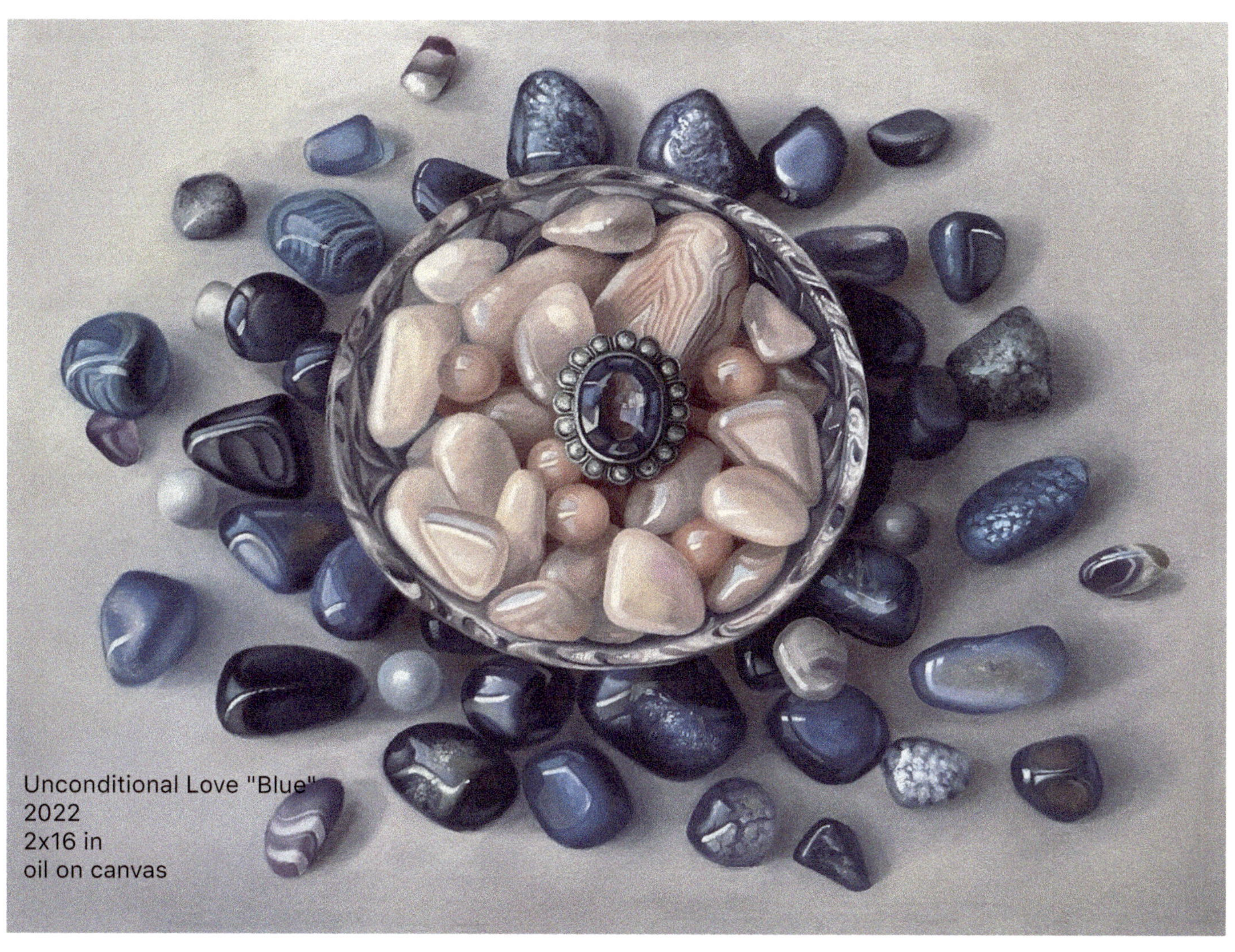

Unconditional Love "Blue"
2022
2x16 in
oil on canvas

Lara Restelli

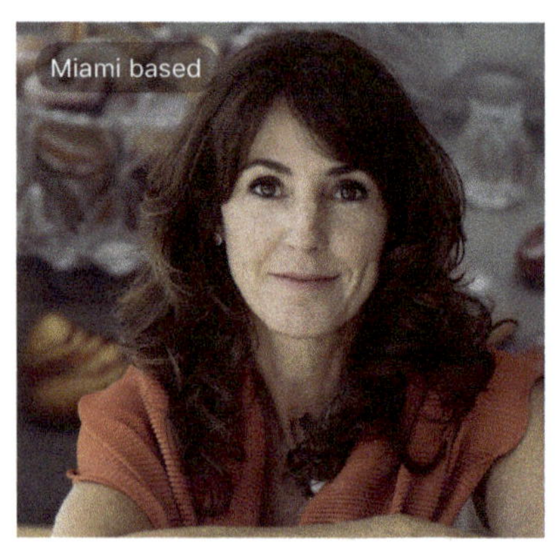

✶ https://www.lararestelli.com
@ artstudio@lararestelli.com
◎ *@lararestelliart*

Nature is my *inspiration*. *Rocks* and *crystals* are my passion.

Lara Restelli discovered the world of stones, gems, and minerals by chance five years ago. Her fascination and admiration for these nature's beauties carried her on a long journey of exploration and discovery. Their exuberant colors and vibrant energy captivated her and drove her to make them the primary subject of her work. After her mother's passing Restelli incorporated heirloom jewelry and objects as a way of honoring their connection beyond their fiscal world. Naturally, color, form, and composition became the pillars of her artistic expression. She paints larger-than-life, realistic paintings of rocks, gems, and crystals that are full of color. Restelli's oil paintings convey a great sense of joy, balance, and serenity, yet they are strong and powerful.

Restelli's mastership in the use of her media, together with a skillful technique, make her art stand out and impress. Her powerful management of feelings, color, and composition results in a final contemporary masterpiece that delights and profoundly connects with the viewer. Lara Restelli is a Miami-based artist who has successfully exhibited in many well-established art shows, including a solo show at MIFA Gallery, Superfine Art Fair, Red Dot Miami Art Basel Week, Art Palm Beach, ArtsParks Miami, and Loyola School of the Arts Miami, among others. Restelli's artwork has also found its way into the homes of many Miami-based private collectors and numerous prestigious condominiums in Miami, FL, like Aria on the Bay, Melody, Square Station, Flagler on the River, and Skyview.

Lara Restelli's art education consists of many years of atelier training within the classical European school of realism.

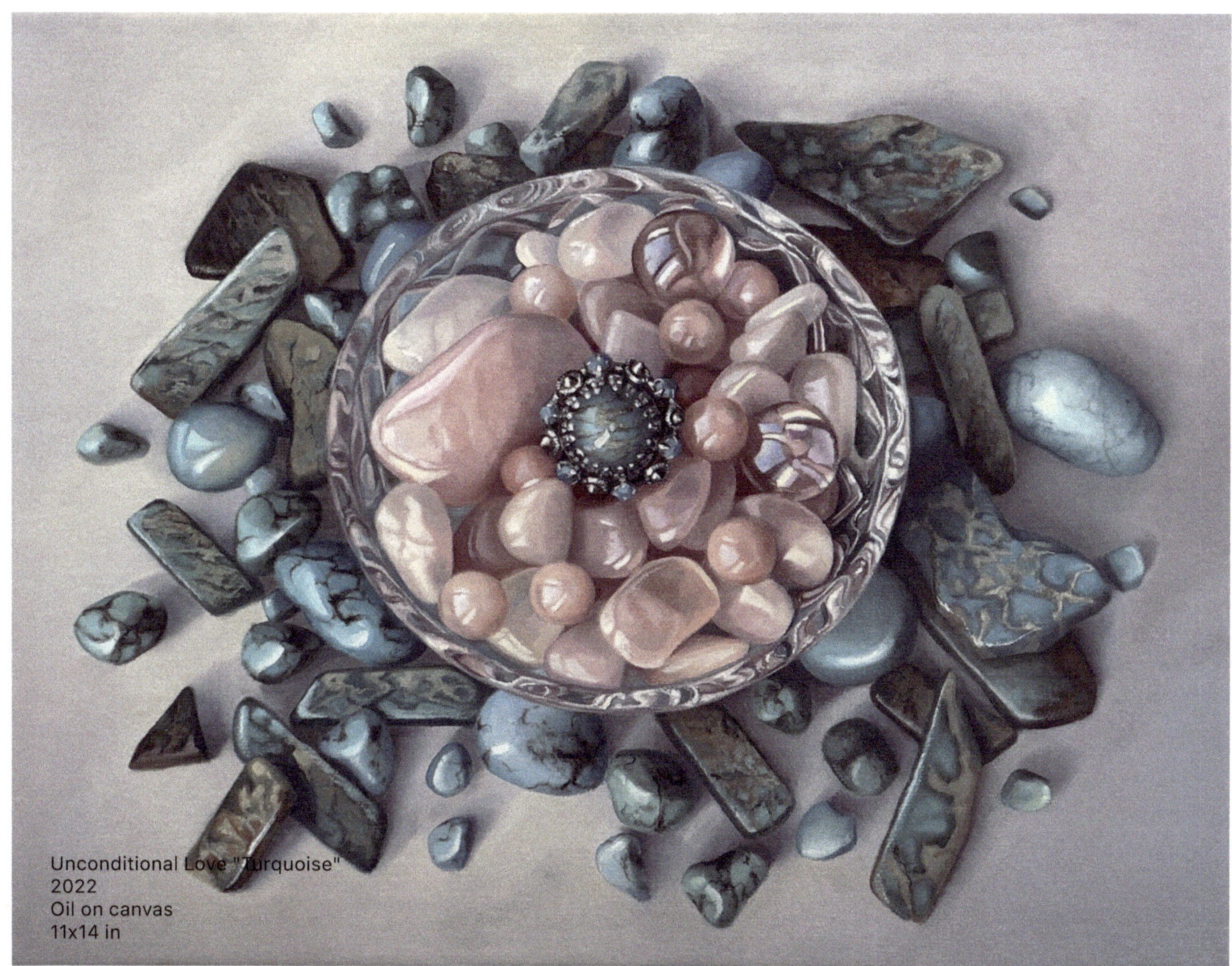

Unconditional Love "Turquoise"
2022
Oil on canvas
11x14 in

What drives you to be an artist?

Creativity! There is a creative energy that needs to come out somehow. The satisfaction of seeing a finished piece of art going to a new home is really fulfilling for an artist.

How would you describe the art that you create and what inspires you?

Nature is my inspiration. Rocks and crystals are my passion. they found a way into my life and taught me about simplicity and beauty. Since then, I've been fascinated by them, learning and admiring their power and properties so much that I turned them into my primary subject matter. I chose to use color, form, and composition as the foundation of my work.
So, now I paint larger-than-life, realistic paintings of rocks, gems, and crystals that are full of color.

I use oil paint as my medium since it is the perfect conduit to achieve my detail-oriented paintings. The sole purpose of my work is to convey the serenity and joy I feel when I paint them.

If you could overcome all of your fears, what would you do with your art?

As an Artist I need to overcome my fears every day in order to share my soul with the world.

When it comes to art making, how important is experimenting vs. sticking to a routine or set of rules?

Experimenting is always part of the creative process. However, to produce high quality classic oil paintings I need to stick to a process that has very specific sets of rules.

What are some of the challenges or experiences that have shaped your artistic journey so far?

Putting together a solo exhibition has been the biggest challenge of my career. There are so many things that need to be accomplish that it can be overwhelming. However, it has been the most satisfactory experience I have ever had.

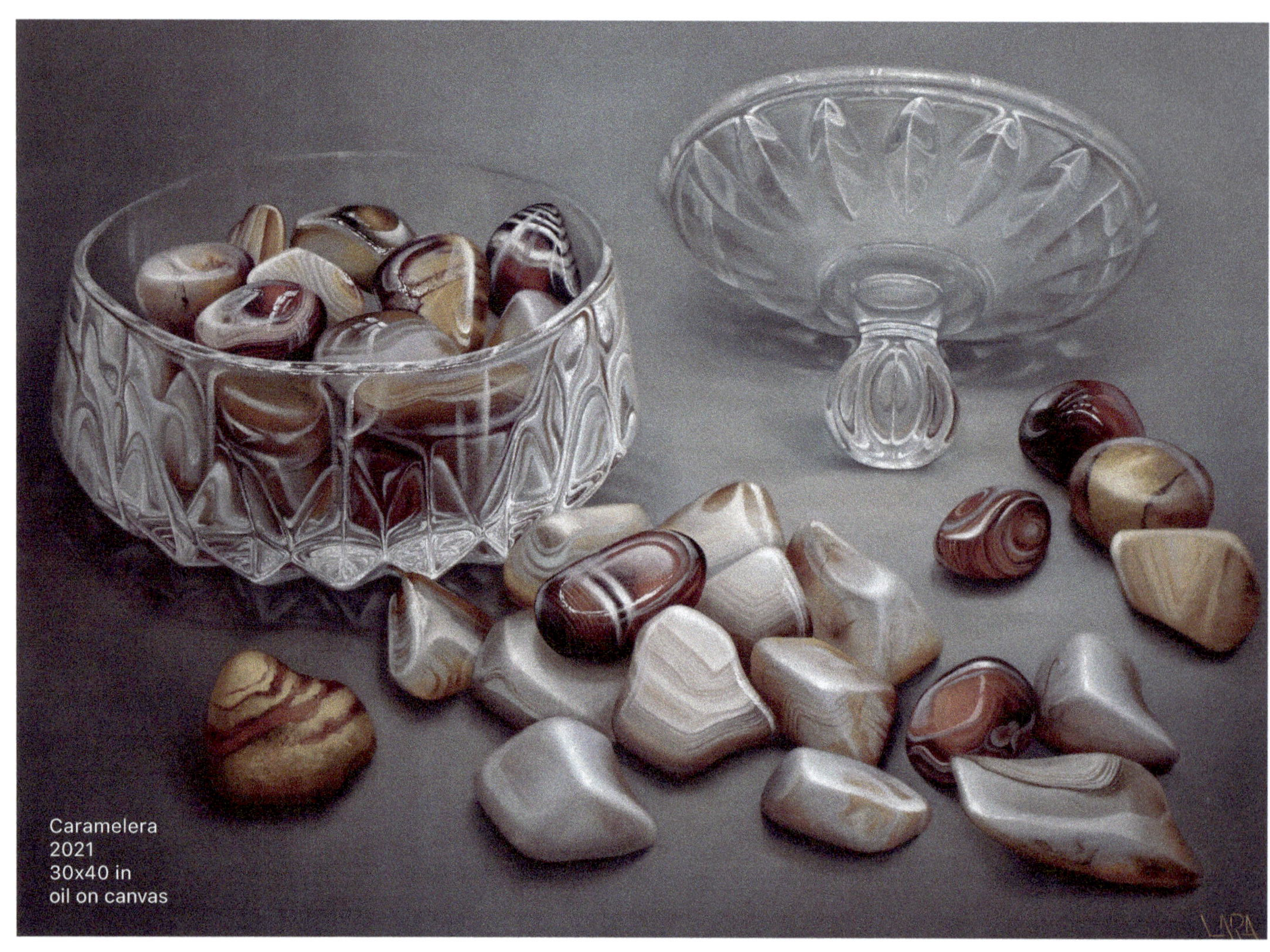

Caramelera
2021
30x40 in
oil on canvas

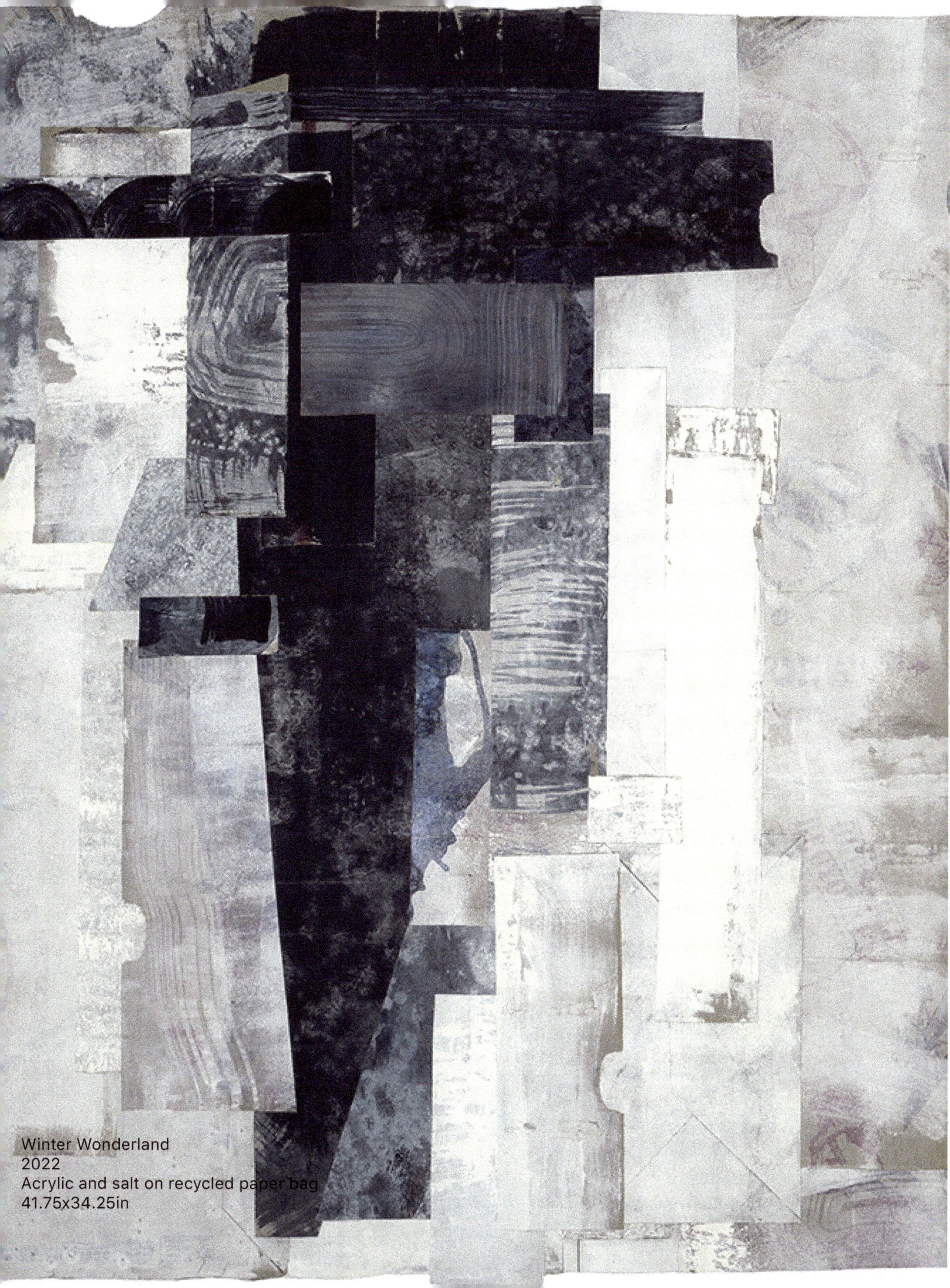

Winter Wonderland
2022
Acrylic and salt on recycled paper bag
41.75x34.25in

Rebecca Youssef

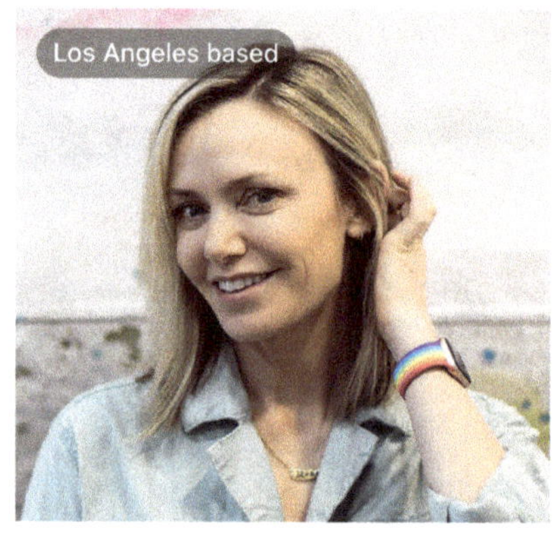

🔗 https://www.rebeccayoussefcom/
@ rebecca@rebeccayoussef.com
⊙ @ rebecca.youssef_ studio

I am *inspired by wild, untouched lands* and carry a deep respect for *hand-crafted art.*

Rebecca Youssef is a Los Angeles-based mixed media artist who was raised on the north shore of O'ahu, Hawaii. Galvanized by the sustainability movement to protect our planet, her work gives new life to discarded paper, boxes and bags by immortalizing them in art, thus honoring their journey from tree to canvas. Rebecca employs a broad range of sustainable practices and natural materials inspired by her love of cultivating native trees.

Rebecca received her BFA from the University of Arizona in Tucson and then moved to Los Angeles to pursue her MA in Art Education at Loyola Marymount University. Following graduate school, Rebecca taught art at various schools across Los Angeles. Currently, she is an artist-in-residence at the 18th Street Arts Center in Santa Monica, California.

For as long as I can remember, I've had my hands in either dirt or paint. My love of process and undervalued materials and the cultivation of trees from seed is what has sustained and given purpose to my work. I am inspired by wild, untouched lands and carry a deep respect for hand-crafted art. Galvanized by the sustainability movement to protect our planet, my work finds a home in the space where art and environmentalism collide.

Whether it's painting on paper I made by hand or on recycled grocery bags, I tell a story through purposeful materials to stimulate reflection on our reciprocity with nature. My use of homemade inks and papers stand in contrast to the commercially made paints and adhesives I use and symbolize our fractured relationship with the natural world.

As a cultivator of California native oak trees, I was conflicted by my love of working with paper. Repurposing and upcycling items destined for the recycle bin and/or landfill has become the cornerstone of my work. It is my fundamental belief that beautiful things can be made by working with the planet, not taking from it. Through my commitment to an environmental and creative consciousness, I am guided towards a more sustainable art practice. When I'm not in the studio, my boots are dusty and my hands are deep in soil working to restore native trees in Los Angeles's urban landscape.

What drives you to be an artist?
Exploring natural processes, elevating salvaged materials from their humble status in an effort towards sustainability is what drives my practice.

How would you describe the art that you create and what inspires you?
For as long as I can remember, I've had my hands in either dirt or paint. My love of process and undervalued materials and the cultivation of trees from seed is what has sustained and given purpose to my work.
I am inspired by wild, untouched lands and carry a deep respect for hand-crafted art. Galvanized by the sustainability movement to protect our planet, my work finds a home in the space where art and environmentalism collide. Whether it's painting on paper I made by hand, recycled cardboard or on grocery bags, I tell a story through purposeful materials to stimulate reflection on our reciprocity with nature.

"The unpredictable nature of exploring new processes is what keeps propelling the work forward."

If you could overcome all of your fears, what would you do with your art?
If I were more fearless, I'd be pursuing galleries more. Even though I'm really proud of the work I create, I don't assume it is for everyone. That lack of confidence about what others think holds me back.

When it comes to art making, how important is experimenting vs. sticking to a routine or set of rules?
Experimentation is a vital part of my practice. The unpredictable nature of exploring new processes is what keeps propelling the work forward. I love the element of surprise experimenting brings. I've discovered many new techniques purely by accident because of this.

What are some of the challenges or experiences that have shaped your artistic journey so far?
The business side of being an artist is challenging for me. Not only are we artists creating the work, but we're also tasked with marketing and selling it, which usually is not in our DNA. However, the art market has evolved and it's now common for artists to sell direct to collector and not go through the traditional channels. There is a certain freedom that comes with being in control of how your work is getting scene.

Agrifolia
2022
acrylic, cyanotype and salt on recycled paper bag
41.25"x40.25"

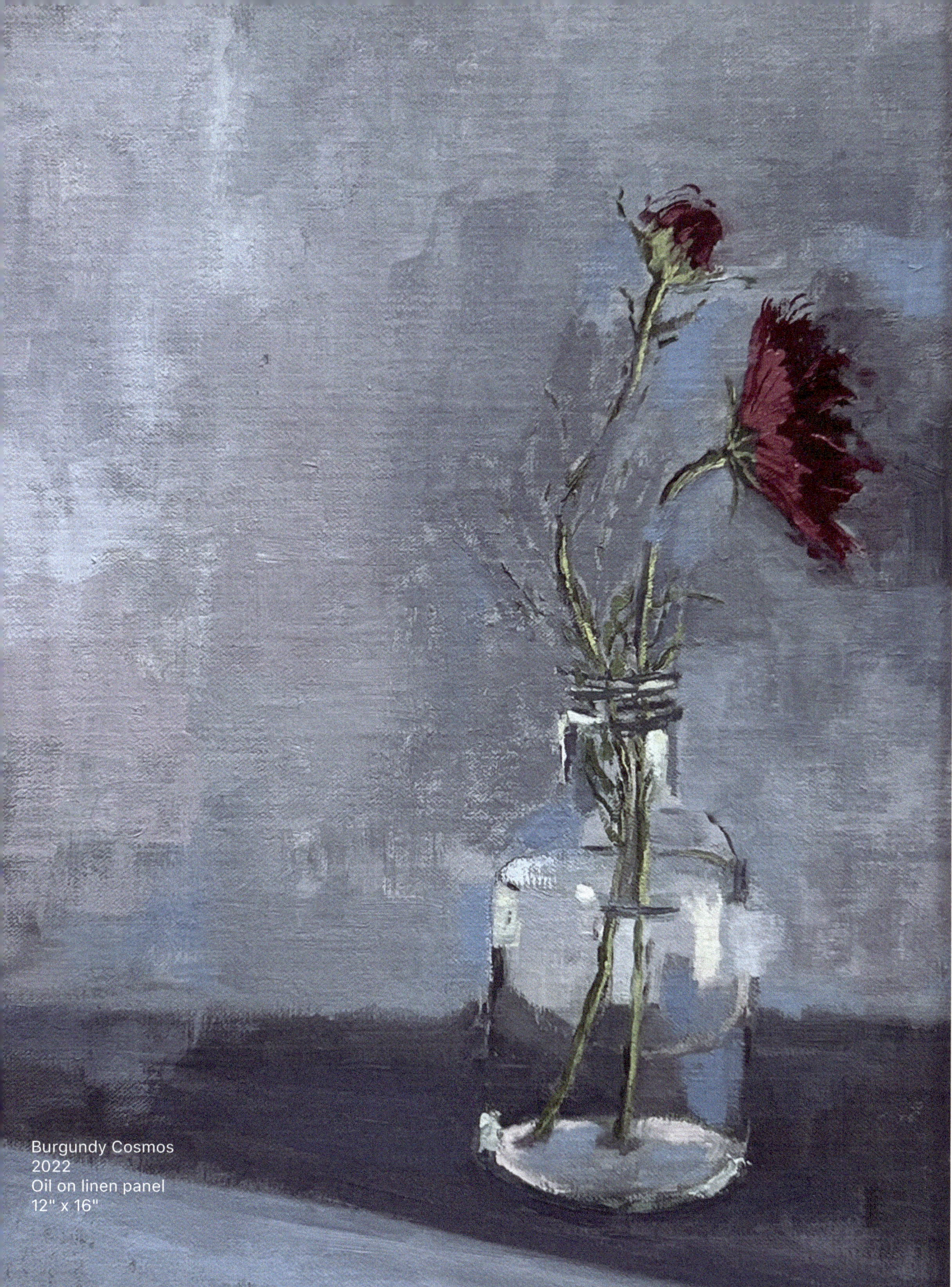
Burgundy Cosmos
2022
Oil on linen panel
12" x 16"

Sioban Scanlon

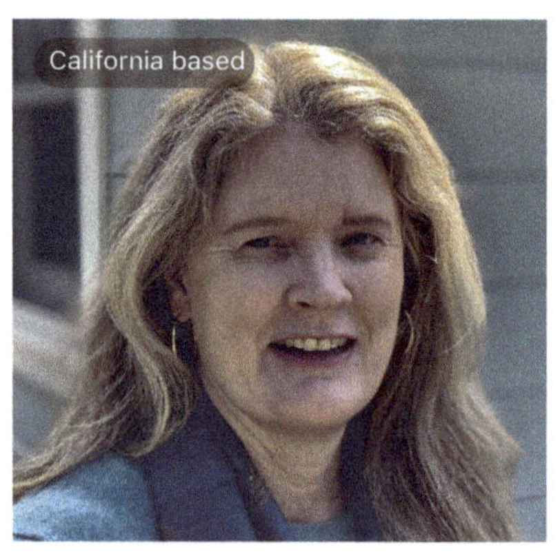

⬈ https://smscanlon.com
@ kristinreed@mac.com
🖸 @siobanscanlon@gmail.com

The *unruly elegance* of *nature* is a deep source of inspiration for her paintings.

Scanlon explores the theme of intimacy in still life, landscape and abstract painting. Her journey into the world of painting and drawing began in a village outside of Aix-en-Provence. Studying painting and drawing at L'Universite Americain d'Aix-en-Provence, she learned to paint in the fields and country lanes of Le Tholonet. This quiet introduction into how to see and how to enter the world of representation and abstraction has informed her work ever since. The unruly elegance of nature is a deep source of inspiration for her paintings. Observation of how an object resides in the surrounding atmosphere is at the heart of her painting practice. Scanlon's ongoing intention is to bring the elegance and visceral beauty of nature into her paintings and to bring joy and peace into the lives of her collectors.
For the past several years, Scanlon has studied painting with several contemporary painters including Carol Lefkowitz, Kathleen Dunphy and Dean Fisher. Her work was accepted into the 2022 National Oil and Acrylic Painters Society Associate Member Exhibition.

Her work was accepted into the 2022 National Oil and Acrylic Painters Society Associate Member Exhibition. In addition, her work was included in a group exhibit for the 2022 Marin Open Studios at The Bay Model in Sausalito, California. Scanlon's work is represented in private collections across the United States.

What drives you to be an artist?

Attempting to mimic and transform the beauty that I see around me each day is strangely intoxicating. The moment of placing brush to canvas feels like stepping into a magical realm where anything is possible. I guess I would say that painting is like taking a chance at running into mystery, magic and joy all at once, every day. Painting just makes me feel more alive and I feel driven to share that aliveness with my viewers.

How would you describe the art that you create and what inspires you?

I'm inspired by the vibrant beauty of nature as well as the quiet resonance of simple objects. I paint still life and landscape paintings in the hopes of sharing that feeling of wonder of the world around me with my viewers. I feel that everything matters. My work is the antithesis to our "whatever" culture. When we feel the wind on our face or when we see the beautiful morning light shine through a green leaf, the feeling of awe and and wonder in that moment matters. That's what my work is about.

If you could overcome all of your fears, what would you do with your art?

If I could overcome all of my fears, I would approach Rizzoli to publish a beautiful volume of my paintings and that book of paintings would accompany the physical paintings at a show in a beautiful gallery in New York City.

"I'm inspired by the vibrant beauty of nature as well as the quiet resonance of simple objects."

When it comes to art making, how important is experimenting vs. sticking to a routine or set of rules?

I think it is important for artists to learn the rules of mark making, composition, values, color and form in order to find their path toward breaking these rules. To me, real vibrancy in a painting occurs when the artist's skill allows her to break out of the rules into more freeform expression of subject. When I look at Antonio Lopez-Garcia's paintings, I see a man who is obsessed with seeing, not with rules. Placing three colors next to each other and having them represent an apple is an act of seeing and ingenuity riding on the backs of all the rules. It boggles the mind to witness great art.

What are some of the challenges or experiences that have shaped your artistic journey so far?

I was deeply influenced by working with Carol Lefkowitz for two years studying watercolor. She not only taught me how to step into the studio with a reverence for the moment, the materials and the subject in front of me, but she also showed me how to let pigment do the talking. It is a challenge to understand that you need to take a back seat at times and allow the painting to emerge. If you want to produce something beautiful, you might have to paint it 30 times, with an open heart. Now that is a challenge, but it is also the journey in front of you. Those lessons are like songs playing in my studio today. I feel very lucky to have the voices of a few amazing artists in my mind when I paint. I also feel blessed when they step out of the room and I'm left with my work alone, allowing the magic of painting to quietly arrive.

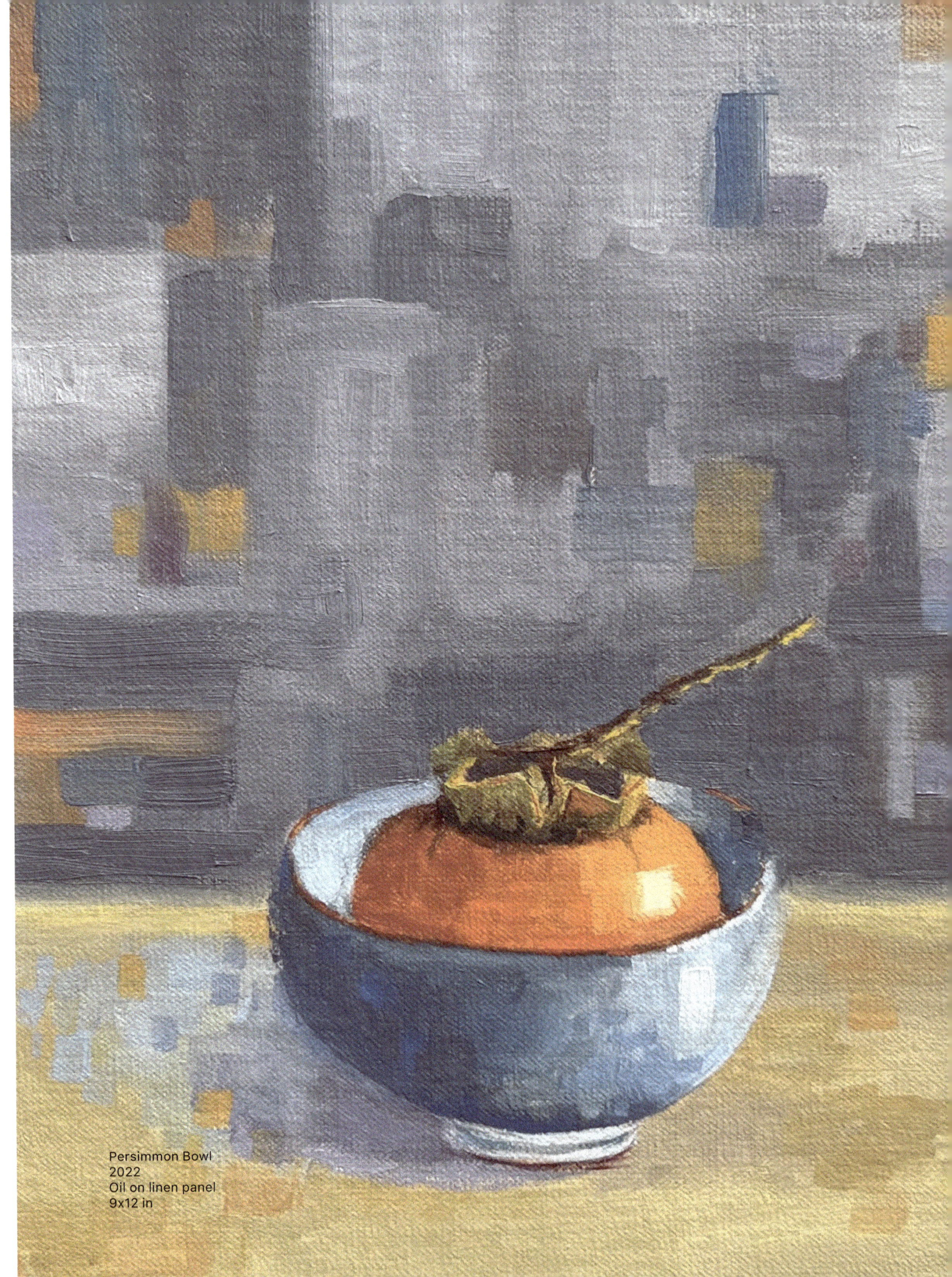

Persimmon Bowl
2022
Oil on linen panel
9x12 in

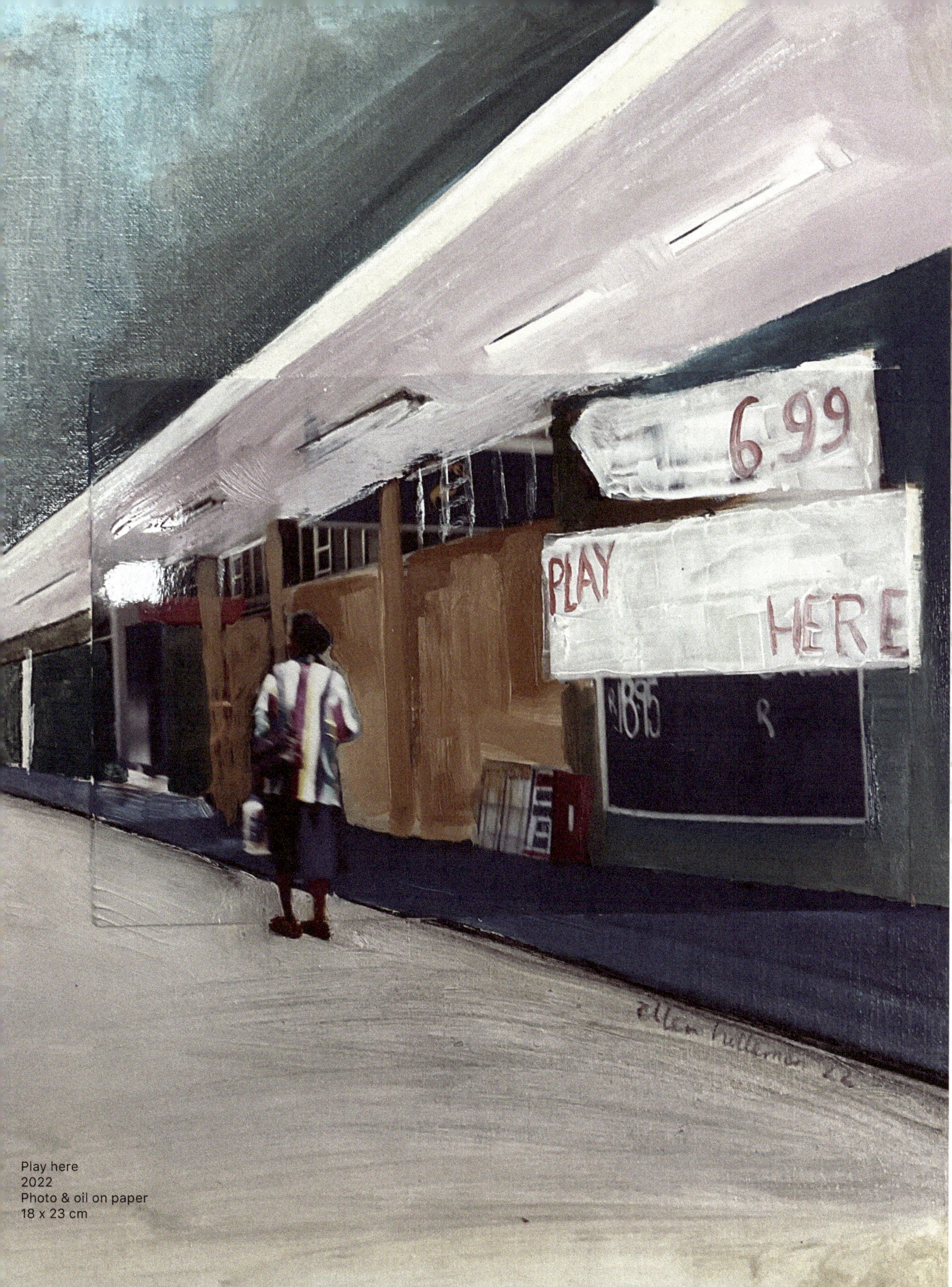

Play here
2022
Photo & oil on paper
18 x 23 cm

Ellen Holleman

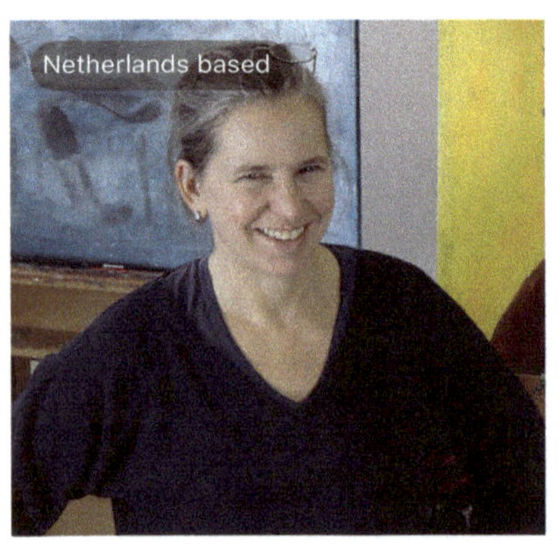

⌂ https://www.ellenholleman.nl
@ info@ellenholleman.nl
◎ *ellen_holleman*

I see the world through a *'paint filter'*, always wondering how to *translate the world* I see around me onto canvas.

Ellen Holleman is a painter, mixed-media visual artist and spatial designer based in the Netherlands. She trained as a spatial designer at the Utrecht School of the Arts (the Netherlands). Ellen prefers working with oil paints and traditional painting techniques, but also enjoys experimenting and using contemporary techniques, like digital collage and photography, as part of her creative process. The themes in her art are strongly affected by her work and experience as an urban design professional.

In 2013, she was invited as an artist in residence at 'tHuisbasis' in Poelenburg, Zaanstad, in collaboration with Sarah Spanton, a UK-based artist. From 2014 through 2017 she was the creative director of IFIKZ, a cultural festival in Zaanstad, where she built an installation on a barge that travelled on the river Zaan as part of the festival's first edition. It moored at sites along the river for a series of storytelling events.

In 2020, after an intense artist retreat, she decided to focus on restarting a professional painting practice, shifting her career from the urban design field towards the arts. The following year, one of her new works was selected for a group show in the St. Maartens basilica, Zaltbommel, and she had her first solo exhibition at the cultural centre De Poorterij in September. In 2022, five paintings were exhibited in an augmented reality pavilion with ArtInside Gallery and she had an online solo show running from April through May. Additionally, three of her artworks were published in issue #5 of The Huts Magazine. This September, her second solo show opened at cultural centre De Poorterij and two of her paintings were featured in Life as a poem, by Cista Art Gallery, London.

In October '22 she participated in the 5th edition of International Artes Exhibition in Turin, Italy, where she was awarded third prize in the figurative paintings section.

Painting, to me, is like magic. To visualize and recreate scenes using only shades and colours never ceases to amaze me. I see the world through a 'paint filter', always wondering how to translate the world I see around me onto canvas. Using oil painting techniques of the old Dutch Masters I build my images with many layers of transparent colours. A ground of pure white gesso reflects the light, which creates the illusion of depth and a rich and intense sensation of colour.

The subjects of my paintings are usually scenes from ordinary, daily life. With an eye for quotidian, urban scenes, I am always collecting images from the places I visit, the journeys I make. With my full attention, I recreate those scenes into artworks that spark a quiet energy or emotion that we can all relate to. Wanting to capture just that one person at that one place in that one specific moment in time. One recurring theme in my work is the contrast of human life in desolate urban landscapes. It reflects my views on the mutual influence of urban spaces on people and vice versa, showing how humans relate to the spaces that surround them. Or, how impossible it can be to relate to those spaces at all – thus addressing and questioning the way we build our cities and societies and the existential solitude that most of us experience at some point in our lives. They also show the intimacy that some are able to create anywhere. To me, it seems that some people have the resilience to feel comfortable with themselves anywhere, regardless of the circumstances, whereas others seem completely lost, lacking the ability to connect. As an observant, I try to visualize this in imaginary narratives.

What drives you to be an artist?

Painting is a magical experience for me. I see the world through a 'paint filter', always wondering how to translate the world I see around me onto canvas. The ability to recreate moments using only shades and colours never ceases to amaze me. It's a deeply fulfilling and mindful process of transforming ideas and thoughts into a visual narrative. Each of my paintings is an invitation to step into the moment and experience it fully. I strive to bring the viewer into the scene, to make them wonder and wanting to understand what is going on.

How would you describe the art that you create and what inspires you?

I'm inspired by the people, places, and moments that make up the urban landscape. My work is a reflection of my passion for exploring the world around me and my desire to capture the beauty of the human experience. Through my art, I hope to spark a deeper connection to the world and to express the beauty and complexities of human relations.

In my work, I draw upon the techniques of the old Dutch Masters, known for their masterful use of light and colour. By layering transparent colours over a white gesso base, I create a sense of depth and richness that brings my paintings to life. This traditional method, combined with my modern perspective, adds a timeless quality to my work and pays homage to the legacy of the Dutch Masters.

If you could overcome all of your fears, what would you do with your art?

My art is a form of self-expression and a way to connect with others. Being an artist requires dedication and commitment, and I am confident that with hard work, my best works are yet to come. I currently don't feel limited by fear, but I recognize the potential for growth and improvement in my art. And if I were completely free from the fear of judgment, it would certainly be easier to share my art with the wider audience.

When it comes to art making, how important is experimenting vs. sticking to a routine or set of rules?

My painting approach is characterized by precision and attention to detail. Sticking to a certain set of technical rules, like a proper preparation of the canvas, absolutely helps me to achieve a desired outcome. Nevertheless, each painting presents its own unique set of challenges and growth opportunities. I embrace the unpredictability of the creative process and view every piece as a learning experience. Also my curious nature drives me to continuously experiment with new materials and themes, essential for my artistic growth. I dedicate time and space for freer exploration, even if the results may not always lead to successful artworks, but aid in my progression as an artist.

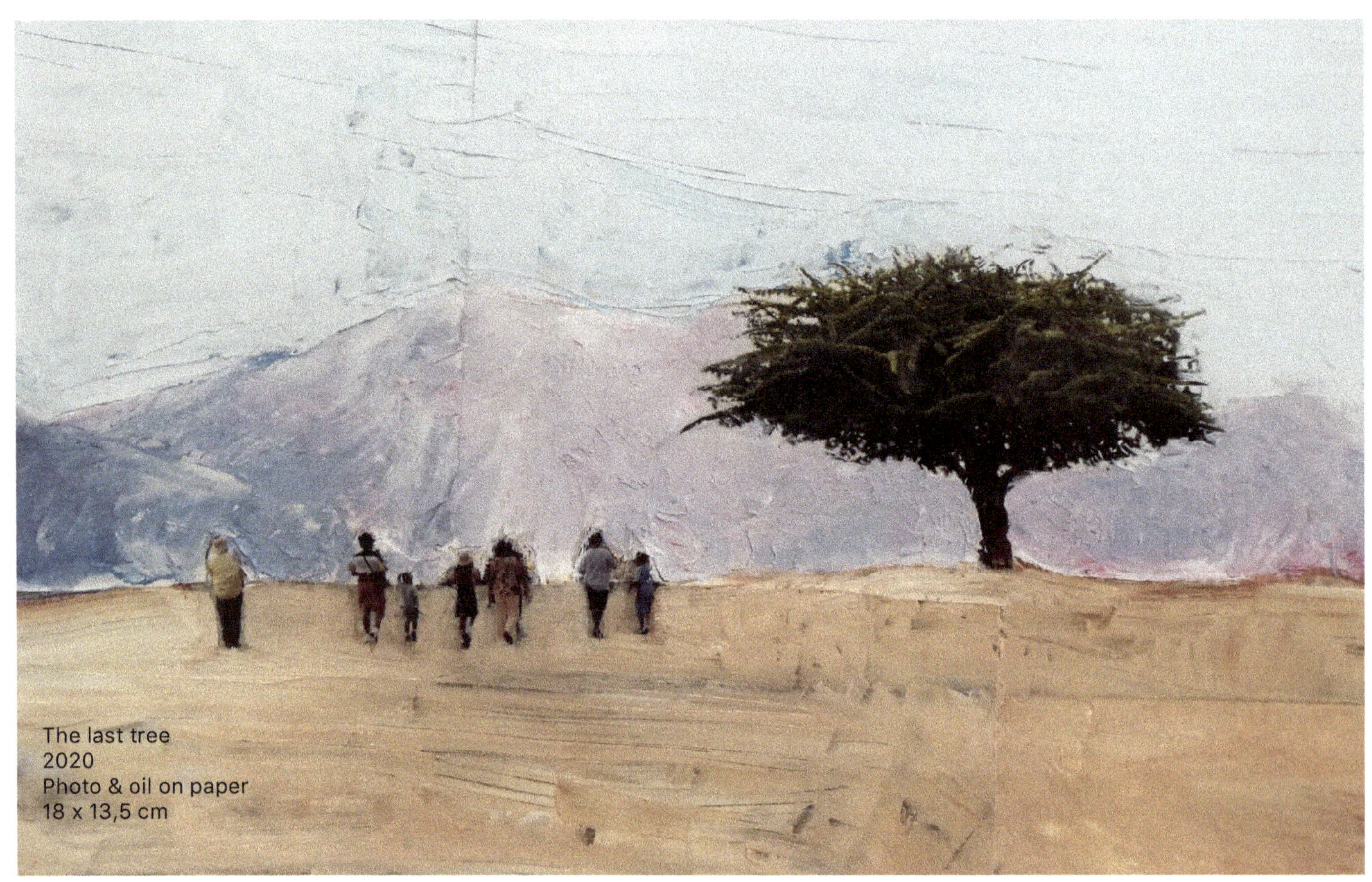

What are some of the challenges or experiences that have shaped your artistic journey so far?

My journey as an artist took nearly 30 years and many twists and turns before I fully committed to painting. Throughout this time, I held various roles - muralist, spatial designer, writer, graphic designer, cultural producer, creative director, business owner, and mother - but my love for painting remained constant. Despite this, I lacked the confidence to share my work with the world. Now, I have found my voice and am eager to share my unique perspective. My diverse experiences and the challenges I faced over the years have shaped me into the artist I am today, and this is reflected in my paintings. I've learned to let the creative process flow, allowing myself time and space to experiment and make mistakes, and to have the freedom to create what I want without worrying about external opinions.

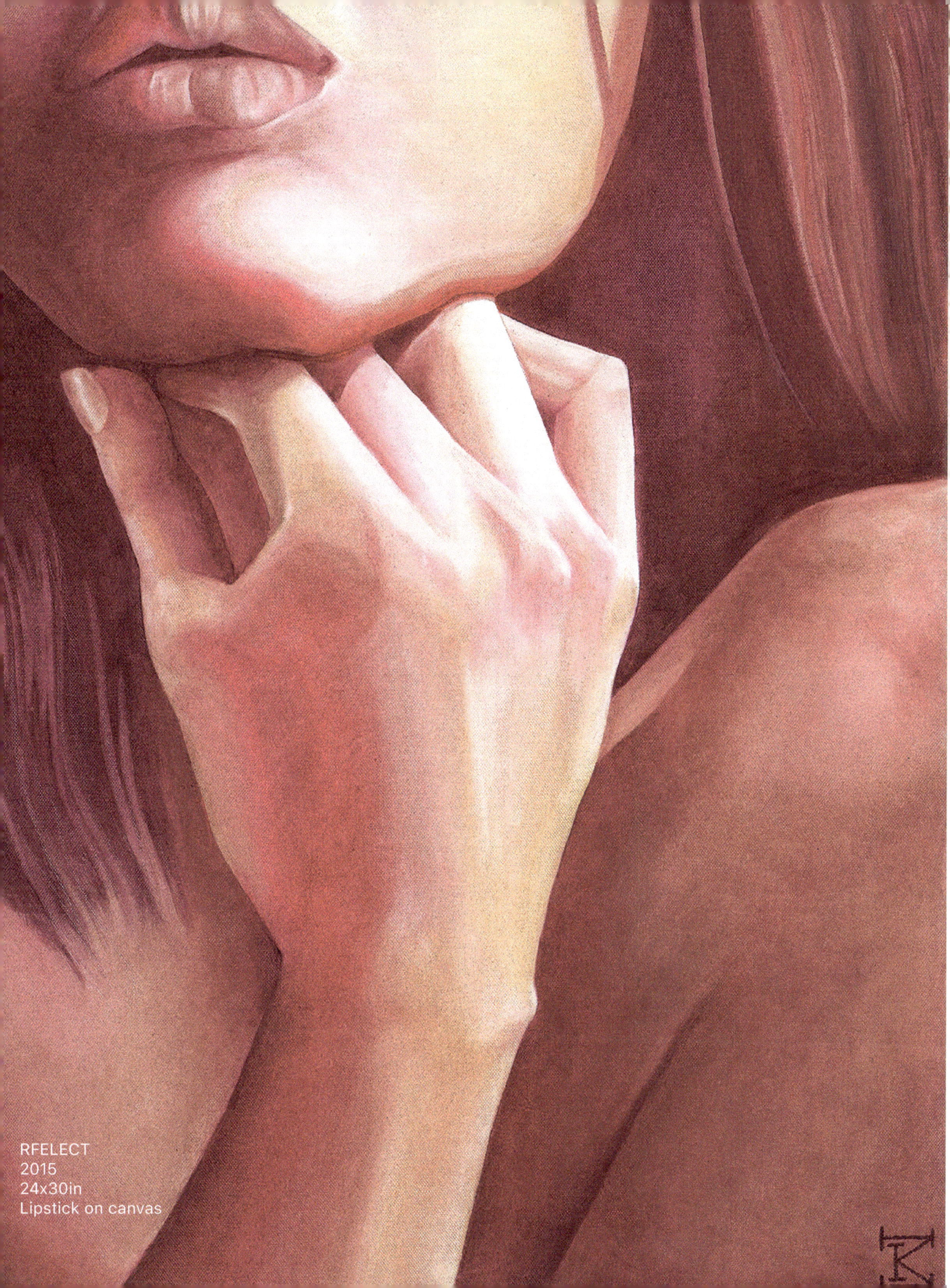
RFELECT
2015
24x30in
Lipstick on canvas

Katherine Mason

My *lipstick series* is a collection of paintings that I created to *support women* who have battled, or are currently *battling, breast cancer.*

I've always had a passion for art but, more importantly, a longing to create and connect with those around me. I moved around for most of my childhood, always experiencing new places, new people, a new life and my art developed as a way to document and understand my ever-changing surroundings. Over the years my passion grew, I pursued art throughout school and eventually received an art scholarship to the University of Oklahoma. Although I loved art, I never saw it as a viable career path. Growing up everyone would always say I was "so talented" but that I can't just be a "starving artist". Unfortunately, that stereotype stuck with me after graduation and as I endured an unfulfilling career in advertising. In 2014 I finally gave in to that relentless urge to create again. I quit my job and focused on my art full-time, painting out of my bedroom until I saved enough money for a studio space in Houston. For the next 3 years I focused on growing my business, building a very diverse portfolio through the creation of personal works as well as commissioned pieces. I experimented with a wide variety of mediums including acrylic, oil, soft pastel, marker, charcoal, and watercolor trying to find my style and purpose. In 2015 I picked up my first lipstick tube and my artistic voice was born. My lipstick series is a collection of paintings that I created to support women who have battled, or are currently battling, breast cancer. When asking women what the hardest part of their journey with cancer had been, they had a shockingly similar answer: They didn't feel beautiful anymore.

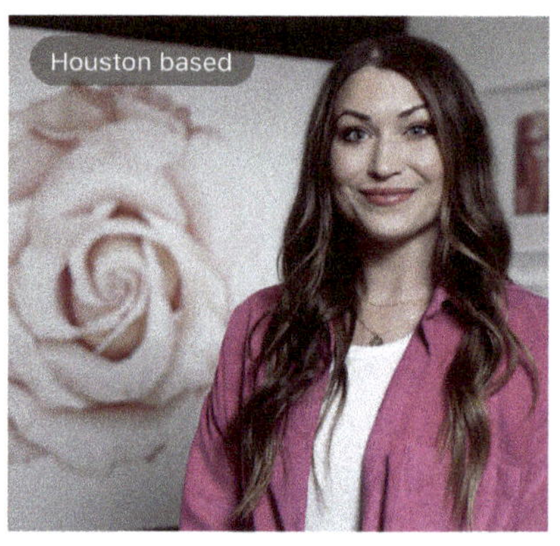

https://www.paintedwithlipstick.com

@paintedwithlipstick

After finding out a good friend was diagnosed with stage 4 breast cancer, I had the opportunity to chat with her and try to better understand the battle she was facing. She told me she had started applying lipstick before her chemotherapy treatments because it was the only thing that made her feel strong and beautiful again. As an artist, I was drawn to the fact that something as small as a tube of lipstick could bring so much joy during such a dark time. From then on, I decided to create this series entirely out of lipstick.

Each painting in this collection tells its own story, either through the title of the piece or the symbolic subject matter of the painting. It embraces beauty and fear, bravery and despair. Cancer is dark and destructive but these women, and the light they exude, take center stage. I want to capture that light.

My series continues to grow thanks to the generosity of those who have donated lipstick in honor and in memory of their loved ones. It is the greatest privilege of my life to take lipstick tubes that once belonged to so many incredible women and incorporate them into my work. I see my paintings, not as the creation of one woman, but but of thousands who have gone bravely before me despite this terrible disease. I know that this is the path that God has set for me, and my hope is that their spirits will live on through my work and continue to make the world a beautiful place. I donate 20% of my proceeds to the National Breast Cancer Foundation in hopes of finding a cure, and in the meantime, reminding women just how beautiful they truly are!

What drives you to be an artist?

I'm not sure that anything "drives" me to be an artist, I have just always been one. Some of the earliest memories I have are of trying to make sense of the world around me through creating. If I'm not bringing beauty into the world and sharing it with others, I simply feel like I'm not living. I know that being an artist is my purpose in life and it's a part of myself that I hope to grow and nurture for as long as God will let me.

How would you describe the art that you create and what inspires you?

I view all of the art I create as an opportunity to share beauty and love with others. It's as simple as that.

My lipstick series, specifically, is a body of work that I have created entirely through the use of donated lipstick tubes. This series honors the remarkable community of breast cancer patients, survivors and their families. Many people have donated lipstick tubes in honor or in memory of their loved ones and it has been an incredible privilege to use these lipsticks to grow my series and in turn, continue to support this community. I would say my greatest inspiration is the love of God. It inspires me to truly just want to be the best person I can be. I want to be a light in this world, which for some is a very dark place. I want to support people, love them, lift them up and encourage them to live a beautiful life and chase their dreams. I want people to know how unique they are, how special, how capable and that they're loved. That is my greatest inspiration.

If you could overcome all of your fears, what would you do with your art?

We all have fears as artists, most of which stem from the unknown or some form of imposter syndrome. I'm sure if fear wasn't an issue I would be much more confident in going out and marketing my work, networking with my target audience, applying for grants and shows, etc. However, if I'm being honest, I wouldn't want to overcome all of my fears. I think fear is a tool to help us grow in our personal development as well as in our faith. When moments of fear or discomfort arise, I pride myself in my ability to overcome those obstacles, which not only strengthens my confidence as a person, but also as a evolving artist.

When it comes to art making, how important is experimenting vs. sticking to a routine or set of rules?

I think it's different for everyone, but personally, there has to be a balance between both structure and experimentation. If I experiment too much, my momentum slows and I tend to not complete as much work...whereas if I have too much structure, I'm producing more but my creativity starts to lack.

Luckily, there's a lot of experimentation throughout my creative process when working with lipstick. That has been one of the most exciting parts of exploring a new medium. It's my job to push the boundaries of lipstick as a medium and see what it's capable of, how to best work with it, develop forms of application and preservation, find unique tools to work with, etc. It's as if I'm exploring uncharted territory which has made my experimentation process very exciting.

What are some of the challenges or experiences that have shaped your artistic journey so far?

There are countless challenges and experiences that have shaped me into the artist I am today and I welcome them all. Obviously learning how to work with lipstick as a creative medium was a huge challenge for me, alongside learning how to properly preserve them. I learned so much about myself through those challenges and grew so much as an artist. I believe obstacles are the best teachers if approached with humility and curiosity, which is easier said than done haha! I hope moving forward, my artistic career is littered with meaningful obstacles and experiences to push me out of my comfort zone and teach me just how resilient and able I am.

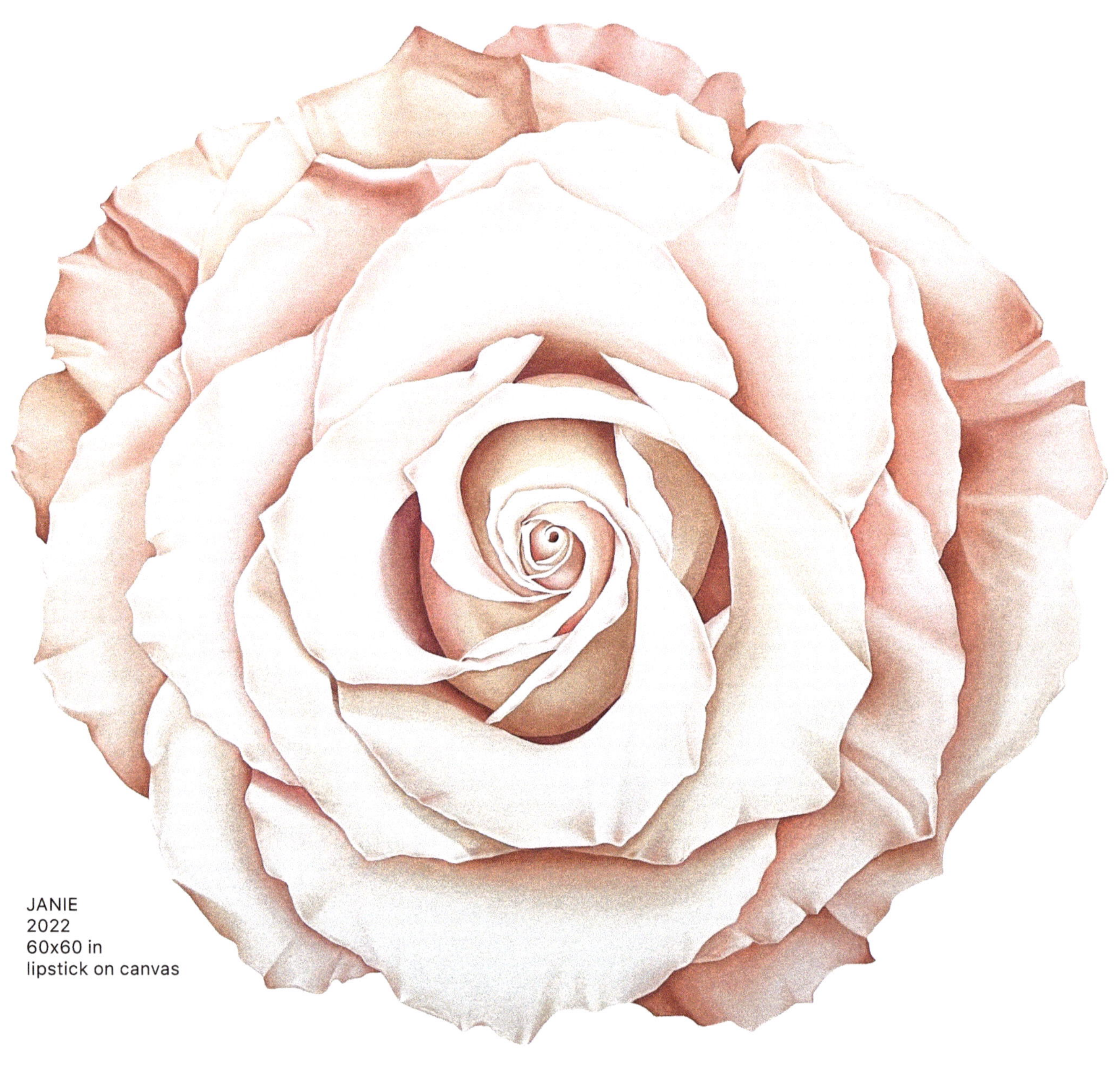

JANIE
2022
60x60 in
lipstick on canvas

"The lipsticks used in the creation of JANIE belonged to the friends, family, and medical team of Janie Moore, a breast cancer survivor who commission this painting."

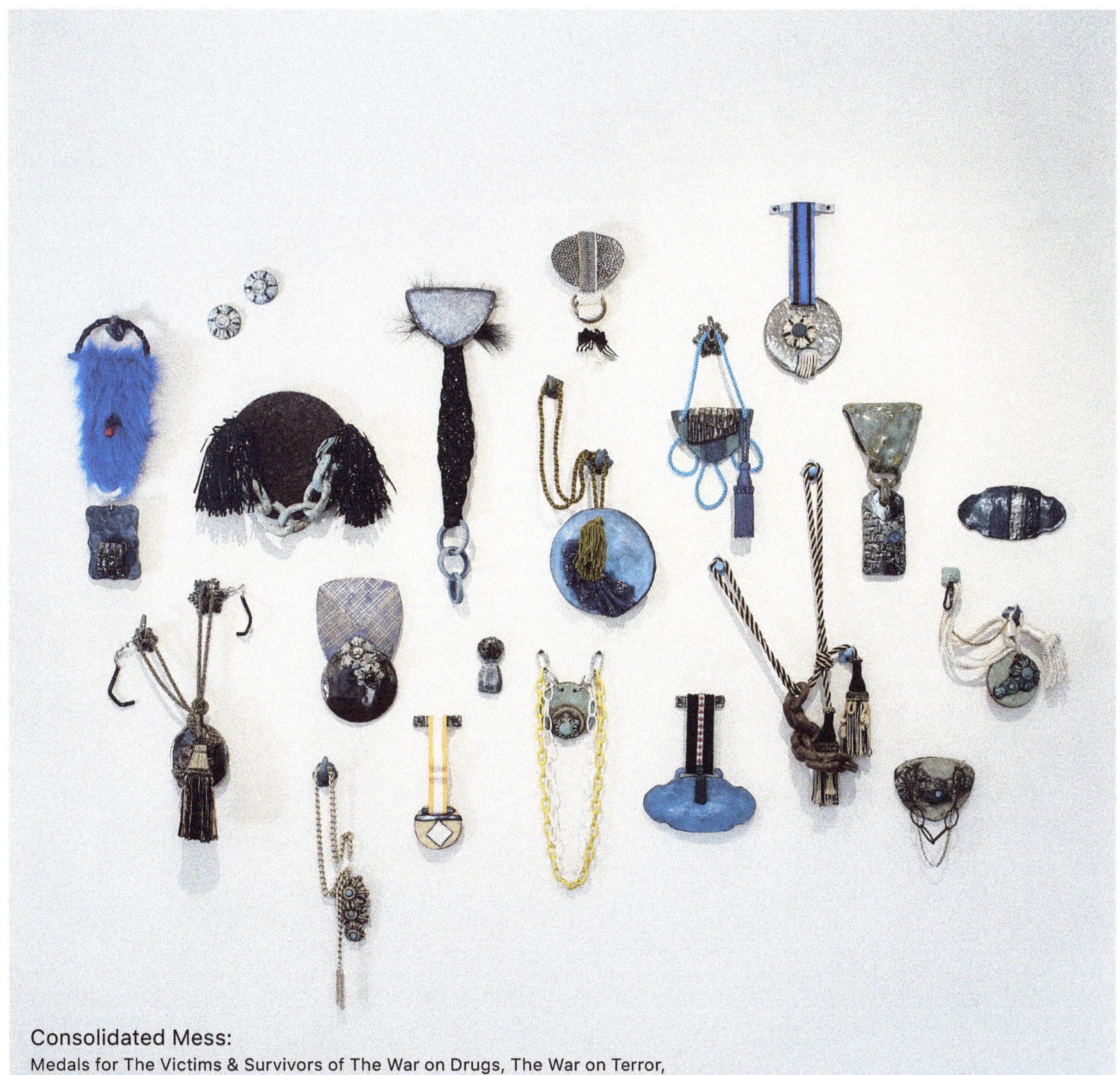

Consolidated Mess:
Medals for The Victims & Survivors of The War on Drugs, The War on Terror,
The Culture Wars, The War on Women, The Covert Wars and The Forgotten Wars.
2022
Glazed Ceramic and Mixed Media,
Approx. 7' x 7' x 5", each component no bigger than 14" x 24" x 5"

Lexa Walsh

I make context-responsive projects, exhibitions and objects *questioning power, value and hierarchy.*

Lexa Walsh is an artist and experience maker based in Oakland, CA.

She is a graduate of Portland State University's Art & Social Practice MFA program and holds a BFA in Ceramics from California College of Arts and Crafts. She was Social Practice Artist in Residence in Portland Art Museum's Education department, received the Southern Exposure's Alternative Exposure Award, the CEC Artslink Award, the Gunk Grant, the de Young Artist Fellowship, and Kala's Print Public Residency Award. Walsh has participated in projects, exhibitions and performances at Apexart, Atlantic Center for the Arts, Cité de la Musique, Exploratorium, de Young Museum, di Rosa Center for Contemporary Art, Exploratorium, Federal Hall, Kala Art Institute, Marin Museum of Contemporary Art, Mills College Art Museum, Oakland Museum of California, NIAD, Portland Art Museum, SFMOMA, Smack Mellon, Taipei Artist Village, Walker Art Center, Williams College Museum of Art, and Yerba Buena Center for the Arts. She has done several international artist residencies, tours and projects.

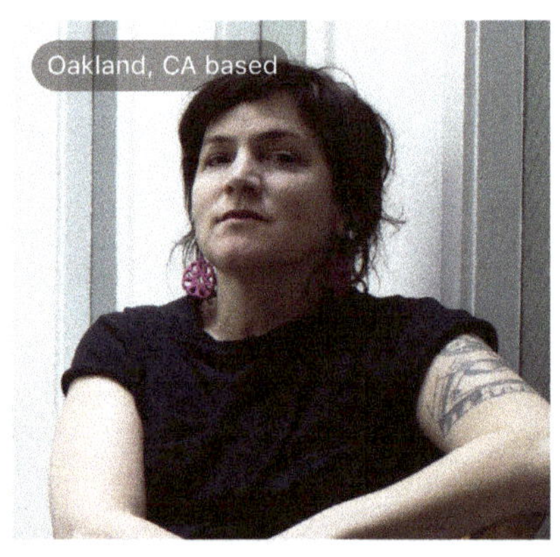

https://lexawalsh.com
lexawalsh@gmail.com
@lexawalshstudios

She founded the 90's experimental music and performance venue the Heinz Afterworld Lounge, worked for many years as a curator and administrator at CESTA, an international art center in Czech republic, whose team created radical curatorial projects to foster cross-cultural understanding. Walsh co-founded and conceived of the all women, all toy instrument ensemble Toychestra. She founded and organizes Oakland Stock, the Oakland branch of the Sunday Soup network micro-granting dinner series that supports artists' projects and the Bay Area Contemporary Arts Archive (BACAA). She is currently Artist in Residence and Grand Central Art Center.

I make context-responsive projects, exhibitions and objects questioning power, value and hierarchy. With a background in both ceramic sculpture and social practice, I create platforms for interaction. My upbringing as the youngest child of fifteen in a house full of trophies that were not mine informs my work, as does practicing collectivity while coming of age in the Bay Area post punk cultural scene of the 1990's.

Currently I am making large collections of ceramic and mixed media award forms: trophies, plaques and medals. Through participation, the public may offer testimonials and dedications to share in an expanded notion of what and who may be celebrated, and why. These are often shared as titles and sound works alongside the objects.

What drives you to be an artist?
Ultimately I am driven by uncovering the grey areas, the in-betweens, the nuanced spaces between unrest and a warm embrace.

How would you describe the art that you create and what inspires you?
With a background in both sculpture and social practice, I make context-responsive, multifaceted projects, exhibitions and objects about hierarchy, power and value. With a background in both sculpture and social practice, I create platforms for participation and interaction across hierarchies, representing multiple voices and inventing new ways of belonging. This can look like a clubhouse surrounded by ceramic medals for Veterans in the former War Room of a WWII Airbase, a wall of awards made of ceramics and mixed media for those who have 'Taken One for the Team', a museum display from thrift store objects, or an exhibition co-designed with progressive nuns. I'm inspired by and regularly do learn from groups of people, situations and places I encounter.

If you could overcome all of your fears, what would you do with your art?
Make larger work with more visual impact and spectacle, to create a sense of wonder.

When it comes to art making, how important is experimenting vs. sticking to a routine or set of rules?
I'm always experimenting!

What are some of the challenges or experiences that have shaped your artistic journey so far?
My upbringing as the youngest of fifteen in a house full of trophies I didn't win, and coming of age in the post punk Bay Area along with living in a radical curatorial collective in Czech republic inform my interests in service, collectivity, exuberance and an ethic of care.

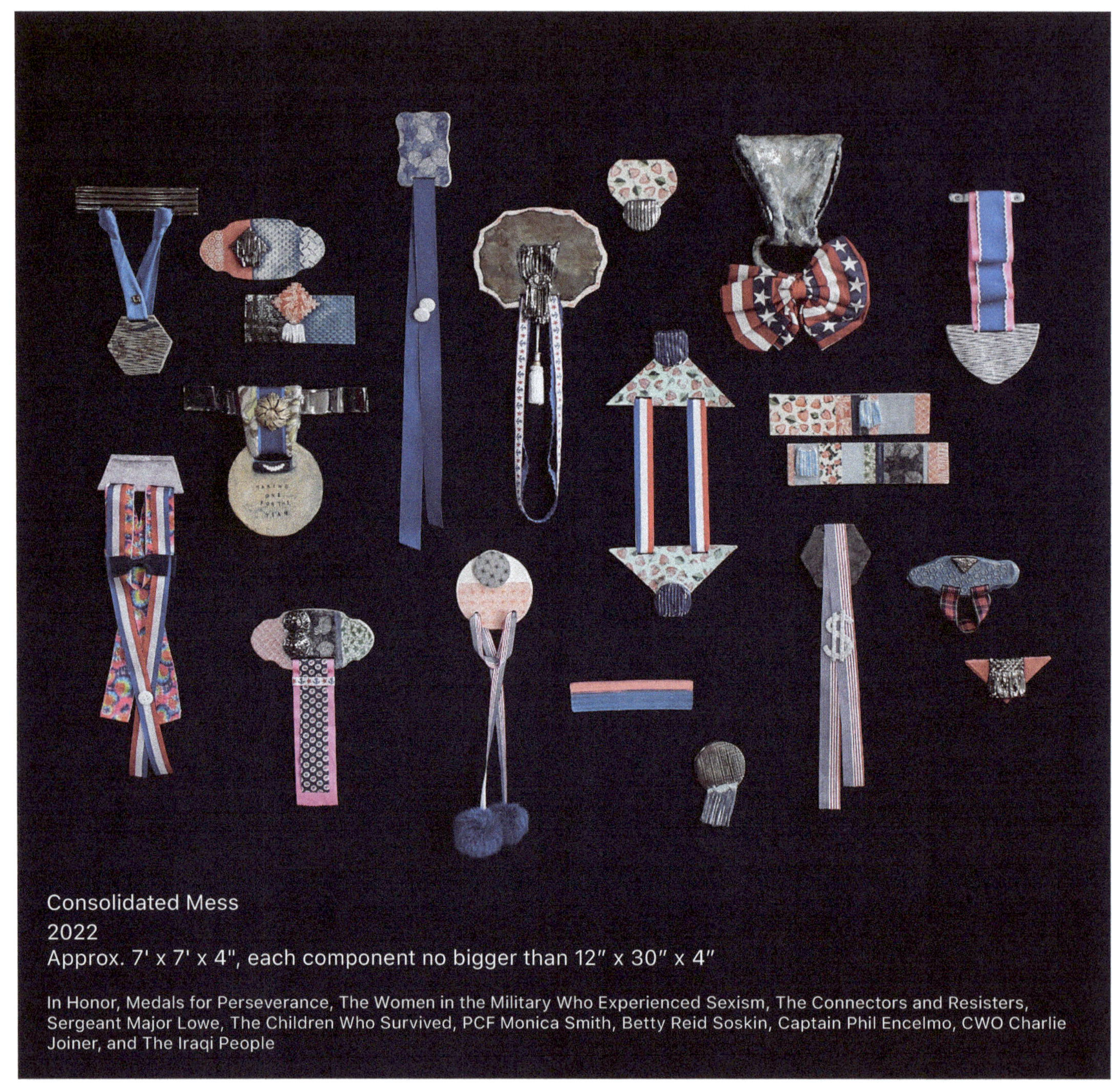

Consolidated Mess
2022
Approx. 7' x 7' x 4", each component no bigger than 12" x 30" x 4"

In Honor, Medals for Perseverance, The Women in the Military Who Experienced Sexism, The Connectors and Resisters, Sergeant Major Lowe, The Children Who Survived, PCF Monica Smith, Betty Reid Soskin, Captain Phil Encelmo, CWO Charlie Joiner, and The Iraqi People

*"Make larger work with more visual impact
and spectacle, to create a sense of wonder."*

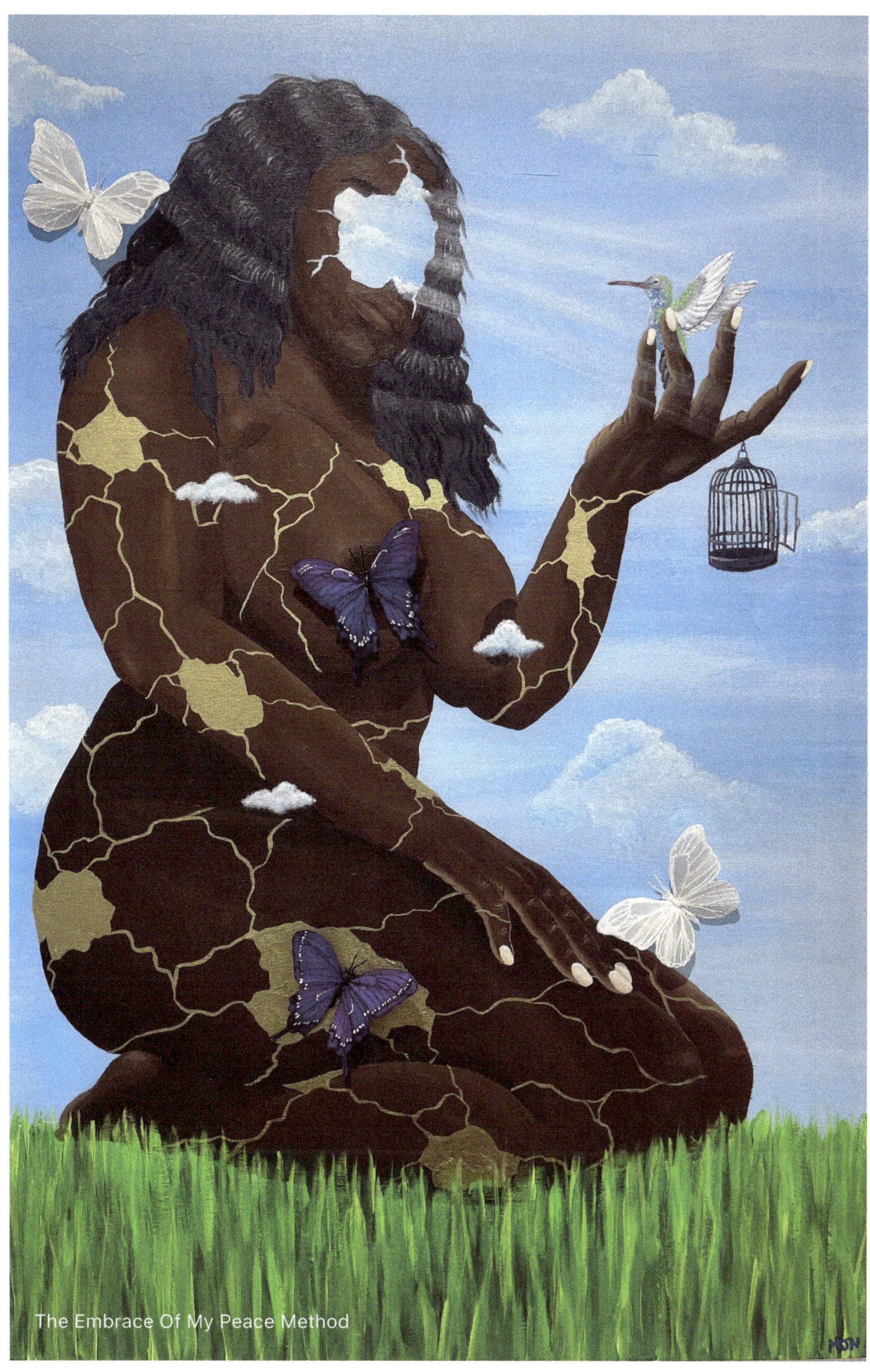

The Embrace Of My Peace Method

Marie-Jose Njoku-Obi

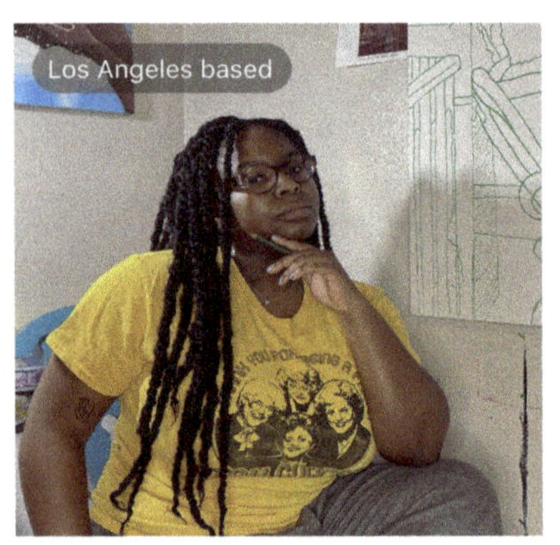

https://www.mariejose-art.com
@ artbymariejose@gmail.com
@ *@mariejose.art*

> We *visualize* and *create scenes* that do not *exist in reality* and therefore allow us to *reimagine our future existence.*

San Francisco born, Inglewood based contemporary artist Marie-Jose began painting in 2016, employing surrealism as a tool for inspiring a previously indiscernible future and occasionally reimagining the past. Along with painting, collage & mixed media are the vehicles for exploring the multiplicity of the Black femme experience.

Influenced by artists such as Salvador Dali, Kerry James Marshall, and the artist's Nigerian heritage, many scenes offer Black figures among dreamlike cloudscapes and thematic metaphors that refer to the intricacy of life, the consequence of introspection, and feelings of vulnerability, hope, and courage. Naming their style as 'Afro-Surrealistic', the work reexamines the pre-conceived barriers of Black liberation. Marie-Jose has participated in numerous art markets and festivals nationwide, and had paintings in the Affordable Art Fair in New York and Aqua Art Miami in Miami Beach in 2022. They have shown work with the LA LGBT Center and the Museum of Science + Industry in Chicago. They were also a recent 2022 Artist in Residence participant in Fukuoka, Japan and made their international debut with an exhibition with Studio Kura.

What drives you to be an artist?
The desire to speak and be heard, the desire to find others to relate to, and the desire to feed my inner child. Visual art is a beautiful language that helps us relate to those around us, and finding purpose in learning and sharing that language is self-fulfilling.

How would you describe the art that you create and what inspires you?
The art I create is figurative and Afro-Surrealist in nature. I like to juxtapose elements into compositions that do not exist in reality. I like to think of surrealism as a tool for liberation, wherein we visualize and create scenes that do not exist in reality and therefore allow us to reimagine our future existence. My approach to the work often includes sourcing metaphoric imagery such as clouds, birds and flowers to help convey a complex range of emotions. I am wholly inspired by my Nigerian heritage, surrealists of the 20th century (like Remedios Varo), and the general Black experience. I take everyday inspiration from nature, books, architectural details, and cloud formations.

If you could overcome all of your fears, what would you do with your art?
I would simply keep creating and never stop. My only fear with my art is feeling like I don't have enough materials to make what I want to make.

When it comes to art making, how important is experimenting vs. sticking to a routine or set of rules?
I like to take some risks with every piece I create. Sticking to a set of rules makes sense once I'm at a sweet spot of a concept I want to exercise. But otherwise, I think pushing the envelope and doing a little experimenting is a good thing and keeps me fresh and creative.

What are some of the challenges or experiences that have shaped your artistic journey so far?
I am so grateful for everything I have encountered thus far - challenges are simply a way to redirect me toward what is meant for me. Though I've heard lots of 'no's, some of the most fulfilling 'yes's' I've had thus far include participation in a couple of international art fairs, and being an artist in residence in Fukuoka, Japan, and getting to exhibit art there as well. I am enjoying the journey of my art practice and cannot wait to see where it goes from here.

" I take everyday inspiration from nature, books, architectural details, and cloud formations"

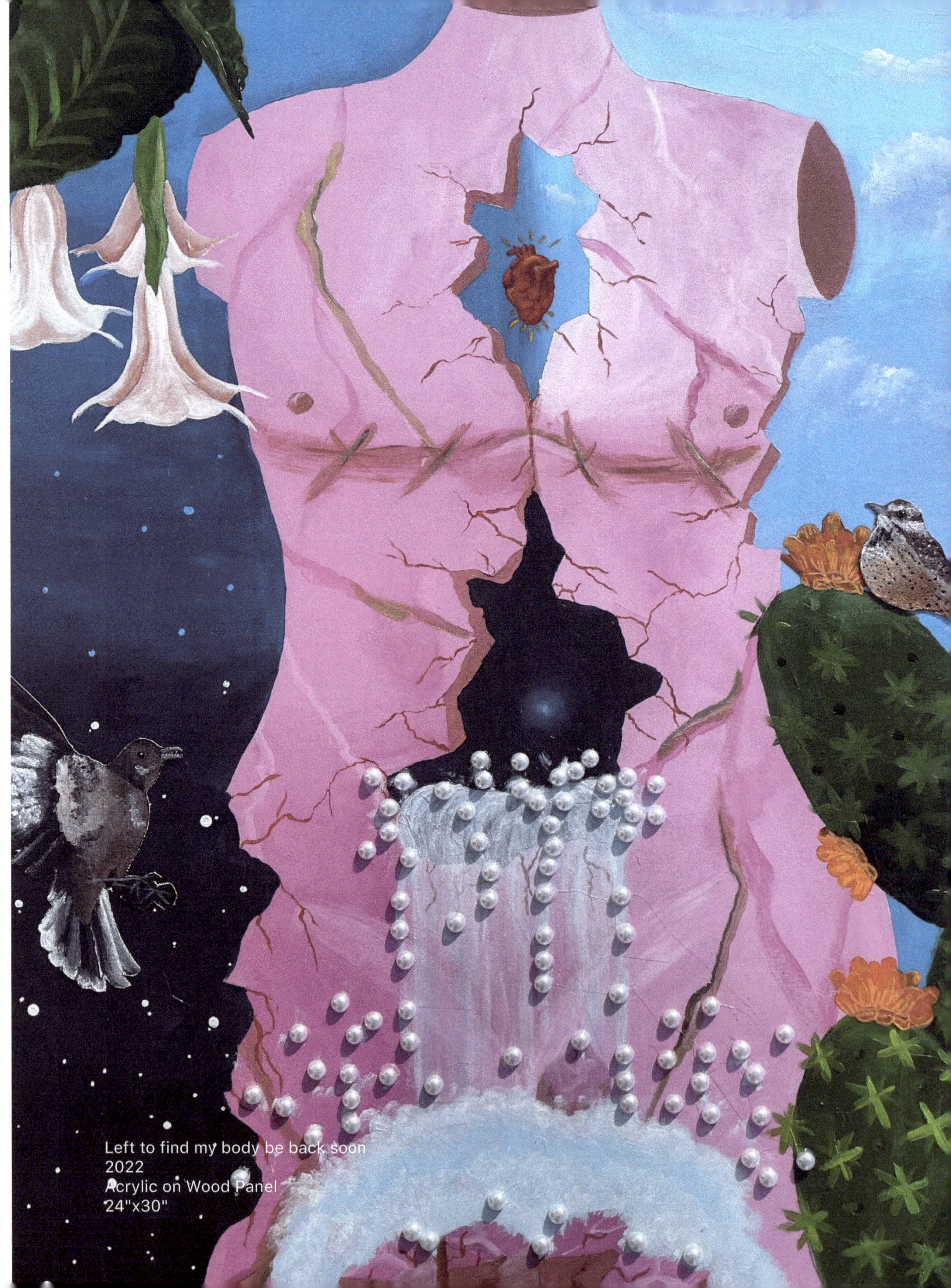

Left to find my body be back soon
2022
Acrylic on Wood Panel
24"x30"

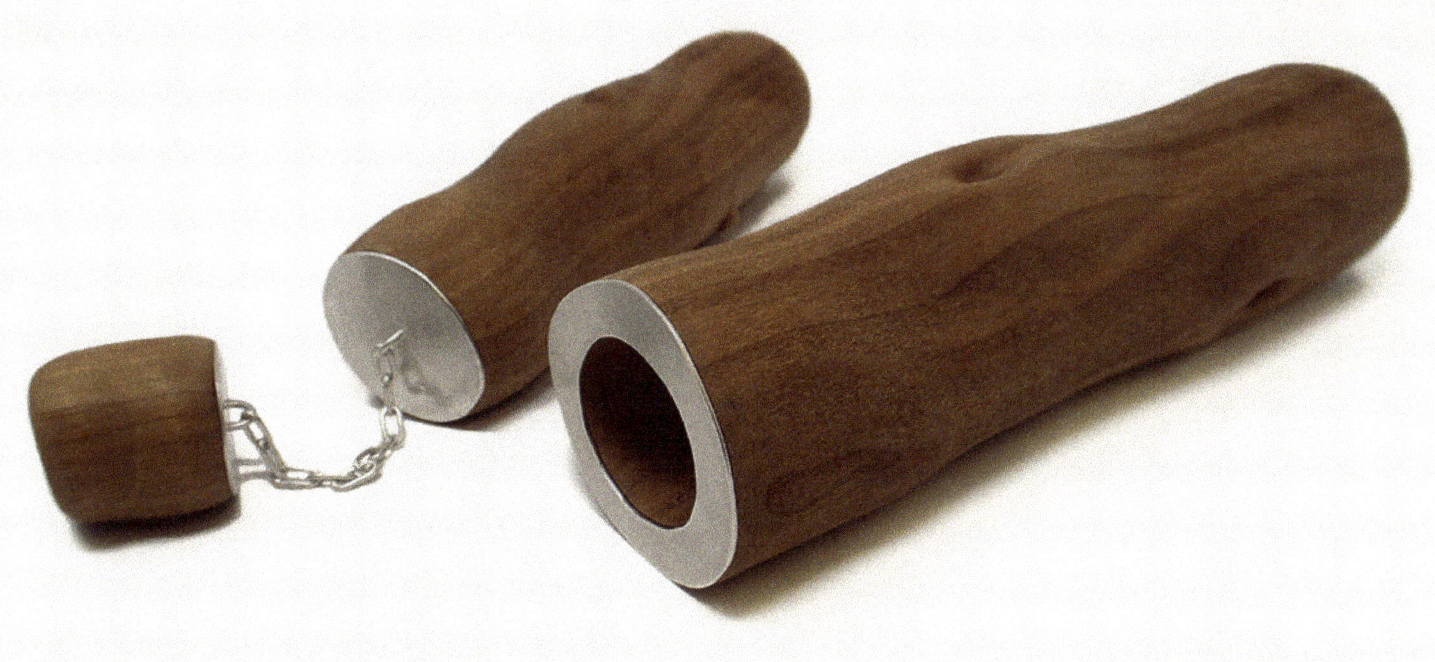

Assumed, cherry wood, sterling silver,
2020
12"x6"x3"

Shuoran Zhou

I get inspired by events I've been through, and art is a means of communication between me and my audience.

Shuoran Zhou was born in Beijing, China, and is an artist currently located in Brooklyn, NY. She graduated with a BFA in Oil Painting from China Academy of Art in 2019, and an MFA in Studio art from Syracuse University. Shuoran's work has been exhibited internationally in China, Spain, Belgium, the United States, as well as in several online exhibitions including ones juried by Robert Ebendorf and Laura Kalman. Aside from being an artist, Shuoran was a jewelry instructor at Syracuse University for two years and is currently teaching introductory jewelry classes and beading classes at Brooklyn Metal Works and 92NY in New York.

With a metalsmithing background, Shuoran found connections with glass beads and uses them as the main material in her current work. She associates the belittled, overrated perception of the beads, the laborious, delicate nature of beading with women's social status, and stereotypical perceptions of gender roles. Shuoran combines beading with metalsmithing techniques to create jewelry and wearable objects that serve as a voice that tells her own stories and communicates to the audience who has similar experiences.

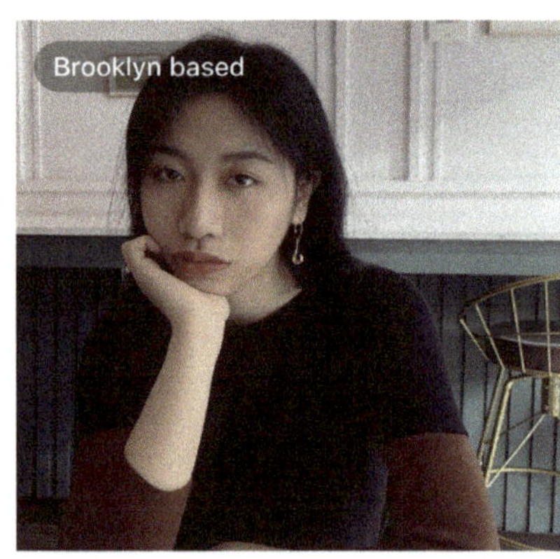

🏹 http://www.kristinreed.com
@ kristinreed@mac.com
◎ @luminousgeometry

Ultimately, Shuoran aims to provoke introspections toward assumptions and oppressive gender expectations of women, leading to understanding, empathy, and equality within the gender context in society.

My work addresses my personal struggles and deals with common stereotypes toward women, and aims to provoke introspection and question those entrenched, stereotypical assumptions. I derive inspiration from my confrontational relationship with my mother, which arises from our differing perspectives and beliefs regarding the roles and aspirations of women. Originated from these unpleasant confrontations, my work embodies the assumptions and norms that affect my life. I make wearable objects with mixed materials to visualize these issues through craft and the property of the material itself, with the hope of resonating with people who have similar struggles to mine and advocating women's autonomy.

What drives you to be an artist?

I never thought I intentionally chose to be an artist, but naturally, I've always been dealing with art--music, designing, painting, and crafting. As an artist, I always feel very grateful that artists are naturally "privileged" with the skill, or mentality, of being able to source from every possible aspect of life as the inspiration of their art practice. Art allows me to "translate", and to see things from different perspectives.

How would you describe the art that you create and what inspires you?

In my opinion, genuineness and authenticity in one's art are always the most convincing, and touching parts. As I follow that belief, my art originates from my personal experiences. I get inspired by events I've been through, and art is a means of communication between me and my audience. Art is like a non-verbal language that tells a story of my own, and is free for interpretation.

" I source inspiration from life, so my life experience is at the core of my art practice."

If you could overcome all of your fears, what would you do with your art?

I'm not clear on what exactly this question means. When it comes to art making, how important is experimenting vs. sticking to a routine or set of rules? I lean more toward experimenting, as it always brings me surprises. I am a very hand-on person, only during the actual process of making things, I would get more inspired or more settle with the original ideas. Set of rules is also important to me, because I thrive under restrictions--the more I know about what I cannot do, the more I get more creative with with I can do.

What are some of the challenges or experiences that have shaped your artistic journey so far?

I source inspiration from life, so my life experience is at the core of my art practice. I came to the US in fall 2019 not expecting what happened later--COVID. The pandemic changed my life plans in a very dramatic way, but also forced me to develop a more adaptable mindset. It taught me to live in the moment as it is essential nowadays. Along this journey, art has been the most loyal company that helped me clear my mind and soothed negative thoughts. Most of the techniques I practice in my art are extremely time-consuming, but very therapeutic for me at the time. I am grateful that art allowed me to find my way to cope with the situation, and that it added such depth to that period of my life.

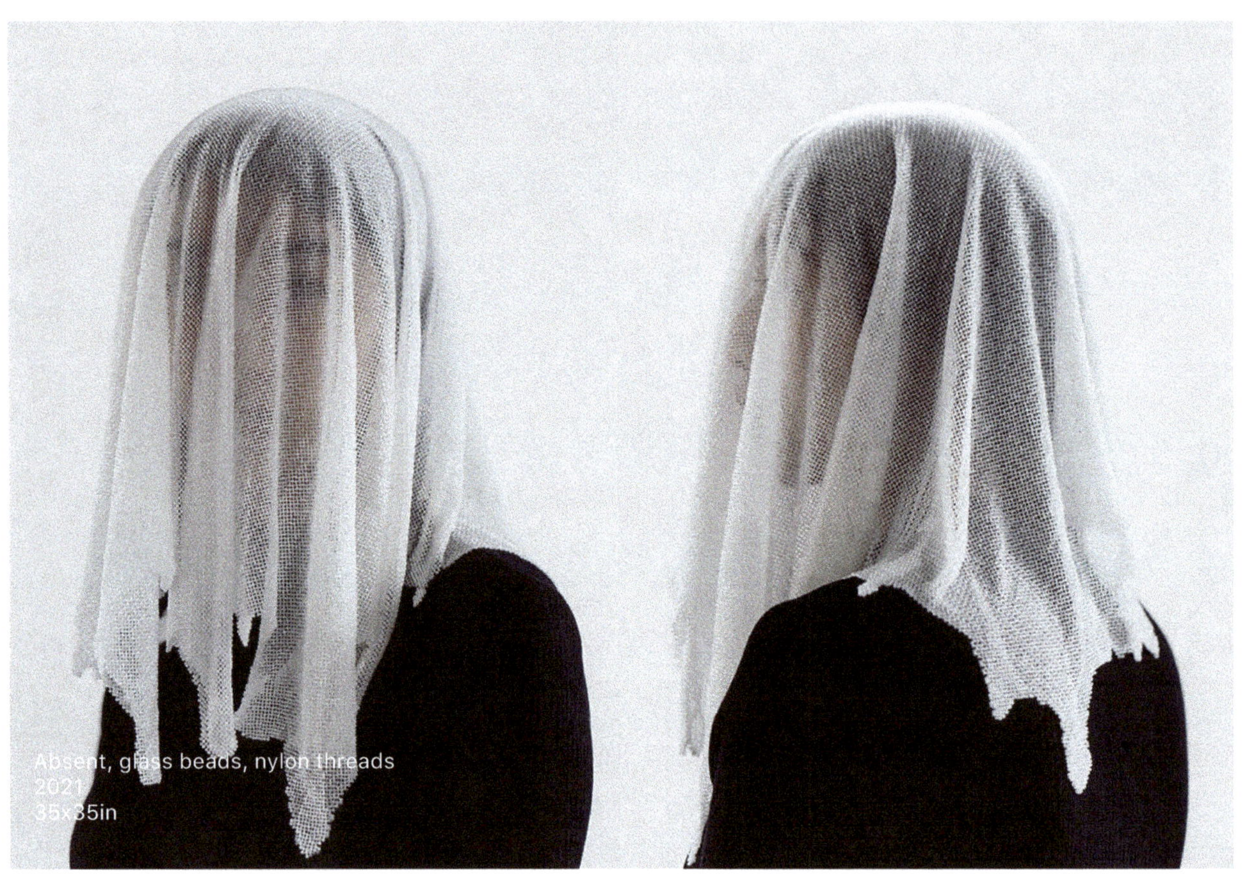

Absent, glass beads, nylon threads
2021
35x35in

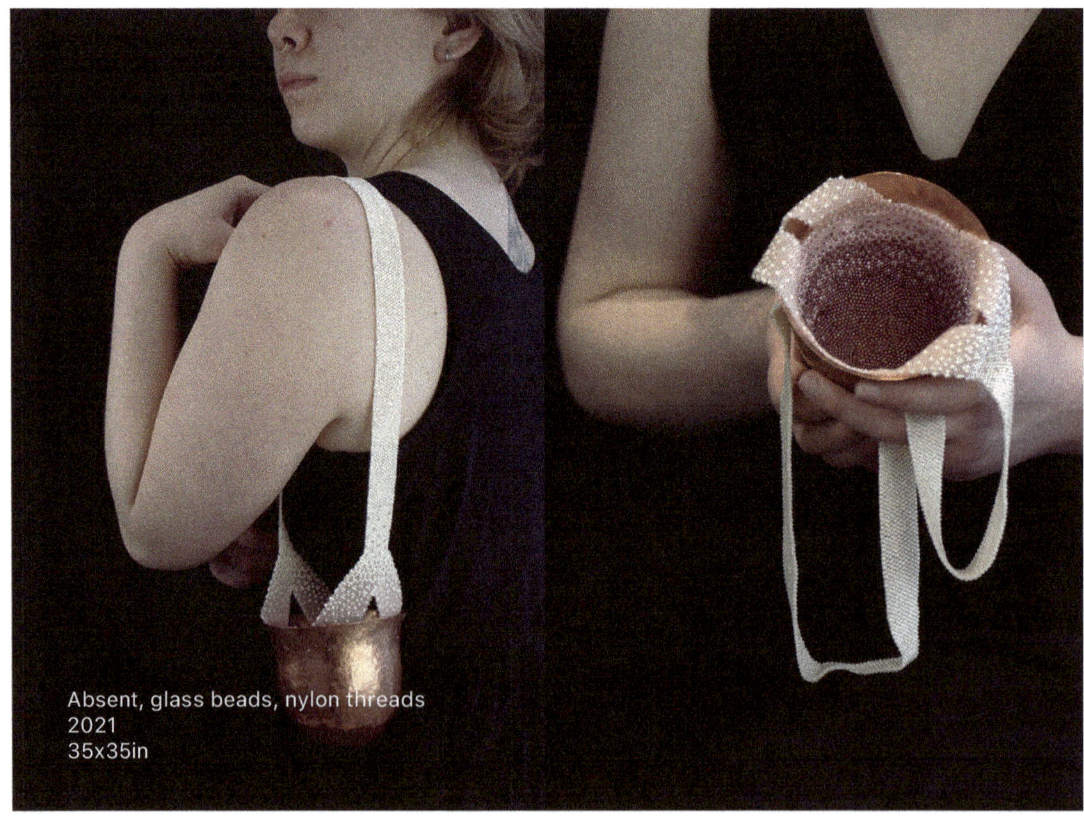

Absent, glass beads, nylon threads
2021
35x35in

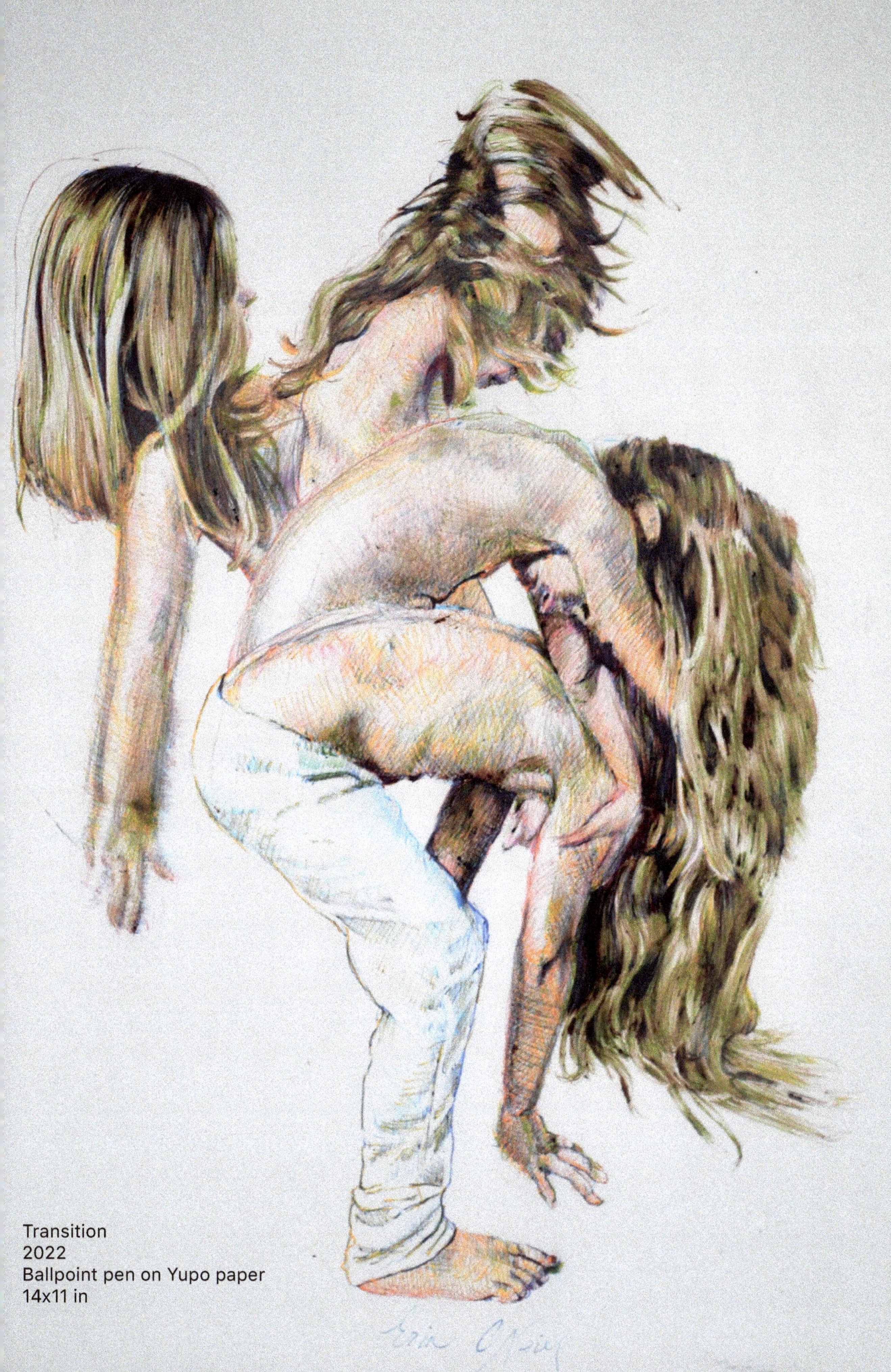

Transition
2022
Ballpoint pen on Yupo paper
14x11 in

Erin ONeill

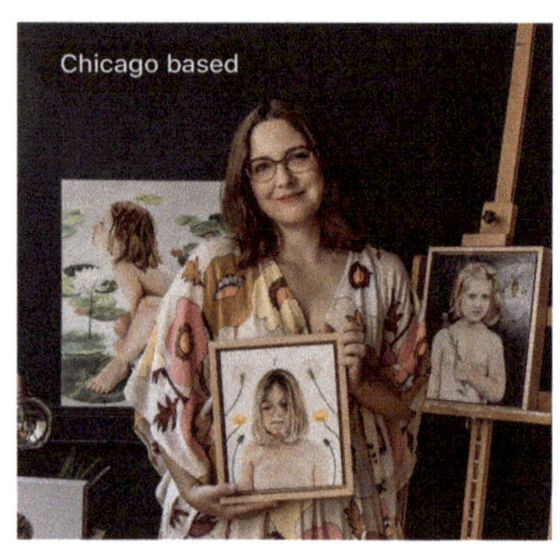

🔗 https://www.erinelizabetho.com
@ erinelizabetho@gmail.com
⌾ *@erinelizabethoart*

I am heavily inspired by *Symbolist art, Photography,* and bearing witness to my Daughter as she grows.

Erin Elizabeth ONeill (b. 1983, St. Louis Missouri) lives and works in Chicago. She received her BFA from the Kansas City Art Institute in 2008.n her paintings and drawings, O'Neill explores the healing power of the inner child while navigating her own generational trauma. Her figures are suspended in negative space creating an intense line of focus between the viewer and the subjects gaze. ONeill plays with collaging her reference images in one space as she tries to depict the duplicity of emotions in the human experience.

What drives you to be an artist?

I'm driven by human connection to be an artist. There is nothing more thrilling than finding a connection to someone else through visual language and feeling as though you are seen.

How would you describe the art that you create and what inspires you?

My paintings are about seeking a connection to my inner child as a way of processing my own experiences of grief and trauma. These paintings and drawings are often using delicate mediums such as watercolor and ballpoint pen. I work best when my materials can be picked up and set down quickly without much planning. I'm inspired by my mental health journey and coming to terms with the loss that I've dealt with throughout my life and how carrying grief is a natural part of our human experience. I am heavily inspired by Symbolist art, Photography, and bearing witness to my Daughter as she grows.

If you could overcome all of your fears, what would you do with your art?

I would make even more art.

When it comes to art making, how important is experimenting vs. sticking to a routine or set of rules?

The unpredictability of my life of raising my daughter, holding a job, managing my diabetes, and my mental health challenges make routines difficult to maintain. Routines tend to give me a lot of anxiety because they can sometimes feel stifling. When a routine is disrupted by my diabetes, or being a caregiver I tend to become weighed down by shame and disappointment. I do much better creating rituals, like setting my space and choosing music to make paintings to. Having my coffee and writing out what I'd like to get done that day. Cleaning up my space and shutting it down for the evening are all things that help me maintain momentum in my process but they leave a great deal of room to try new things.

What are some of the challenges or experiences that have shaped your artistic journey so far?

My work is very intertwined with my experiences as someone living with chronic illness and raising a daughter with my partner while trying to break cycles of generational trauma and understand my own neurodivergence. Challenging as all that is, my biggest challenge has been getting out of my own way and letting go of expectations about how my life as an artist is supposed to look. These expectations and beliefs about myself have kept me out of the studio, from sharing my art or putting myself out there. I'm having to really build a lot of blind trust in myself in order to keep putting one foot in front of the other. Unsurprisingly, it's this unlearning experience that has pushed my work the farthest I've taken it in recent years.

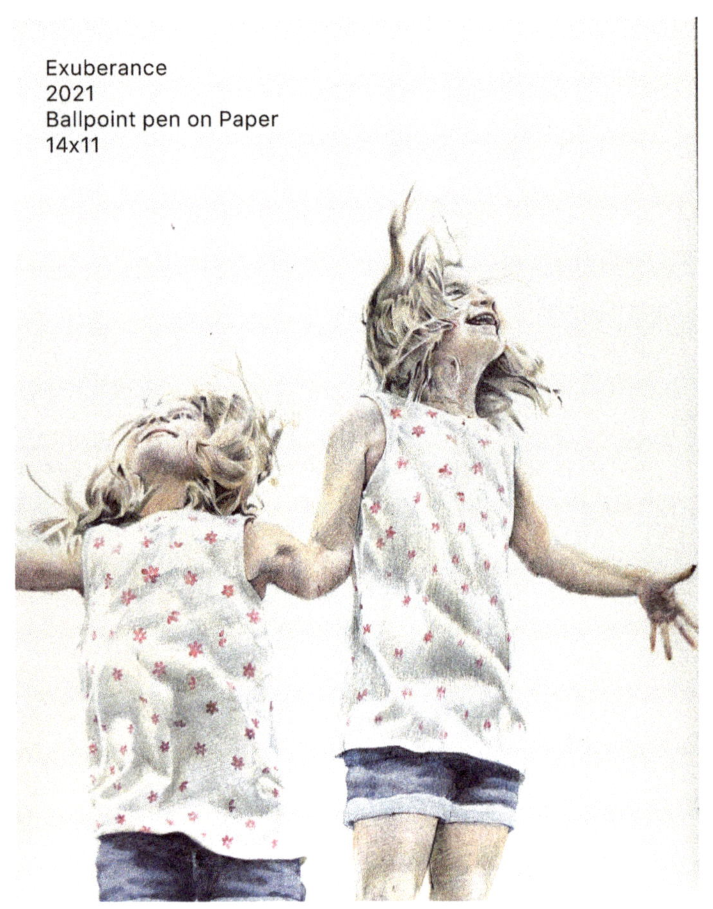

Exuberance
2021
Ballpoint pen on Paper
14x11

"It's the persistent 'why' moments I find myself working through as an artist. The ones that don't leave me alone."

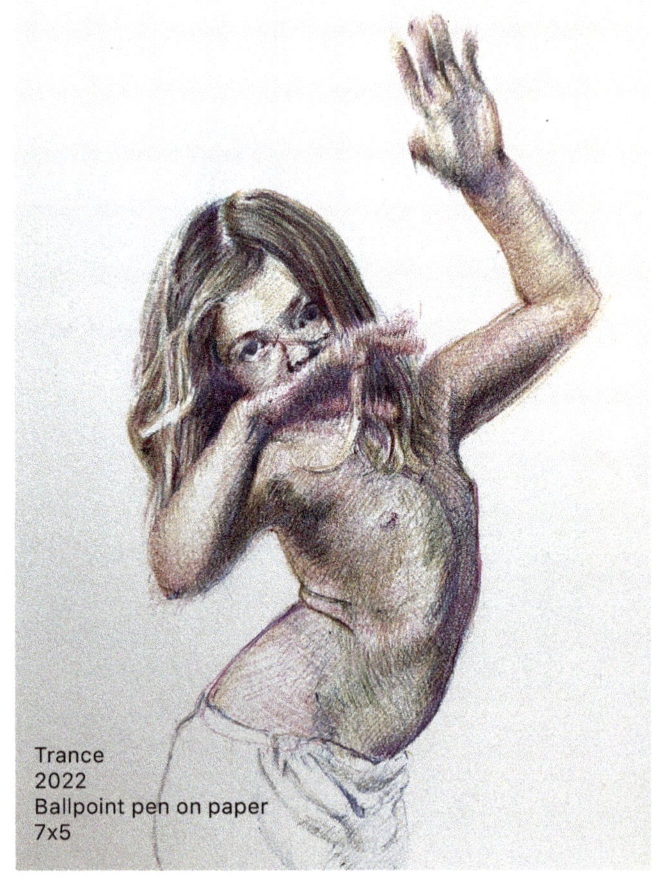

Trance
2022
Ballpoint pen on paper
7x5

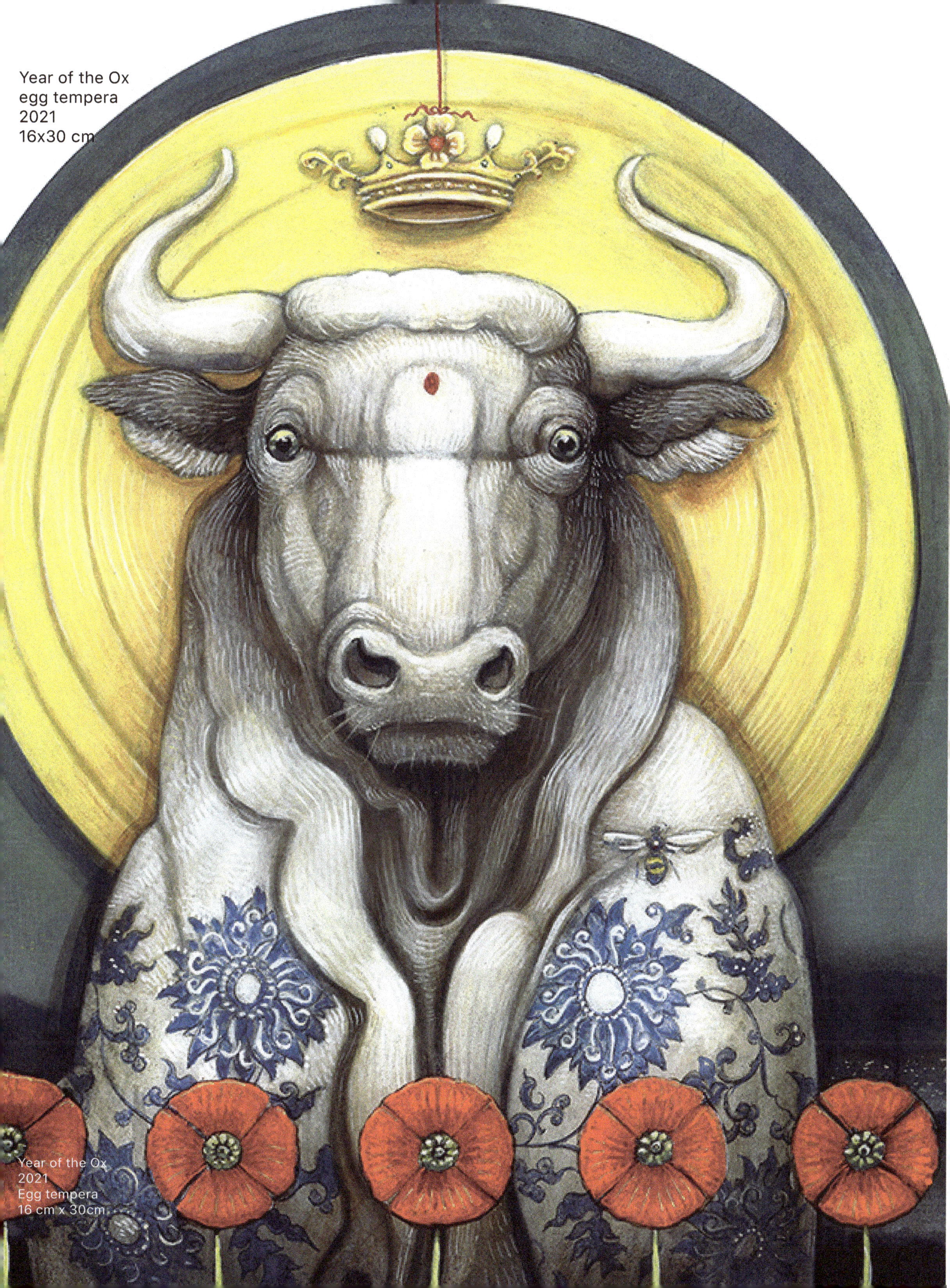

Year of the Ox
egg tempera
2021
16x30 cm

Year of the Ox
2021
Egg tempera
16 cm x 30cm.

E. E. Kono

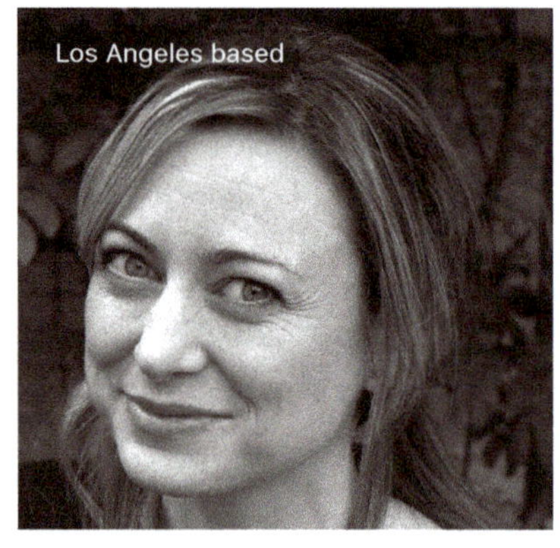

🕊 https://www.eekono.com/
@ eekono@eekono.com
◎ @e.e.kono

My work encourages reflection on how we are *connected* to *nature, the past, and each other.*

Growing up, E. E. Kono's family split their time between a diverse international community and small-town, middle America. The experience led to a life-long curiosity for how stories and symbols create meaning that is then interwoven between societies. Initially, this inspired a career in children's literature, writing and illustrating picture books. Now, she explores that imagery using ancient techniques and materials to create detailed, precise paintings that connect universal symbols and mythologies encountered in her travels and through the mixed heritage of her family.

While she is a self-taught painter, Kono studied art history at the University of Hull (England) and The University of Iowa (Iowa City, IA). She has studied traditional egg tempera techniques under the guidance of artist Koo Schadler. Although Kono is focusing on fine art, she is also an award-winning author and illustrator. Kono's work is collected internationally and is in the collection of the Mazza Museum (Findley, OH). Her work has also been exhibited in notable venues, including La Luz de Jesus (Los Angeles, CA), Modern Eden (San Francisco, CA), Beinart Gallery (Melbourne Australia), and Riverside Art Museum (Riverside, California).

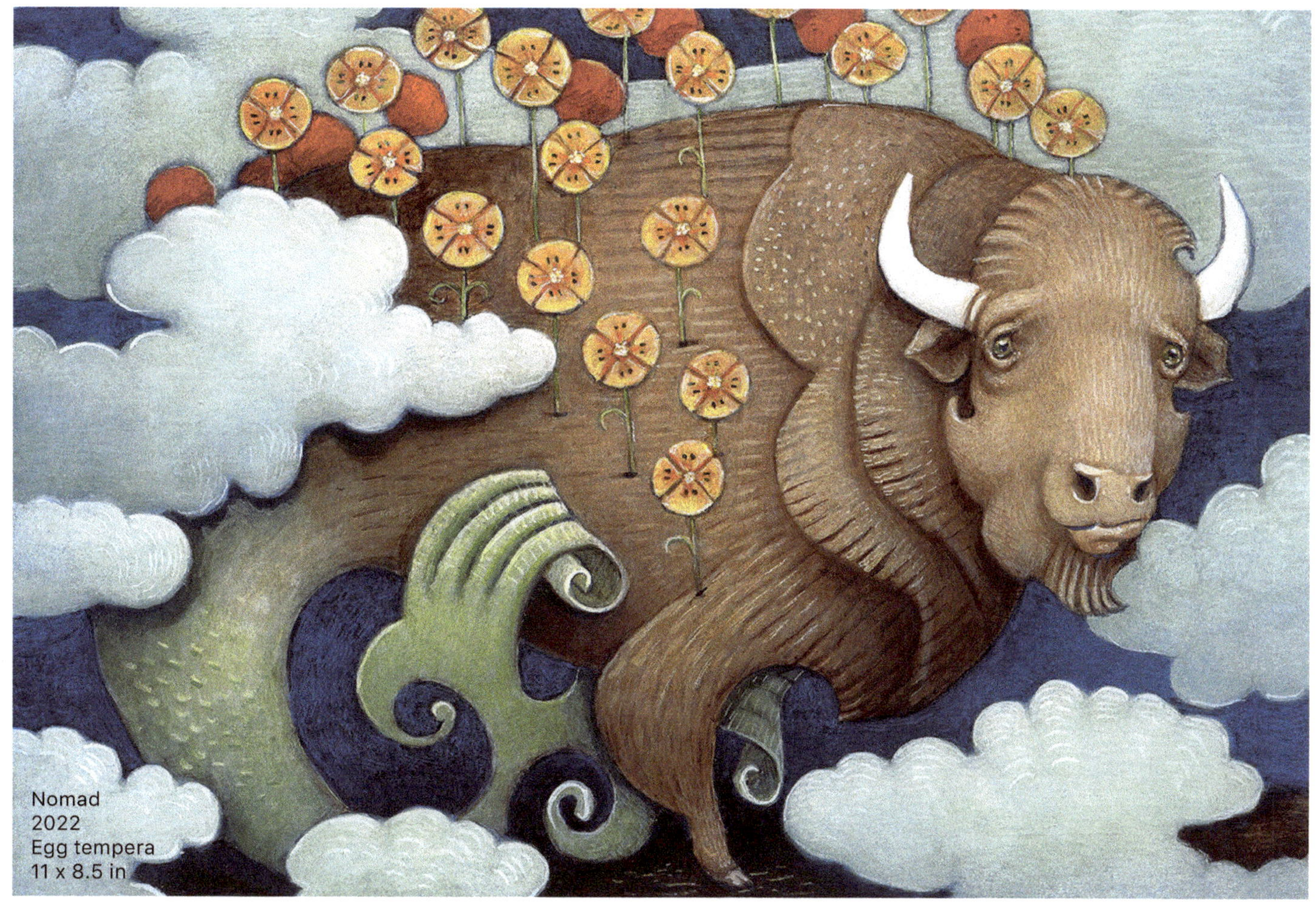

I'm interested in the fluidity of culture and time. Growing up, we spent our summers in a diverse international community and the rest of the year in Irish Catholic, middle America. I became intrigued by how stories and symbols create meaning and tap into a collective unconscious that is interwoven between societies and across time. The foundation for my practice is silverpoint, which forms the base of each painting. I've chosen this method to acknowledge the key role precious metals have played in establishing trade routes and developing the modern world. Egg tempera combines ground pigments with egg yolk and water. The pigments are sourced from across the globe, each telling a unique tale of its place of origin and history while uniting to create the artist's pallet. Egg tempera has been used for thousands of years, yet it is commonly associated with the early renaissance, a transitional era that parallels our own. My work encourages reflection on how we are connected to nature, the past, and each other.

What drives you to be an artist?
I once saw being an artist as having a career. But I've come to realize that being an artist is simply how I see, interact, and interpret the world.

I've learned that one of the ways that I can best contribute to others is to create and share visual connections. That is the purpose that drives me to improve my skills and deepen my practice.

How would you describe the art that you create and what inspires you?
My practice explores the fluidity of culture and time. I'm interested in how stories and symbols create meaning that's passed from one society to another, transcending cultures and offering a connection between diverse viewpoints.

I work primarily in egg tempera. Each of my paintings begins with a fully rendered metal point drawing on traditional gesso ground. I've chosen this method to acknowledge the key role that precious metals have played in the foundation of western culture and as the catalyst of global trade, capitalism, and colonialism. Ground pigments, sourced from across the globe and chosen for their specific historical and geographic significance, are mixed with egg yolk and water. The paint is then applied in hundreds of semi-translucent layers using a slow meditative process that connects directly to artists of the past.

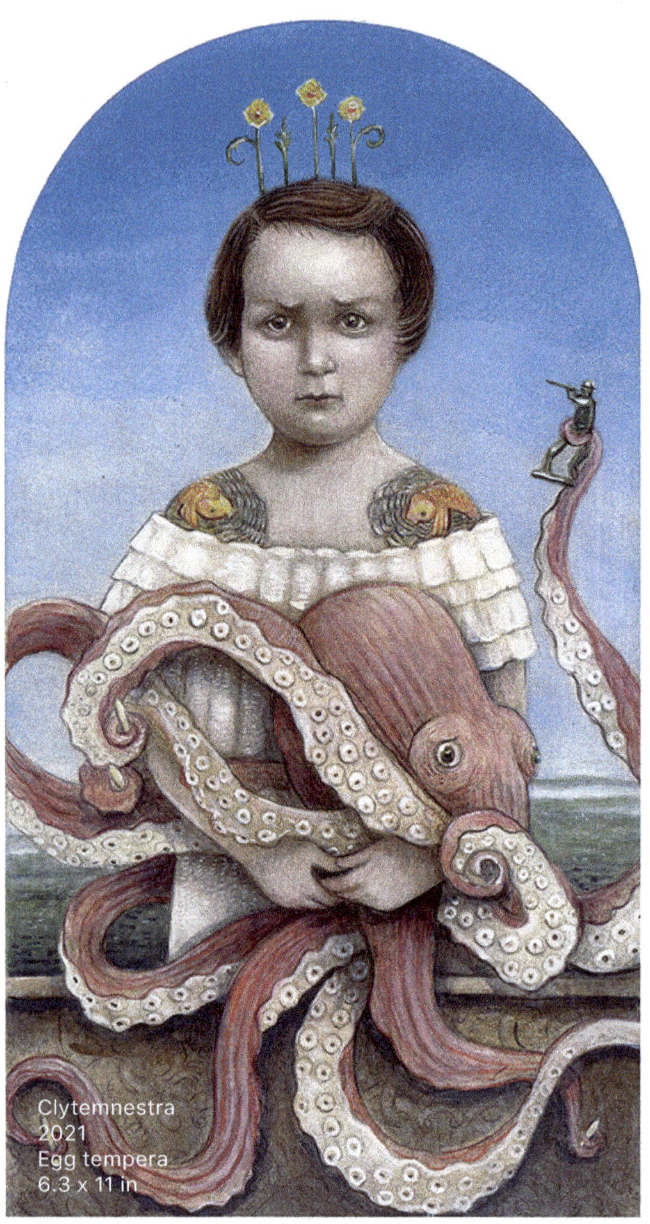

Clytemnestra
2021
Egg tempera
6.3 x 11 in

"My practice explores the fluidity of culture and time."

While used for thousands of years, egg tempera is most often associated with the early renaissance, an era that formed the foundation of the modern world. It's a period that parallels our own when the introduction of innovative technologies led to wide-ranging social disruption. By returning to the medium, I hope to highlight the cyclical nature of time and our roles in shaping the coming age.

If you could overcome all of your fears, what would you do with your art?

My dream is to create large-scale installations. I'd love to explore light, shadow, and sculptural elements to create an immersive experience that better contextualizes the imagery in my paintings.

When it comes to art making, how important is experimenting vs. sticking to a routine or set of rules?

Because I'm drawn to traditional mediums there are rules and steps that must be followed. Metal-point doesn't adhere without certain preparations. Each dry pigment requires a subtly different amount of egg binder. If the rules are ignored, the painting or drawing will disintegrate. Craft is important to me. It's a way to connect to the past. But we don't live in the past. Subject-wise it's vital to question who made the rules and why. Experimentation, and the willingness to fail, are key to creating anything worthwhile.

What are some of the challenges or experiences that have shaped your artistic journey so far?

Growing up middle class in middle America I didn't see fine art as a viable career. Despite receiving a scholarship for studio art to university, I actively avoided it, studying art history instead. I then went on to a career in commercial illustration. But, despite making a paycheck, it wasn't a good fit. Every vision was edited by committee and I lost my love for the process. Once I decided to stop thinking of creation as a commodity it became far more meaningful.

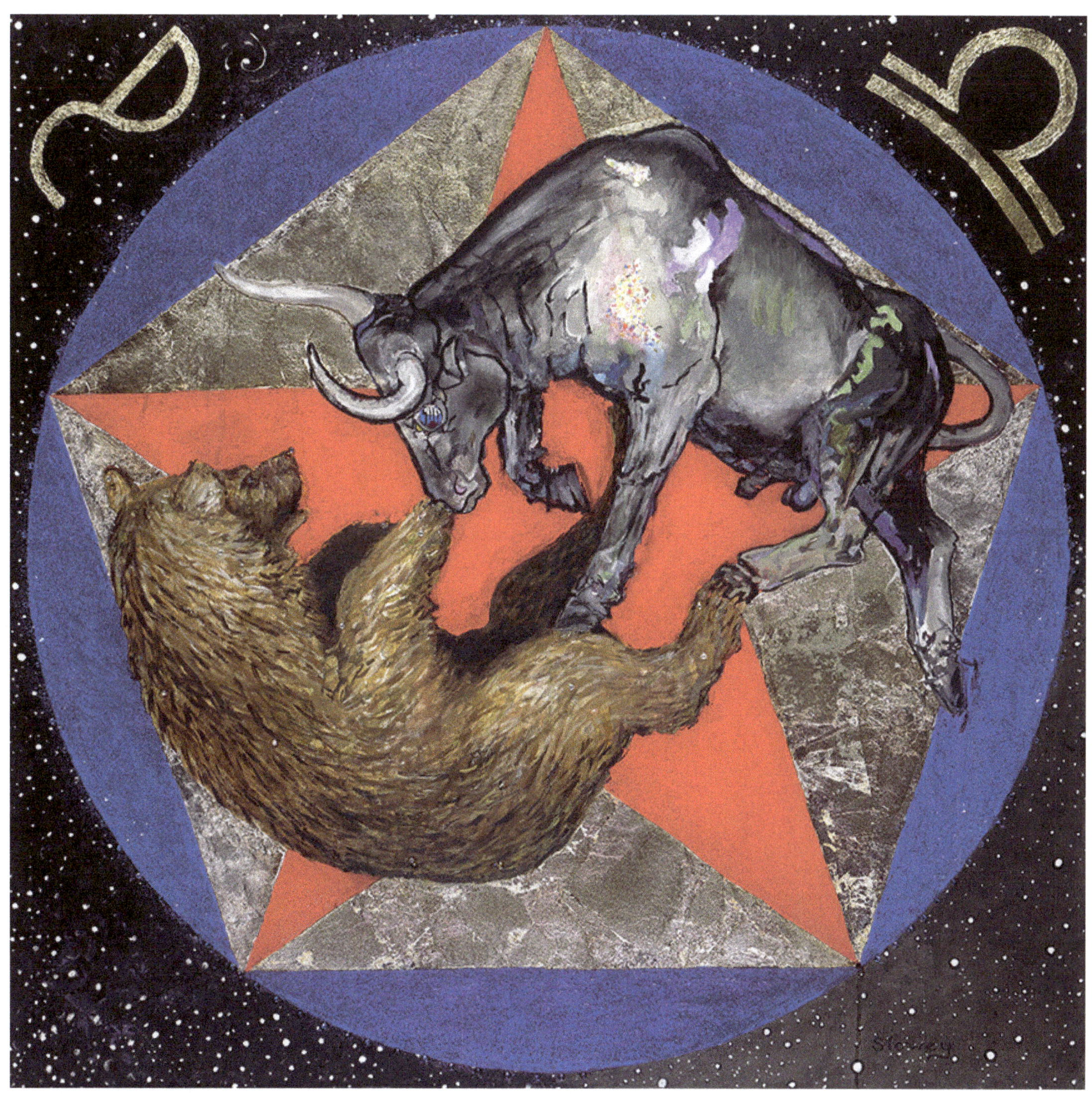

Polaris North Star
2019
Oil on canvas w crystals
36 x 36 inches

Debi Slowey Raguso

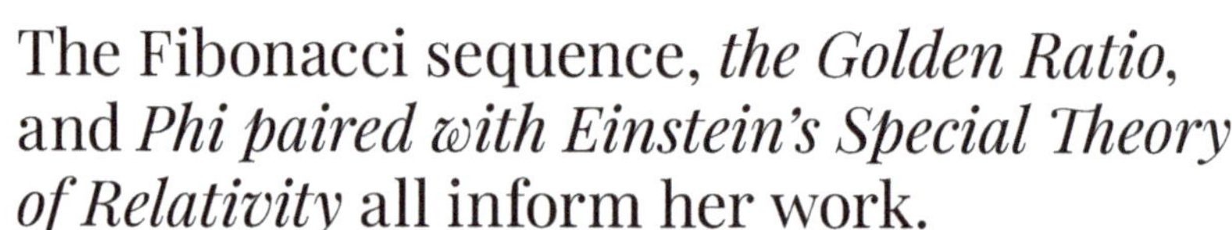

The Fibonacci sequence, *the Golden Ratio,* and *Phi paired with Einstein's Special Theory of Relativity* all inform her work.

🔗 https://www.debslowey.com
@ debslowey@gmail.com
📷 *@debslowey*

Deb Slowey's paintings engage the viewer with stories about myths and legends, living in a moment, in an imagined space, yet rooted in mathematical principles and formulas. The Fibonacci sequence, the Golden Ratio, and Phi paired with Einstein's Special Theory of Relativity all inform her work. The stories can take place in the past or the future.

Deb Slowey lives and works in the Tampa Bay region of Florida. She studied painting at the Pennsylvania Academy of Fine Art, aesthetics at the Barnes Foundation School of Art, and printmaking at Bob Blackburn's PMW. For nearly two decades, Slowey lived and worked in the Chelsea neighborhood of New York City under the mentorship of Will Barnet.

Slowey had solo exhibitions at notable galleries such as Chuck Levitan Gallery (New York, NY) and The Stone House Museum (Hasbrouck, NY). Her work is also in prominent permanent collections such as the US Embassy in Paris, France, The Printmaking Workshop Collection (New York, NY), St. Mary's College (Maryland), Parana Curitiba (Brazil), and many more. She has also been a Registered Nurse for nearly two decades.

What drives you to be an artist?

To be an artist fulfills my need to say that we are more than our physical beings of individual consciousness. We are energy down to vibrating electrons that compose our body's cells.

What happens to this energy when we sleep? Why do we need sleep stages, especially the dream state of REM? What becomes of us when we no longer need sleep or feel pain? Why is grief predictable in those connected with our energy when our energy changes at death? Energy is not stable without reflection, attraction or repulsion. Life energy requires the other. When I die I want my energy to still reflect on someone that sees and loves something I have created with my heart/soul. is to create and share visual connections. That is the purpose that drives me to improve my skills and deepen my practice.

How would you describe the art that you create and what inspires you?

I love color, and as a child in the 60's was significantly influenced by the hippy flower children that would gather in the backpark that my childhood yard spilled into. From the colorful clothes to the music lyrics of Bob Dylan and Carol King their "love-ins" were more fun to watch than playing with toys on a Saturday afternoon. Because of these childhood encounters, I took an interest in the 60s counterculture as a young adult influenced by psychedelics. I don't need to repeat the tripping experience. However, I will always question if the colors I hallucinated and that I can still use were nature expanded or are part of the energy from my imagination.

In recent years I started basing my compositions on the Fibonacci sequence. I had thought I was mainly making compositions by intuition or instinct, but as I discovered in music, there are mathematical reasons for my actions. I decided to study the Fibonacci idea and combine it purposely with what I put energetically and with physicality in my paintings.

If you could overcome all of your fears, what would you do with your art?

I would get my work out there more if I thought I would always be accepted. I would not put something "out there if I did not believe in it." My biggest fear is the disappointment of acceptance followed by an error that the judgment was incorrect and with a follow-up rejection. That rejection reminds me of protests I made in childhood when picking teams; if you chose someone, I wanted everyone to agree that you couldn't change the choice.

When it comes to art making, how important is experimenting vs. sticking to a routine or set of rules?

This choice is a tricky question. Both- I love experimenting, yet I know how to begin a painting and when it is completed routinely. Experimentation throughout the creation is necessary to keep the process fun; fun is important to me!

I love getting new tools and keeping up and incorporating the latest gadget or processes. These tools, when used well, make the paintings as a whole different and fresh from each other.

What are some of the challenges or experiences that have shaped your artistic journey so far?

I always credit other creative people I have been with on my journey as my most crucial experience; I love people! They have helped me so much.

As a teen, I knew that running around Wyeth country landscape painting was fun but only sustainable for a short time without camaraderie and friendships. I wanted and went to the city and found fellowship for four years with the students and teachers at PAFA, after which I moved to Manhattan. I had a very engaging life in NYC among the art and extraordinary people in the art circles they privileged me to. After 20 years, I decided that I wanted to live where the weather was warm, and the cost of living was more manageable, so I moved to Florida after realizing that the internet and travel would keep me connected.

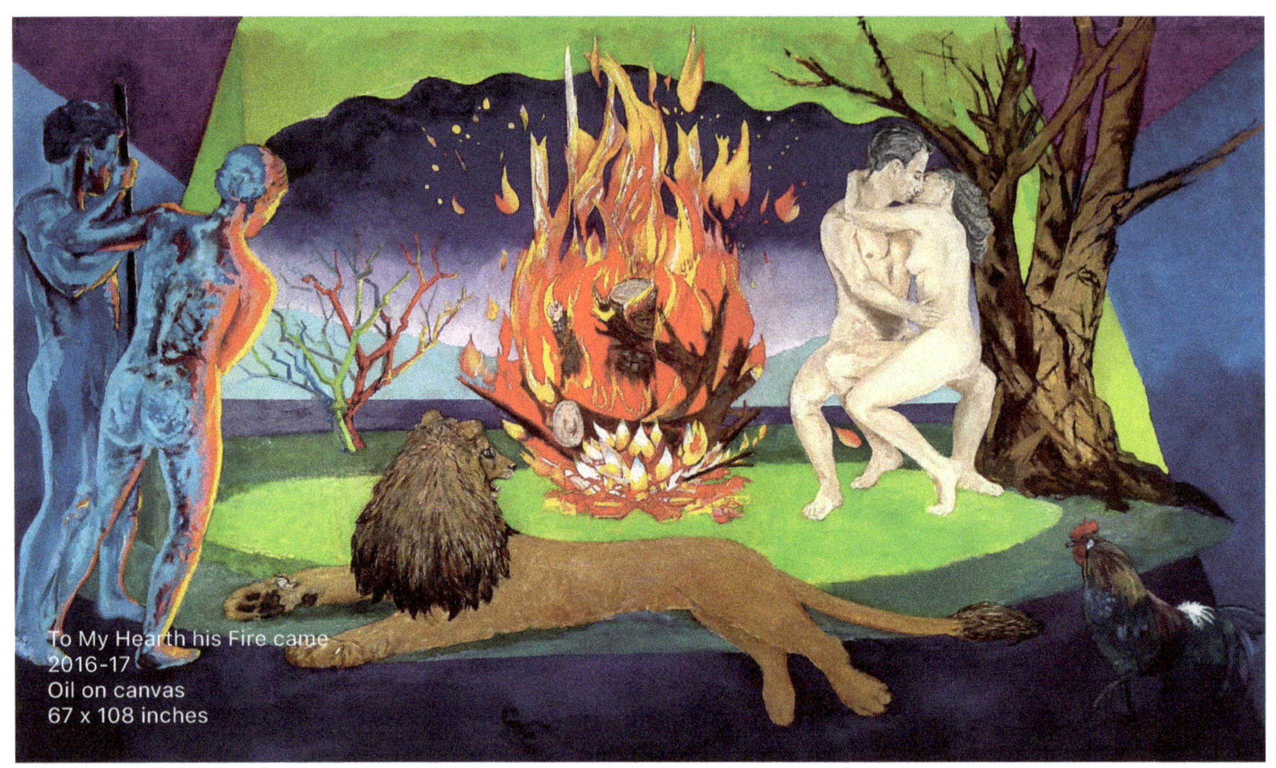

To My Hearth his Fire came
2016-17
Oil on canvas
67 x 108 inches

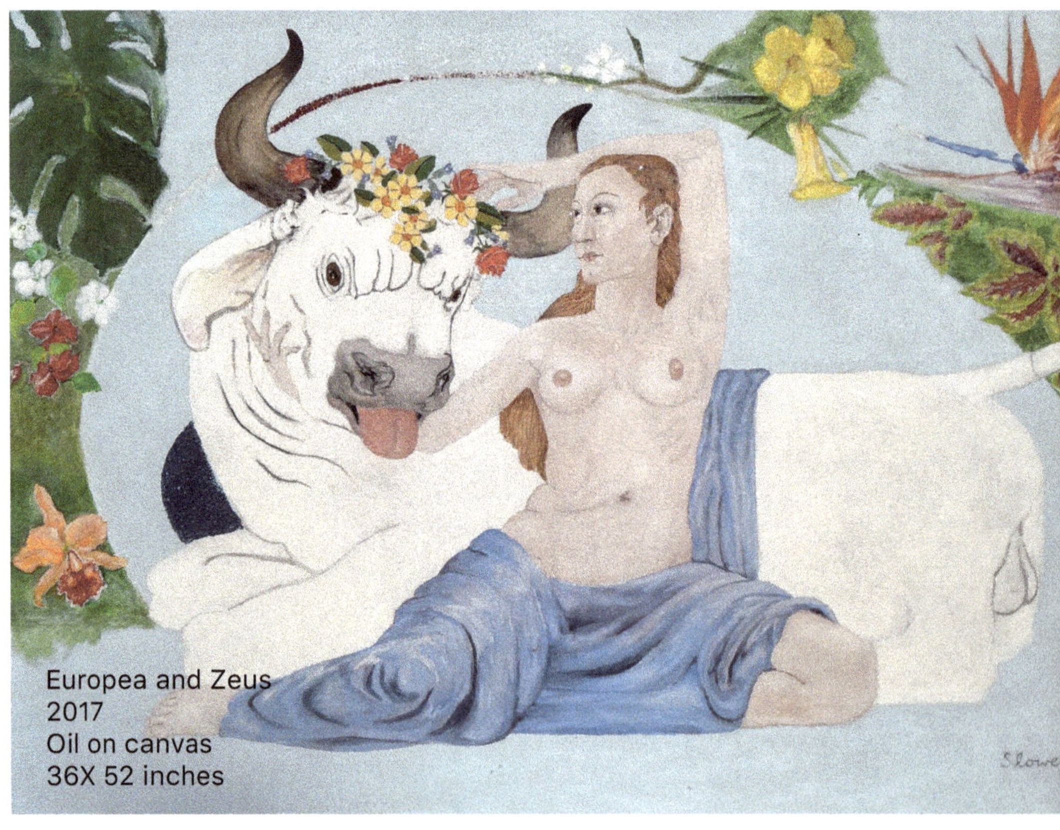

Europea and Zeus
2017
Oil on canvas
36X 52 inches

"I would not put something "out there if I did not believe in it."

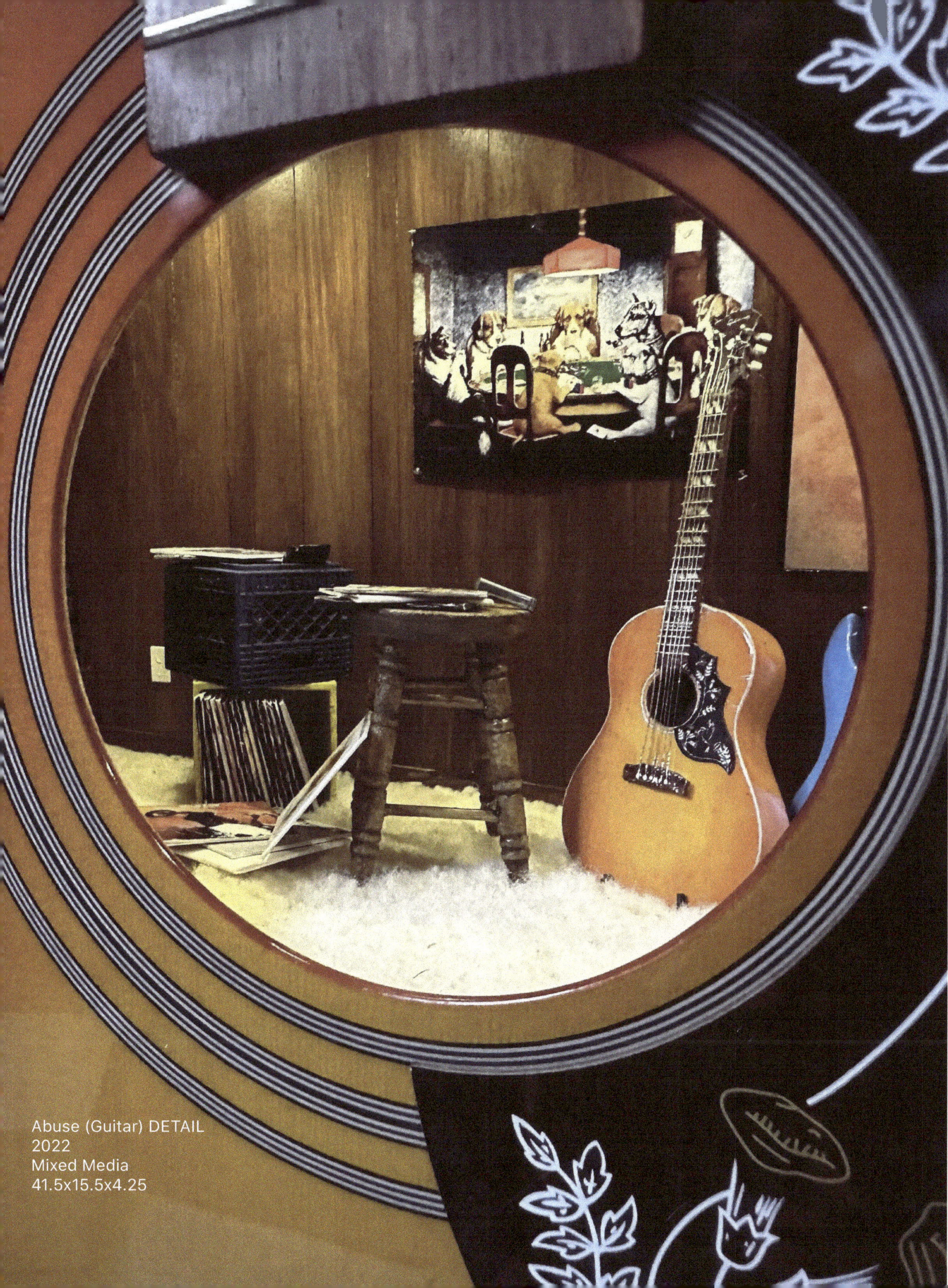

Abuse (Guitar) DETAIL
2022
Mixed Media
41.5x15.5x4.25

Joanne Steinhardt

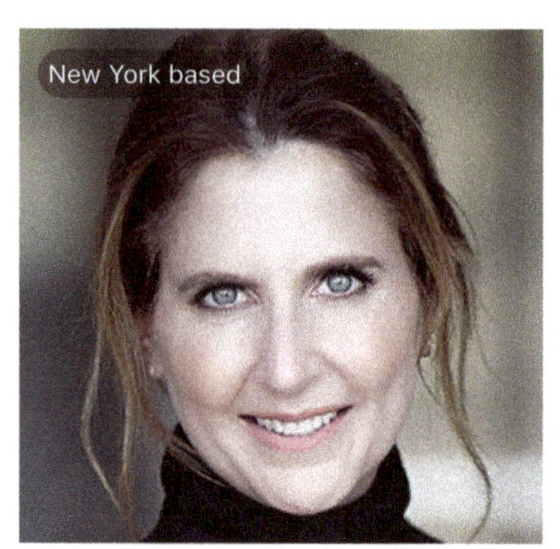

http://www.JoanneSteinhardt.com
@ joannesteinhardtstudio@gmail.com
@joannesteinhardt

I used to *fear the viewer, the market, the critics,* etcetera but I have *let a lot of that go.*

Joanne Steinhardt lives and works in the Greater New York City Metro Area. She holds a Master of Fine Arts from the Maine College of Art and a Bachelor of Science in Photography from the RIT School of Photographic Arts and Sciences. Steinhardt's work has been exhibited at The Equity Gallery, Carter Burden, The Tampa Museum of Art, Polk County Museum, and Covivant Gallery. She has been Artist in Residence at Willow Brook Farm and Art Center in New Hampshire and done several residencies in US and Europe. She has lectured and led workshops at numerous institutions around the US and abroad, including Parsons School for Design, University of Florida, NYU Tisch ITP, the Harrison School for the Arts, and La Biennale del fin del Mundo in Ushuaia, Argentina. Previously, Steinhardt achieved tenure in both the Art and Communication Departments at the University of Tampa where she conceived a multidisciplinary Electronic Media Art and Technology Program designed to support those interested in a self-directed academic Major combining art, communication, English, music, computer information systems, and entrepreneurship.

In a series of painstaking, tiny sculptural recreations that inhabit the tragedies of her family, from abortion and abuse to disease and beyond, Joanne Steinhardt's intimate portrayal of rooted obsession attempts to refill our deepest human absences, opening a peephole into an emotionally wrenching, embodied state of disembodiment. Object attachment, the experience a person has when they feel an emotional fettering to an inanimate object, is at the core of Steinhardt's projects. Psychologically, we imbue possessions with deep meaning to fill a void. She collects objects that were the point of attachment for another, repairs, repurpose, and sometimes, literally, furnishes them. The physical is transferred, and the arduous combination of collection, creation, research, and production, means each piece takes months and years to create. Like ancestral altars, these objects become familiar sites of displacement and refuge.

What drives you to be an artist?

I am driven as an artist to build a connection between me and the world around me. For me, the need to make is two-fold. On one side of it is the making. I use the process of making to deeply examine issues and topics that affect me at any given point in time. For example, interpersonal relationships, reproductive rights, obsession, and usefulness of people and things that have outlived their societal "use." The other side is using the work created to drive community discussion, engage in open dialog, and inspire others. Showing the work is a part of it but teaching, participating in panels, lectures, workshops, delivering master classes, and such is where the real purpose of my practice lives. For me, making without engagement is an incomplete process.

How would you describe the art that you create and what inspires you?

My artwork is (and always has been) deeply personal at times bordering on sentimental. I have always examined interpersonal communication and relationships, whether it be with another or that which we nurture within ourselves. From making paper from the lint collected from individuals' laundry, to intertwined narratives etched in glass, books whose content-material-form all marry, drawing with thread on rags that have outlived their purpose, or building tiny environments that represent the effects of object obsession I am inspired by relationships (both good and bad) and driven by the materials I use. In turn, I look for the broader themes that reach into the larger discussions of culture and society.

I am most inspired by the conversations the work generates; the stories I am told and the people who readily choose to share themselves with me as a result of viewing / interacting with a piece.

If you could overcome all of your fears, what would you do with your art?

I used to fear the viewer, the market, the critics, etcetera but I have let a lot of that go. The fear that I maintain is the fear of somehow not fitting into the set definitions within the art world. If I could overcome that, I think I would be more prolific because I would spend less time figuring out how to fit in and more time just creating and making.

When it comes to art making, how important is experimenting vs. sticking to a routine or set of rules?

For me it is all about experimentation! There is a joke in the studio that "there is no YouTube video for that." I let the combination of the idea/message and material drive the creation process and everything else after that is about experimentation. Problem solving is an important component to my overall making process.

What are some of the challenges or experiences that have shaped your artistic journey so far?

There have been several significant challenges/ experiences along the way. Having children definitely reshaped how I view the world. I am lucky to have had some amazing advisors, mentors, and collaborators each who have had significant impact. But if I had to pick one overarching challenge, it would be the theft of an entire body of work that had been my single creative focus from 2012 to 2019. This event forced me to question literally everything causing significant change in me. I cannot say I have moved past it, but I have learned to live with the loss, embrace it, and use it to move forward.

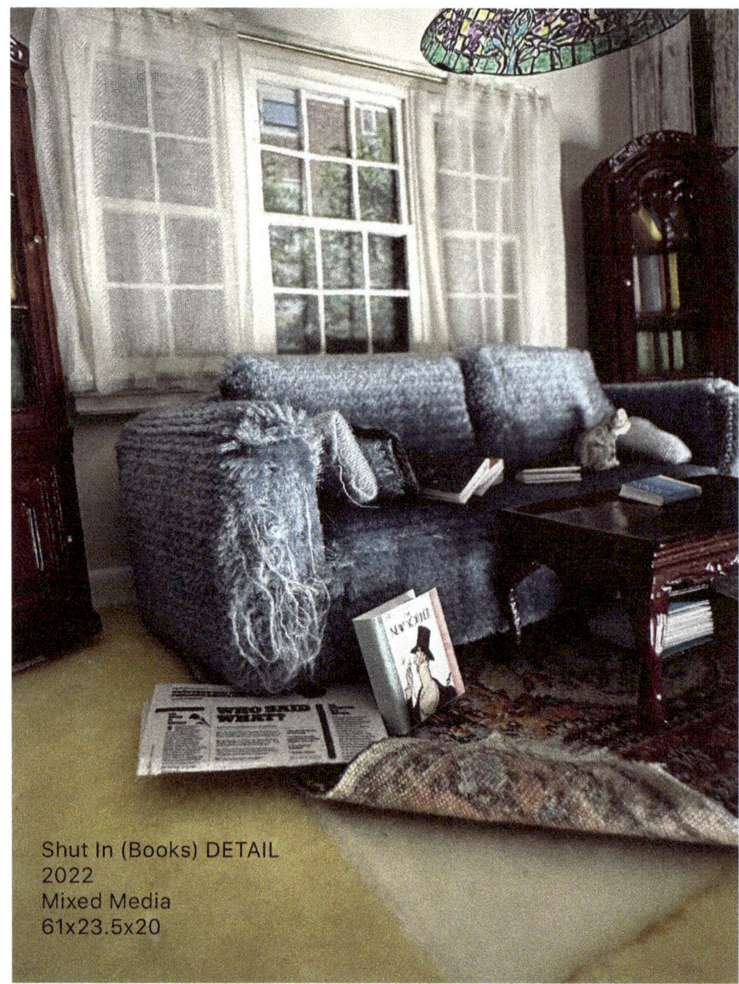

Shut In (Books) DETAIL
2022
Mixed Media
61x23.5x20

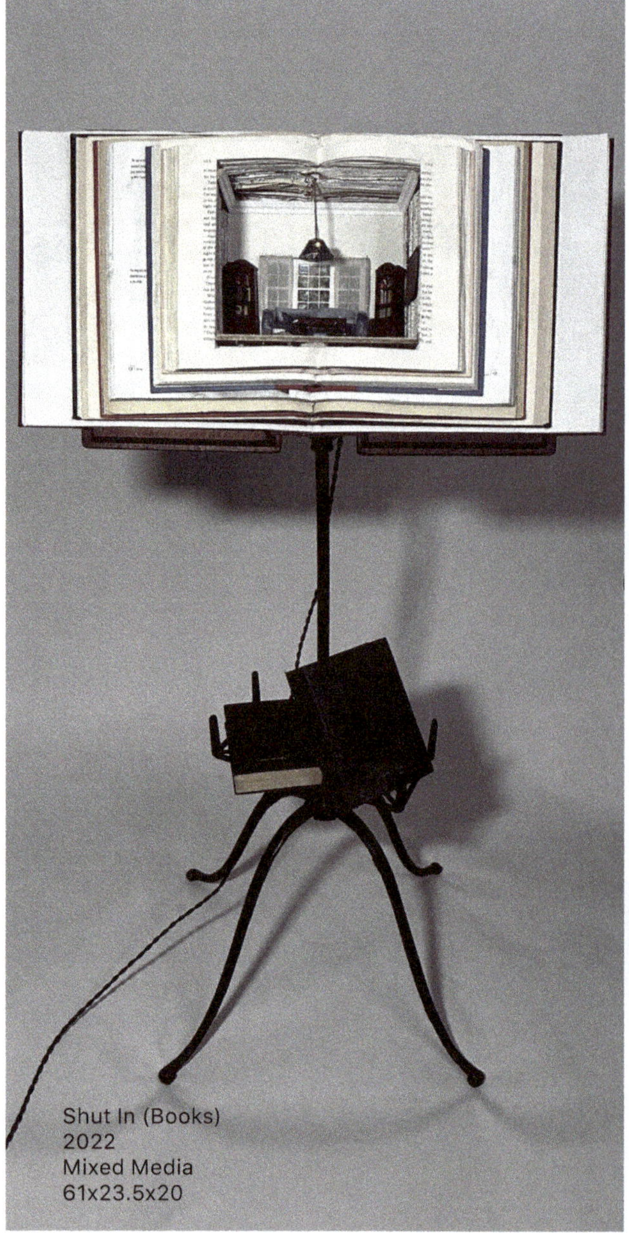

Shut In (Books)
2022
Mixed Media
61x23.5x20

"Problem solving is an important component to my overall making process."

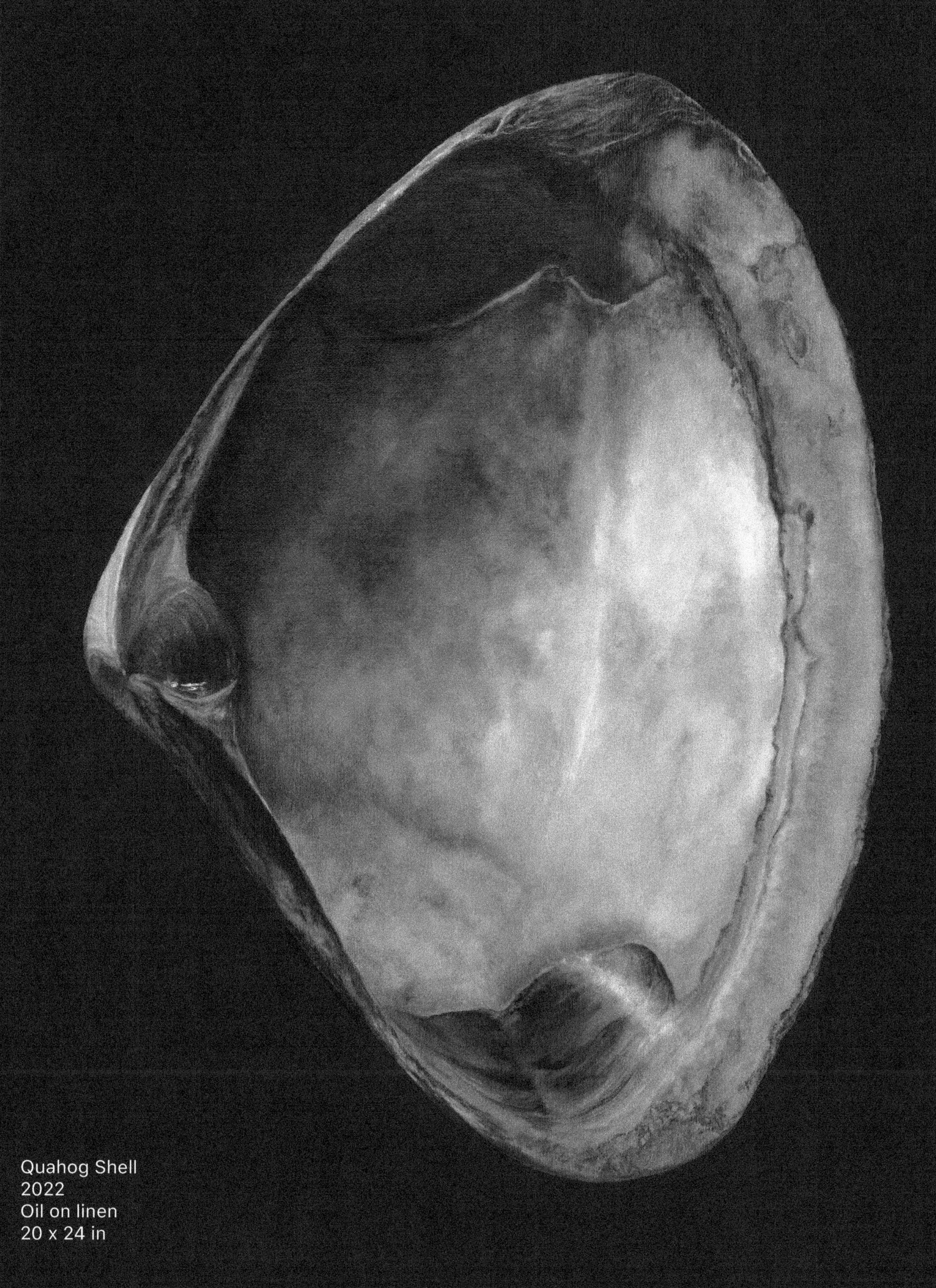

Quahog Shell
2022
Oil on linen
20 x 24 in

Sarah Verardo

The act of painting my subject is more than study and is ultimately a *reflection or meditative practice.*

Sarah Verardo is a contemporary oil painter based in Providence, Rhode Island. Having grown up in coastal New England, the ocean has always been a familiar representation of home. After living in New York City for 14 years, Sarah returned to Rhode Island, connecting with the seaside New England environment in a different way as an adult. The idea of home, and in particular proximity to the ocean, changed from a pacifying comfort to become more of a spiritual and reflective touchstone. Through her work, Sarah pays homage to the role her environment has had in her personal evolution through both trying and celebratory times in her life.

Sarah graduated from Georgetown University with a BA in Government and, when not painting, works in digital marketing. She is an Elected Artist at the Art League of Rhode Island. Her work has been featured in juried exhibitions with the Art League of Rhode Island and the California Art League. Sarah's work belongs to private collections within the United States and internationally.

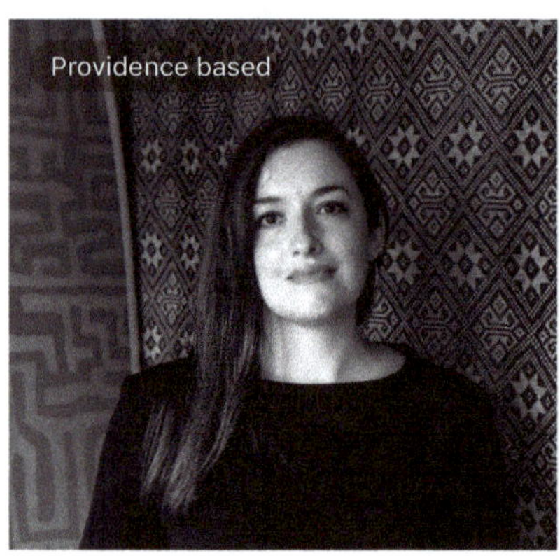

https://www.sarahverardoart.com
@ sarah@sarahverardoart.com
@sarahverardo_art

My subjects are organic, with complexities and layers. There are intricacies that I don't pick up on until I'm well into my painting process. The act of painting my subject is more than study and is ultimately a reflection or meditative practice. I am able to take the time to truly consider my subject, and through that process, I am more considerate of my own presence and the presence of the environment around me. My hope is that when someone views my work, they are also inspired to stop and be more mindful of their surroundings and step outside of themselves.

I consider the opportunity I have to paint to be a gift. It continues to afford me the chance to be a more mindful person, and if I'm able to share that experience with just a handful of people, then it is well worth any effort.

What drives you to be an artist?

I did not start painting until I was almost 40. I was a creative kid, took some art classes in college, but it never once occurred to me that being an artist was a viable career path. I worked in marketing for almost 20 years, and I liked it, but looking back I realize now that I did not understand true fulfillment until I started painting. I go to bed at night thinking about the next time I get to paint, and that feels incredibly fortunate. I suppose I'm driven to be an artist because I have the benefit of hindsight, and I can appreciate what it means to really love what you do. I am eternally grateful that I have found my purpose.

How would you describe the art that you create and what inspires you?

The art I create is always a study and sort of a meditation. I paint the things around me in nature, isolating a piece that's usually overlooked. My subjects are things I pick up on the beaches of Rhode Island, where I live. I gravitate to pieces that are broken and weathered by nature, exposing details and intricacies that are usually overlooked and unappreciated. Painting my subjects allows me to be more present, and my hope is that my paintings inspire others to be more aware themselves.

If you could overcome all of your fears, what would you do with your art?

I feel like I am forced to overcome my fears and inhibitions every day. I'm absolutely terrified every time I share my art, post on Instagram, or reach out to a complete stranger. I constantly push myself out of my own comfort zone, so it's hard to identify what more I would do.

When it comes to art making, how important is experimenting vs. sticking to a routine or set of rules?

I think evolution is incredibly important to any individual. No one has it all figured out a day one – especially artists. My first paintings were seascapes, and at the time, I couldn't imagine painting anything else. Now I've just finished an oversized still life of a rock. Life is unpredictable, and it would be incredibly boring if I knew what and how I was going to paint for the rest of my life. It can be hard in the social media age to be willing to be a bit messy, but that's usually where the best ideas are born.

What are some of the challenges or experiences that have shaped your artistic journey so far?

Like a lot of people, my artistic journey took off during the pandemic when I had the time and inclination to start a new hobby. What has really shaped my journey, however, was navigating my grief after the death of my father. I think I have gained a lot of perspective through that experience, and it has been my greatest motivation for living a purposeful life. My art is an expression of this purpose.

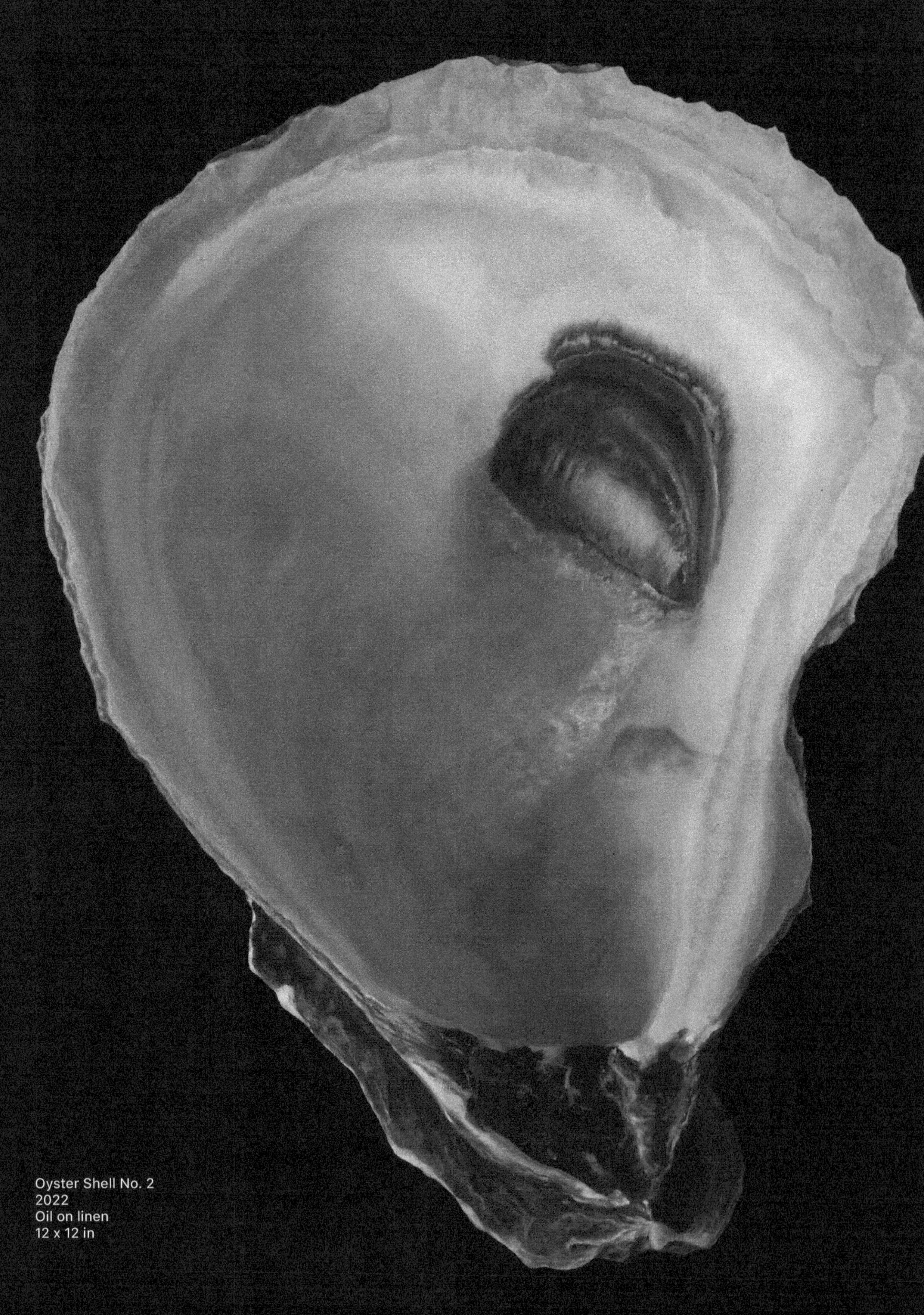

Oyster Shell No. 2
2022
Oil on linen
12 x 12 in

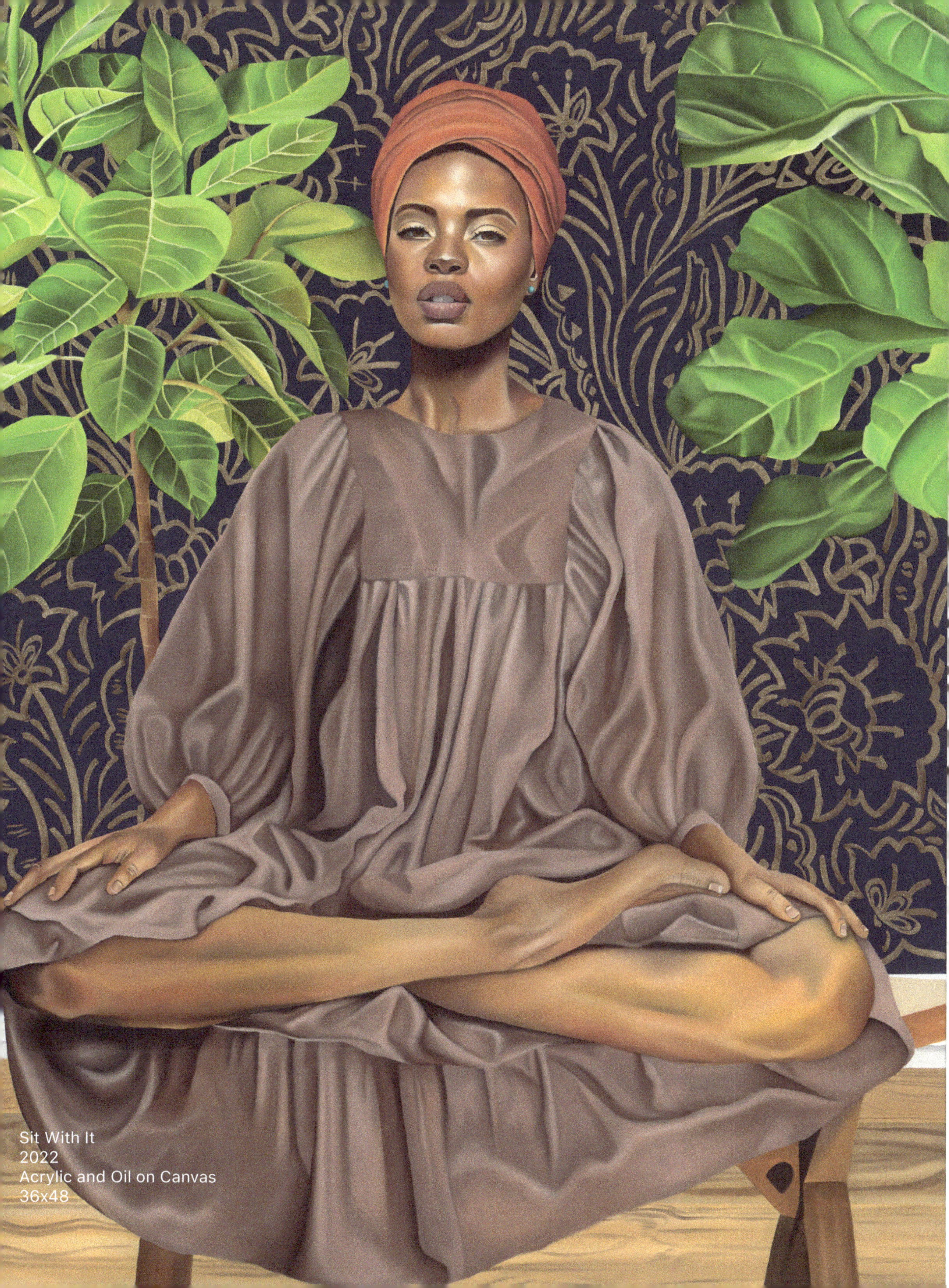

Sit With It
2022
Acrylic and Oil on Canvas
36x48

Taylor Bamgbose

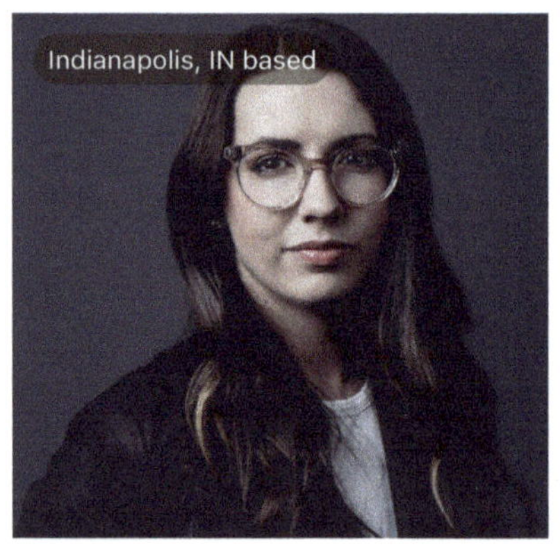

🌐 https://www.taylorbamgbose.com
@ taylor@taylorbamgbose.com
📷 *@taylorbamgbose*

My hope is that my work creates greater awareness of our *thoughts, emotions, and behavioral patterns.*

Taylor Bamgbose is a self-taught visual artist based in ITaylor Bamgbose is a self-taught visual artist based in Indianapolis, IN. Also a certified life coach, she works at the intersection of art and mental health. Her vibrant figurative paintings take the audience on a journey of guided self-reflection, inviting the viewer to explore how their thoughts, emotions, beliefs, and behaviors are working under the surface to shape their lived experience. In the four years she's been working as an artist, she has completed three major bodies of work; Verses, a poetry-inspired collection; State of Mind, which explores the nuances of everyday emotions; and Deal With It, which tackles how we cope with big emotions, for better or worse.

Taylor's work has won several awards, including "Best of Show" at two juried competitions. In 2022, she was awarded the Robert D. Beckmann, Jr. Emerging Artist Fellowship through the Indianapolis Arts Council. She was also selected for the Hoosier Women Artists Program, an initiative of the Indiana Arts Commission. Her work has been displayed in the Indiana Statehouse and in vinyl murals throughout the city of Indianapolis, as well as featured in several art publications, including I Like Your Work's Spring Exhibition Catalog, Create! Magazine, New Visionary Magazine, and Divide Magazine.

What drives you to be an artist?

I've always been a very visual person. Even back in school, I learned the best when a concept was illustrated to me, rather than simply spoken. And I think that's what I love most about being an artist, and what drives me to create work—I want to create visual representations that help people absorb and integrate a message or a concept. I want my paintings to be able to serve as touchpoints in people's daily lives, providing a tangible reminder or challenge or encouragement every time they see them.

How would you describe the art that you create and what inspires you?

The art I create is designed to help my audience explore their inner world—the thoughts, emotions, beliefs, and behaviors that shape who they are, how they experience themselves, and how they show up in the world. Though my main subject is women, I illustrate realities that are often universal to the human experience, regardless of gender, race, or nationality. And at the same time, the specific ways we have lived these realities is also entirely unique and personal. Through my work, I hope to provide a compassionate, non-judgmental space for people to feel seen, understood, and connected to one another, and to grow in self-awareness.

While I have always been fascinated by psychology and human behavior, I am predominantly inspired by my experiences as a certified life coach. Being in that space not only has made me more aware of my own inner life, but has also given me a window into our common struggles—our emotional wounds, limiting beliefs, self-sabotaging behaviors, and coping mechanisms. I've had the privilege to be in many vulnerable and healing environments, and I hope to bring some of this encouragement to my audience through my art.

If you could overcome all of your fears, what would you do with your art?

If I could work through my fear, I would love to find more ways to combine all the things I love—art, coaching, and writing. I already do this in my solo shows, where I pair paintings that are inspired by topics from coaching with pretty extensive wall labels. These labels tell a little bit about each piece, but almost always include some reflective questions, so each person who views the work can personalize it to their own experience.

I have a dream of doing something like an illustrated coffee table book of essays, or something along those lines in the future. For me, my art practice isn't just about selling art. It's about helping the people who encounter my work build a deeper, healthier relationship with themselves (and others by extension). It's about truly flourishing, and finding the emotional freedom to become the best version of ourselves.

When it comes to art making, how important is experimenting vs. sticking to a routine or set of rules?

I'm primarily a self-taught artist, so I haven't historically felt bound by many "rules" in my art making. I like to approach a painting intuitively, choosing colors that feel right rather than being constrained by convention or photo-realism. Everything has an advantage and disadvantage, so I'm sure there is much I could learn from the rules of art, such as color theory, composition, and more, but I have found my way this far mainly through experimentation.

While I don't focus on rules, I do have a routine in how I approach a new body of work. I like to come up with a broad message or focus, then brainstorm individual concepts that support that idea. Once I've generated some possible titles, I start to create visuals to go along with each. I mock up each painting on my iPad using Procreate, and then once I've tinkered to my heart's content and I am happy with the cohesiveness of the collection, I sketch the images on canvas and begin to paint.

What are some of the challenges or experiences that have shaped your artistic journey so far?

I don't have much formal art training, and I never imagined myself becoming a full-time artist, so I've had to contend with the occasional flare-up of imposter syndrome. It took me a while to introduce myself as an artist with joy and confidence. This journey has also required me to confront some limiting beliefs about money, providing value, and personal worth. I've also had the most incredible experiences through art in the 4 years I've been working. My work has been the conduit to some inspiring, encouraging, vulnerable conversations, and has allowed me to connect with others on a deep and beautiful level. It's also given me immense joy to know that so many people have chosen to have my work in their homes—to live their lives with it, to cherish it, and to let it enhance their day to day.

I've felt incredibly supported in my art journey so far, and the thing I love most about it is the experience of being my most authentic self. I've been in a lot of jobs and a lot of spaces that didn't feel right, and each one of them has made me appreciate and treasure the life I'm living now all the more.

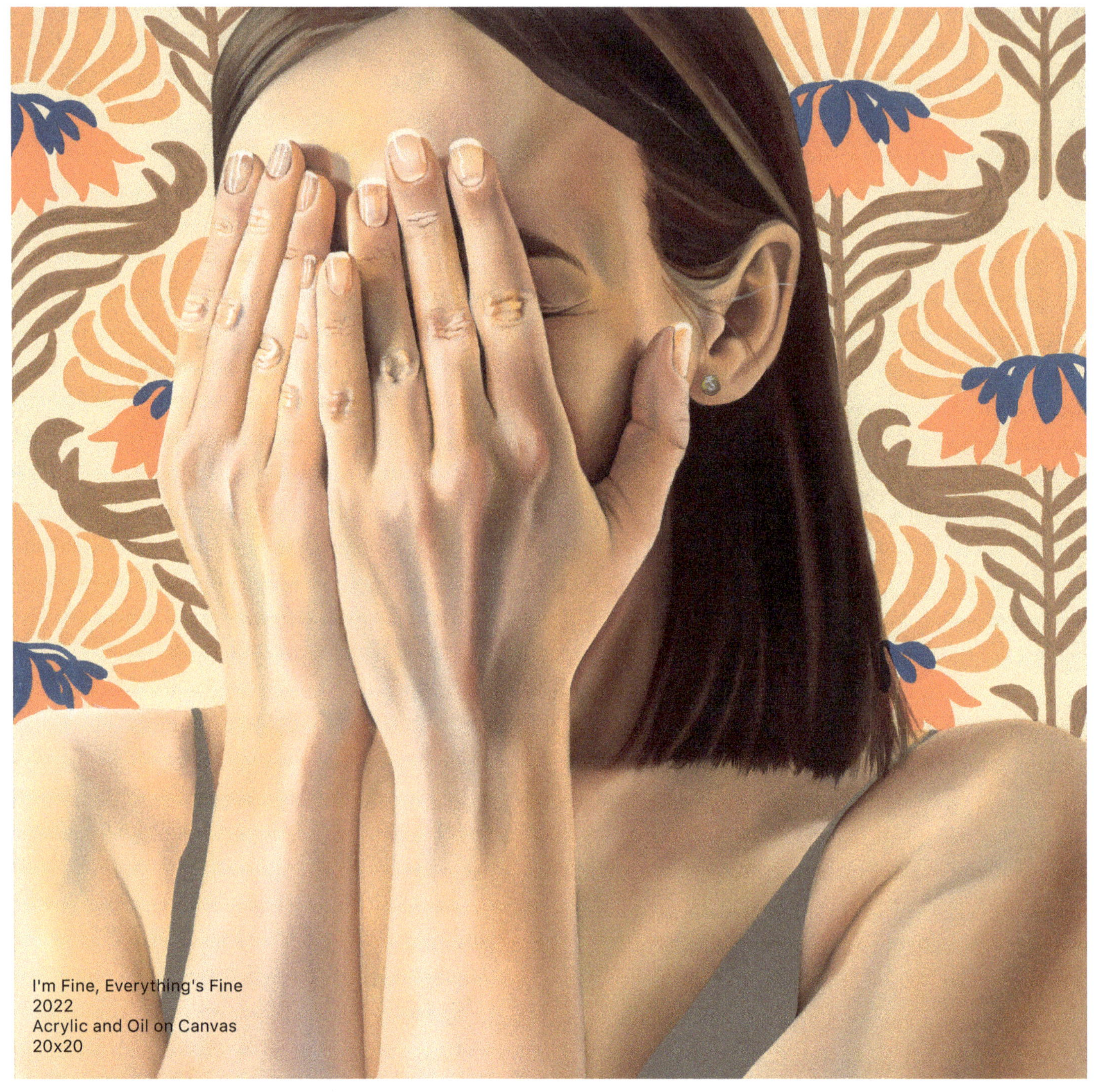

"I'm primarily a self-taught artist, so I haven't historically felt bound by many "rules" in my art making."

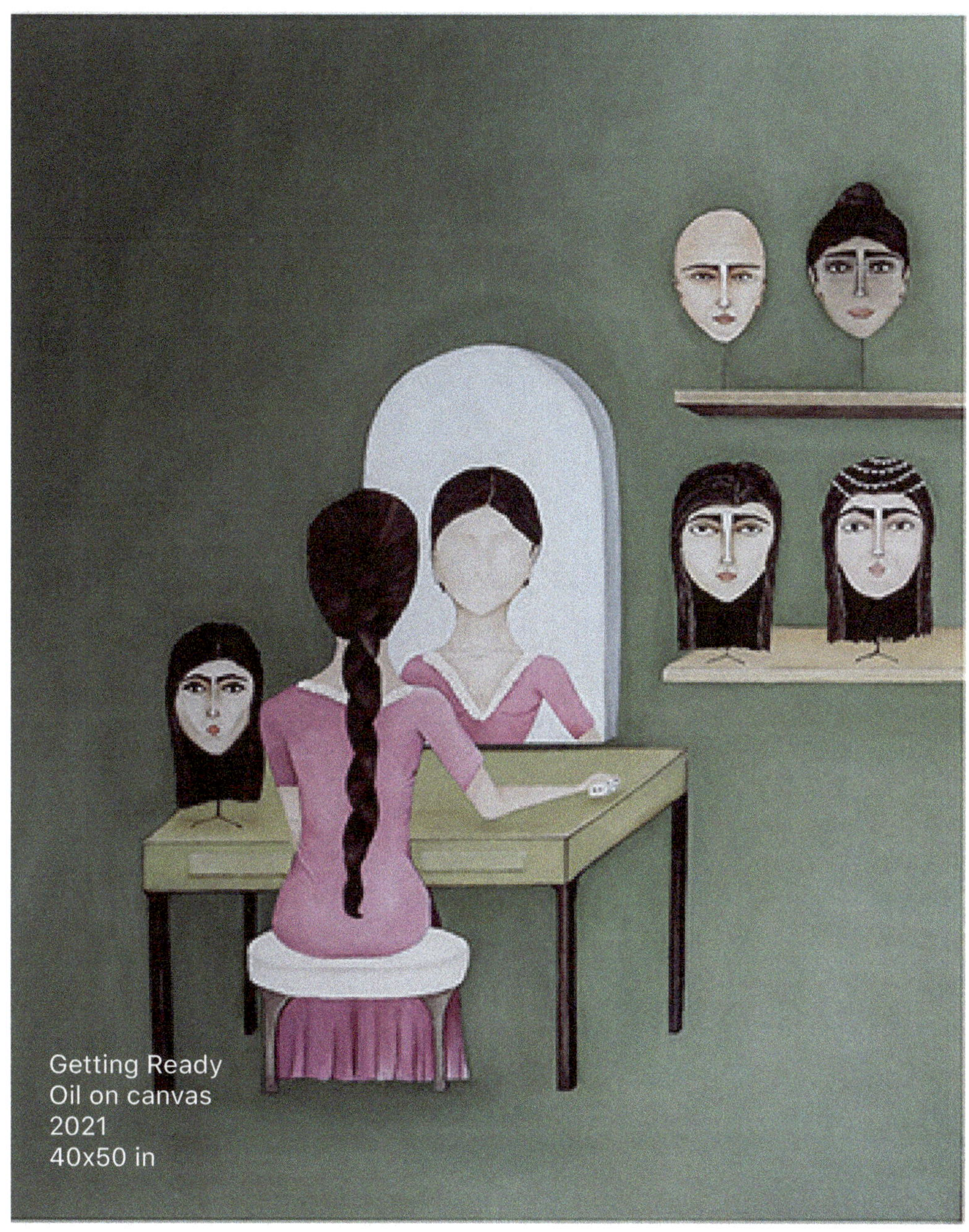

Getting Ready
Oil on canvas
2021
40x50 in

Sarrah Zadeh

There has always been a *burning desire,* an *energy beyond myself* that has always impelled me to *create.*

Sarrah Zadeh is a conceptual surrealist artist working primarily with oil paint. Zadeh finds inspiration from human connections and behaviors, and recently she has been exploring the intangible world of the subconsciousness. Her artworks narrate stories, bringing to light social taboos and norms, particularly the role of the women our society, allowing us to contemplate and question our social situations and surroundings. Originally from Iran, Sarrah Zadeh, has been living in the States since the age of ten, and for the past 15 years, she has been dividing her time between Colombia and USA. She holds a BA in Art from University of Houston.

I have always been intrigued not only by humanity and the role social standards play on human behavior, but also by the duality in nature and our subconsciousness. As an artist I believe my role is to tell a story, to create art that makes people think, ask questions, and in turn make them feel.

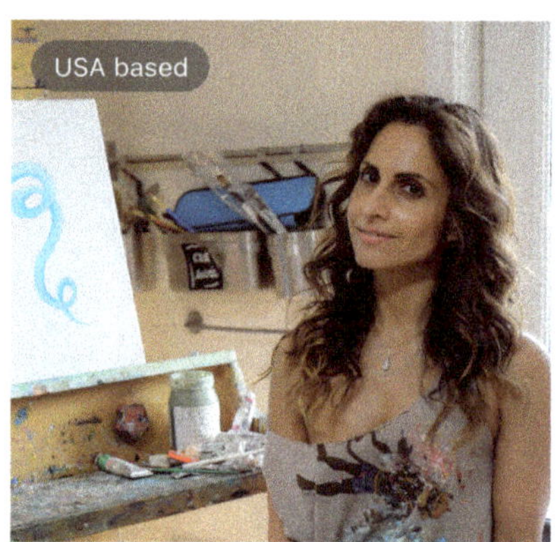

@ zadehsarrah@gmail.com
@sarrahzadehart

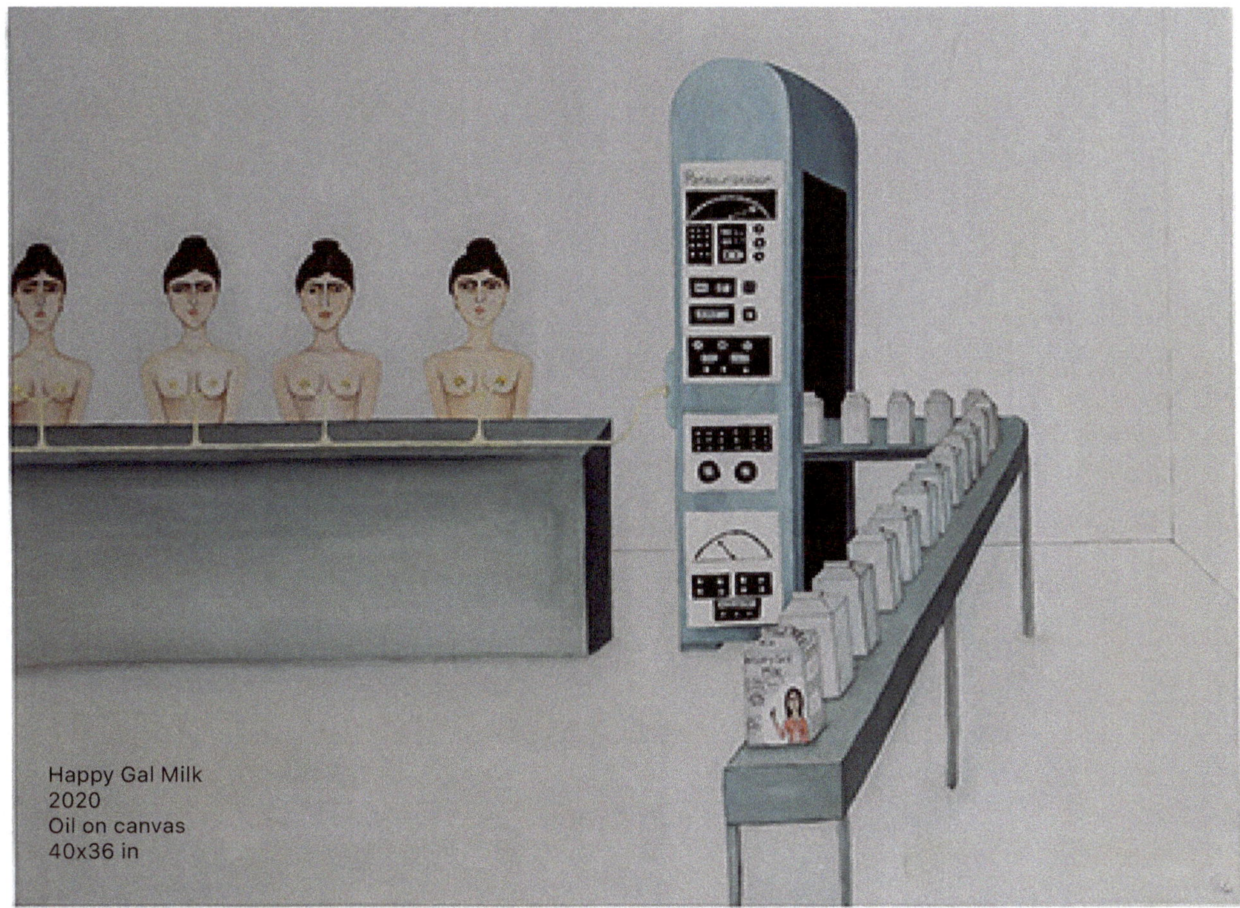

Happy Gal Milk
2020
Oil on canvas
40x36 in

What drives you to be an artist?

There has always been a burning desire, an energy beyond myself that has always impelled me to create. Even during my lowest lows, when I am physically, mentally, and emotionally depleted, there is always this powerful desire pulling me to tell stories, to give life to what I see and feel.

How would you describe the art that you create and what inspires you?

I would describe my art as arousing, in the terms of arousing a question about ourselves, believes, and our surrounding. My art is about telling a story in order to make the viewer ask questions, to face their own feelings and thoughts about the story being told.

If you could overcome all of your fears, what would you do with your art?

I think the last fear I need to overcome is having a solo show. This idea that I would be the only artist showing and having people view and comment on my artwork, is still a fearful idea for me.

When it comes to art making, how important is experimenting vs. sticking to a routine or set of rules?

As a self-taught artist I view experimentation in art making a key element in order to evolve in ones work and as an artist.

What are some of the challenges or experiences that have shaped your artistic journey so far?

One of the biggest challenges for me had been letting go of fear. I come from an environment where being an artist was not considered a true profession, and this fear of whether or not I would be able to live comfortably while creating authentic artwork had always guided my art career.

I have learned over the recent years to let go of this fear, and to believe in my intuition, the process, and to create art that is true to whom I am as a person and as an artist.

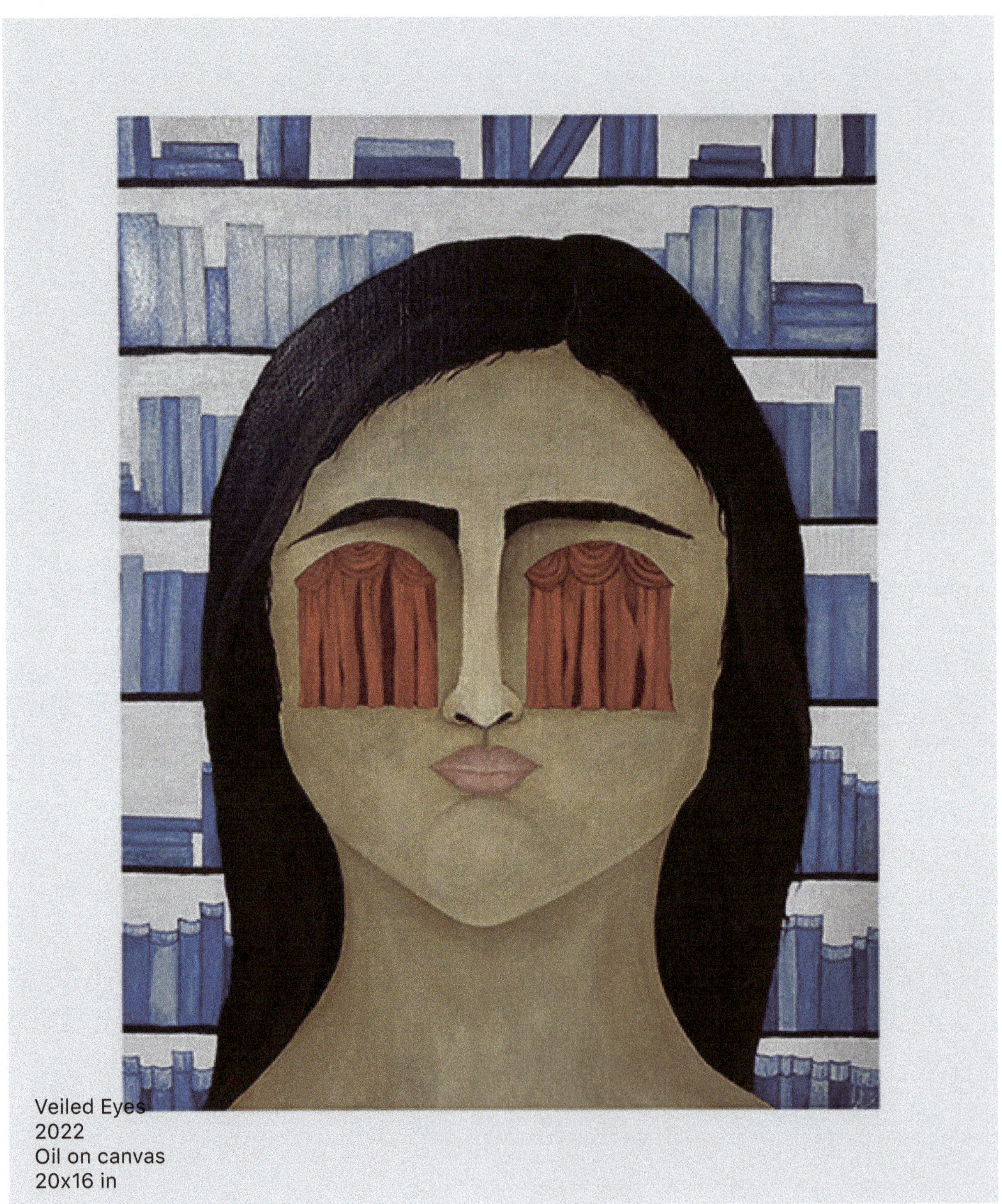

Veiled Eyes
2022
Oil on canvas
20x16 in

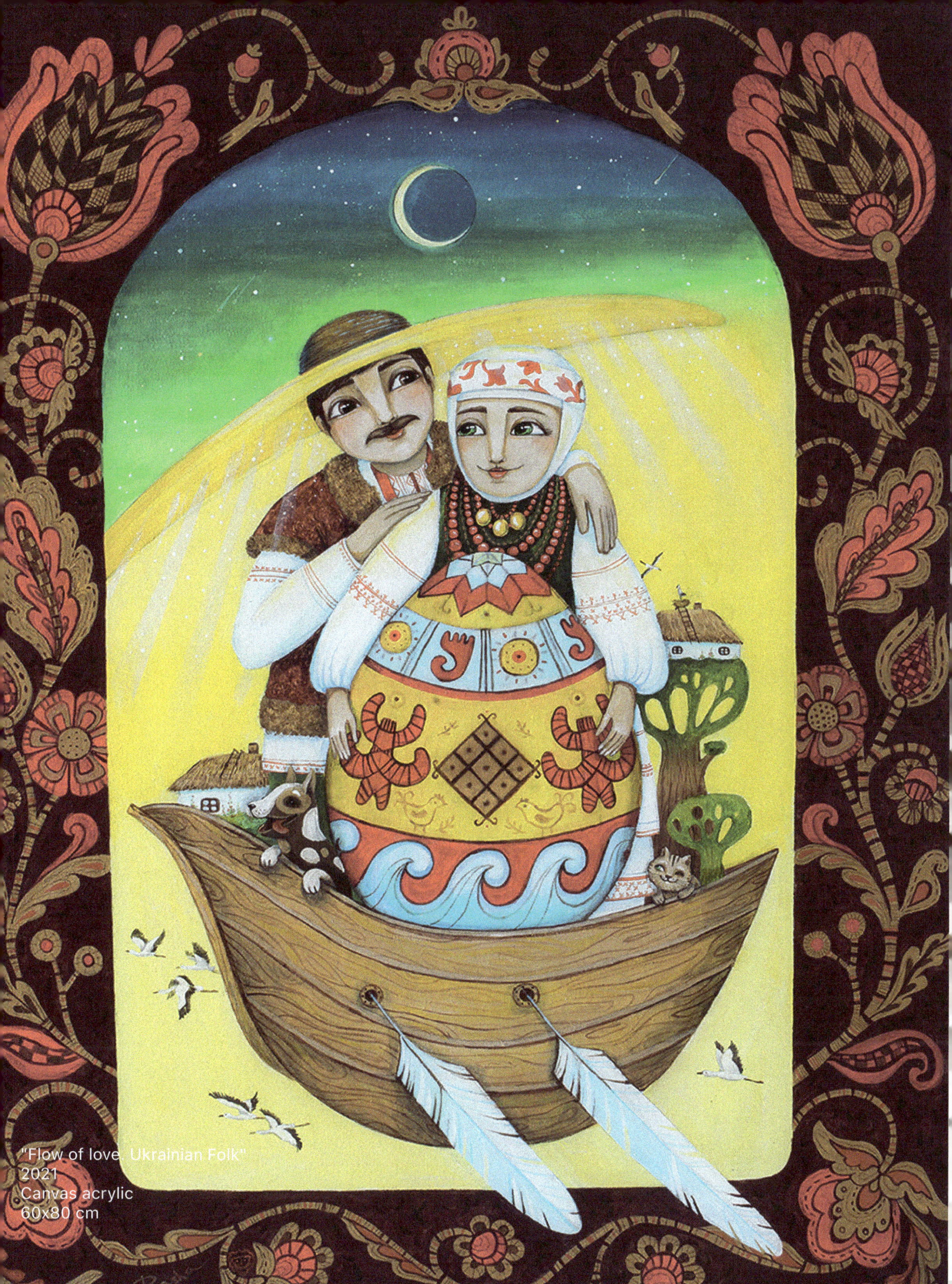
"Flow of love. Ukrainian Folk"
2021
Canvas acrylic
60x80 cm

Aleksandra Paranchenko

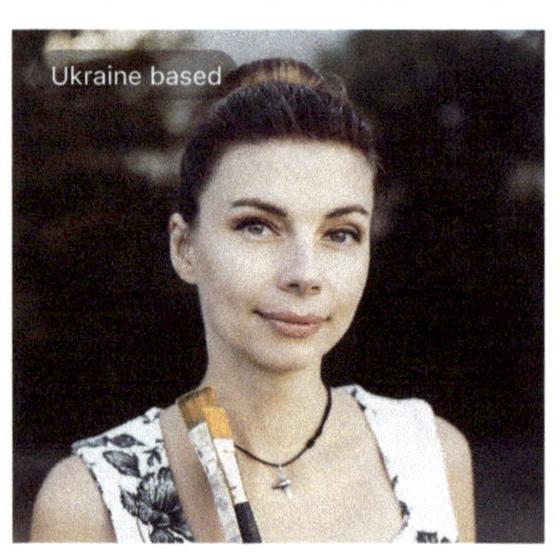

✍ www.artparanchenko.com
@ paranchenko.art@gmail.com
⊙ *@paranchenko.art*

I am feeling happiness, drawing it.

Aleksandra was born and lived in a small town Kherson in southern Ukraine. Since childhood, as soon as Aleksandra learned to hold a pencil in her hand, she began to create. I can't stop creating! - she says. Aleksandra tries to draw as soon as images come to her mind. There are days when there are too many, and then she sketches to capture the ideas. Inspiration comes from many sources, one could say that life itself inspires her.

Aleksandra's work has different themes, but what unites them is beauty and love for the world. Aleksandra always starts new work only in a good mood and creates only good subjects. She says – "I am a living person and, feeling and seeing pain, and injustice, I can also be sad. But I don't see the point in multiplying those emotions by making hard pictures - that's my principled position. "

With her art she is in dialogue with the inner child of each viewer, addressing the soul itself and reminding that life is happiness. And it is in each of us. Waking up in the morning is a great joy because there are blank canvases waiting for me." - she says.

Aleksandra has a higher art education and professionally engaged in creative work for over 16 years. The basic direction of creativity is painting, book illustration and murals.

What drives you to be an artist?

I had a happy childhood in a very difficult time, the country was on the brink of poverty. But wonderful parents who taught me to be happy and to see the beauty around me. When I saw people with frowns, I always wanted to show them that there were many reasons to be happy. Maybe that's why I became an artist.

How would you describe the art that you create and what inspires you?

I'm not an art historian, so it's difficult to describe my art. But I can tell you what my art is about. I always paint in a good mood and only positive stories. Very often they are fantasy stories, fairy tales and fantastic creatures. I want people to smile when they look at my paintings, to put them in a positive mood. I want one to feel like a happy child with a pure heart and a great imagination again. When I draw, I often talk to the characters in the picture, I imagine how they live and what their character is like. I like that and I smile and enjoy working on the story. I think this is important because I believe that the mood and energy of the artist stays on the canvas and then the painting emits that energy. Therefore, in each of my work, the wish for happiness and joy. I am inspired by life itself. I could create all day long, ideas come to me like radio waves. You just need to tune in to the right vibrations and be grateful to the world for every opportunity. The process of creating art is magic.

If you could overcome all of your fears, what would you do with your art?

I've been doing art for so long that I've gotten used to ignoring fears and am always free in my art. After all, fear is just the uncertainty of the future, and when you are sure of yourself and know that you will find a solution. You stop being afraid and begin to act. Only through everyday work can you overcome fear and be free to express yourself.

When it comes to art making, how important is experimenting vs. sticking to a routine or set of rules?

Experimenting in creativity is always very important, as well as adhering to the rules. Only in the harmony of these opposites can a good result be achieved. I am constantly learning classical art techniques and improving my skills, but at the same time, I am also exploring modern trends and experimenting. Sometimes it's good, sometimes not so good, but that's the way forward.

What are some of the challenges or experiences that have shaped your artistic journey so far?

Now there is a war going on in my country and I had to leave my home. It greatly influenced my creative path. Art has always been one way of dealing with a crisis. In times of war, it is especially important because it awakens feelings. In my case, it's the great opportunity for my to show the people the culture of Ukraine, and to show what we are fighting for. And as I said before, art to me is first and foremost a way of awakening the most positive feelings in people. Such as love, compassion, the value of life and the value of nature.

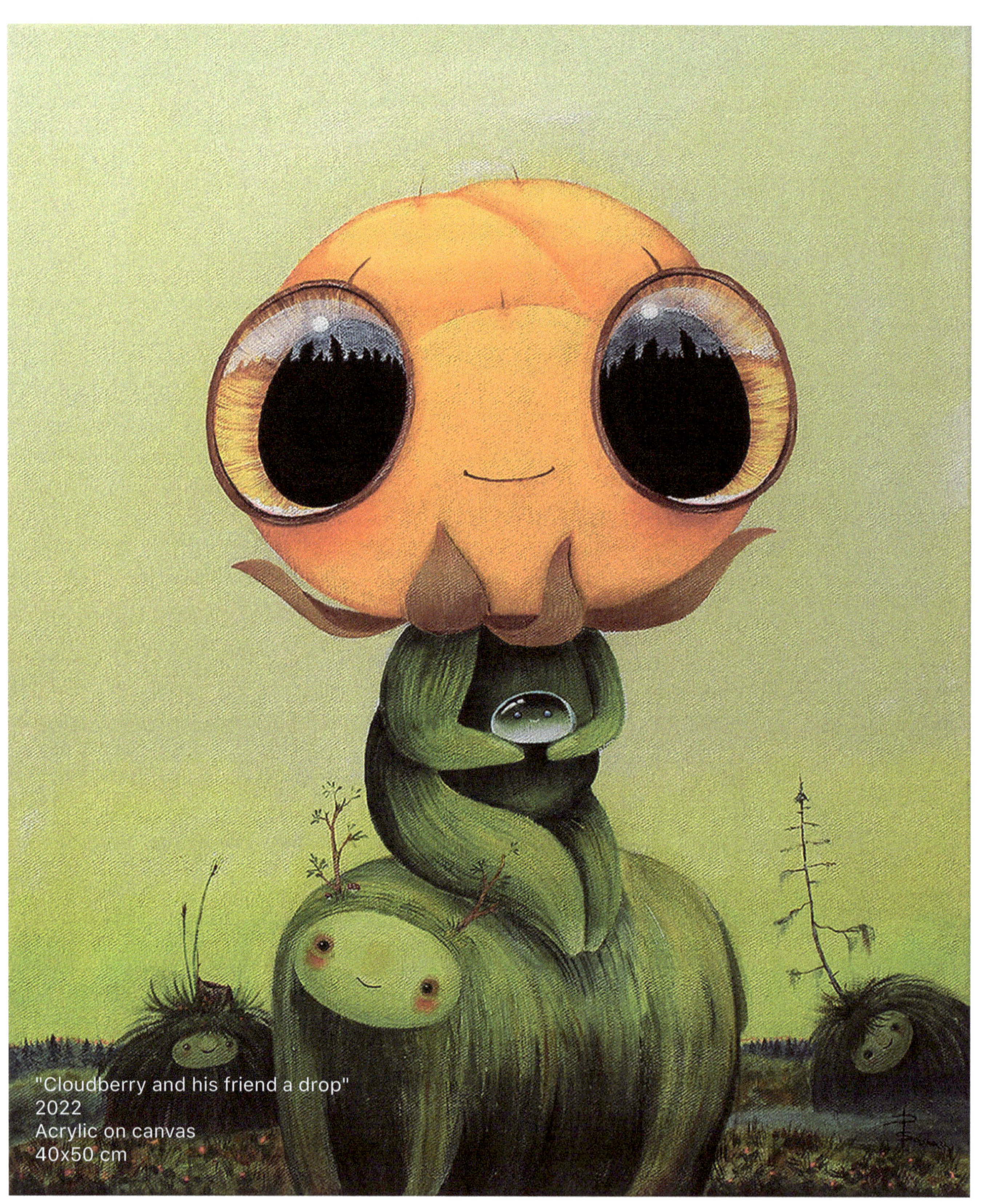

"Cloudberry and his friend a drop"
2022
Acrylic on canvas
40x50 cm

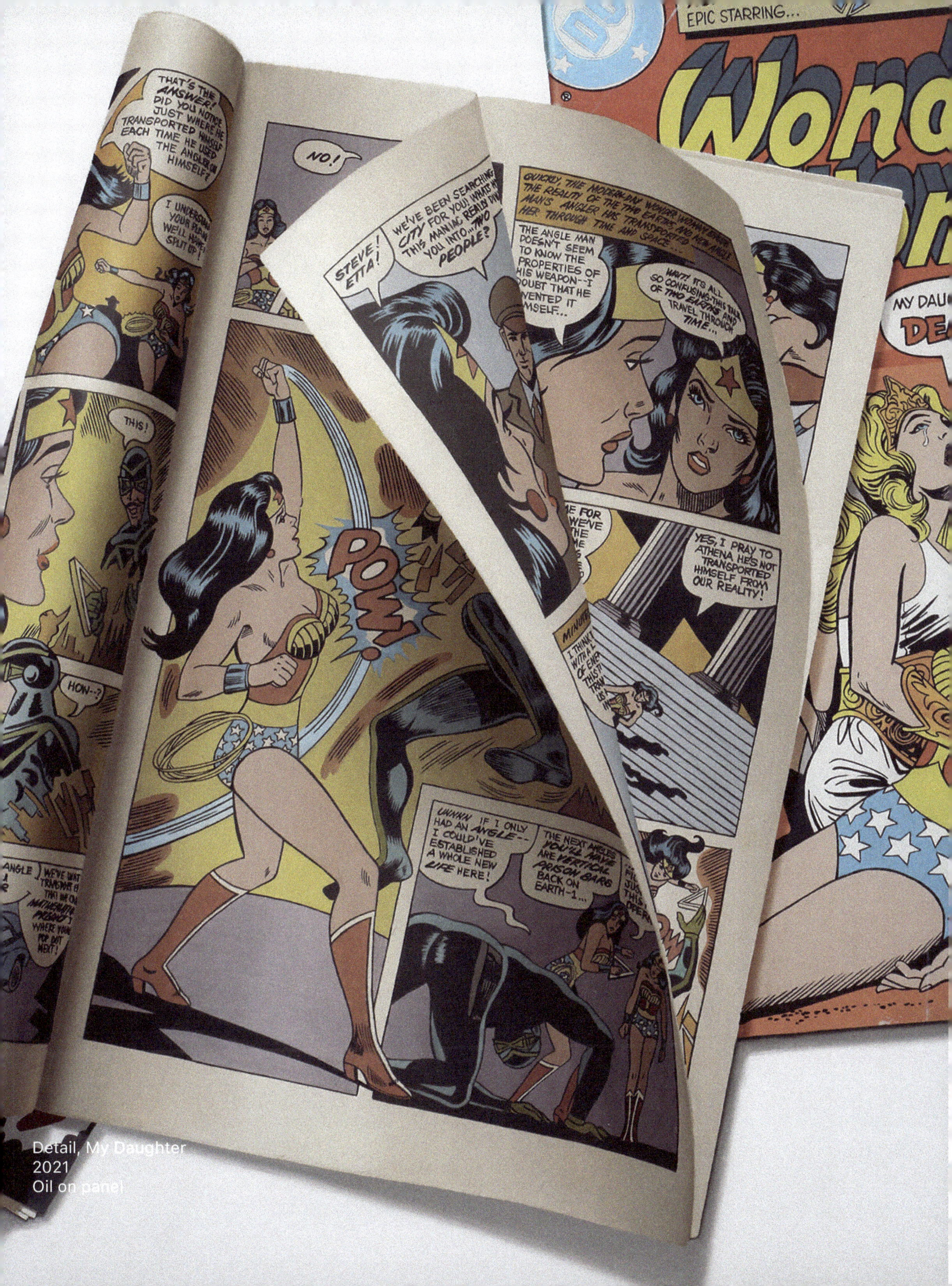

Detail, My Daughter
2021
Oil on panel

Sharon Moody

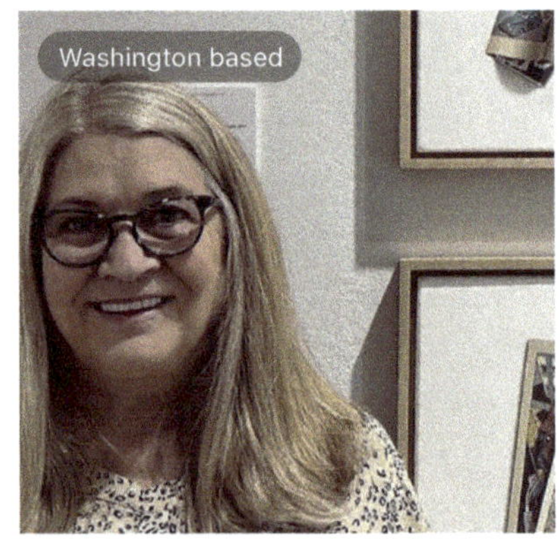

www.sharonmoody.com
sharonlmoody@outlook.com
@sharonmoodyart.

The *movements* that most fascinated and enthralled me were *Pop art* and *Photorealism*

Sharon Moody was born in Florida and grew up in North Carolina; after a BA in Fine Art degree from Appalachian State University, she worked in Washington, DC where she exhibited her figurative drawings at the Washington Women's Art Center. She then moved to NJ where she won a painting fellowship from the NJ State Council on the Arts for her photorealist paintings of small-town streets. Later returning to the DC area with her family, she earned an MFA in painting from George Washington University where she was the Morris Louis Fellow. As part of her technical training, she copied masterworks at the National Gallery of Art. She has been a teaching artist for most of her career, combining studio practice with teaching at George Washington University and later at Georgetown University.

Multiple series of paintings of still life subjects evolved into her current specialization in *trompe l'oeil* compositions of vintage comic books, which have been exhibited nationally and internationally and have been acquired by numerous private and public collections, including the Schwartz Art Collection at Harvard, Crystal Bridges Museum of American Art, DC Commission on the Arts and Humanities Art Bank and others.

When I was coming of age, the singular and linear path of art history which had culminated in the triumph of Modernism in the twentieth century was fragmenting into multiple channels of art. Called Pluralism at the time, there were many simultaneous movements and styles, an expansion of what was considered "fine" art, a new appreciation for previously unheard voices, and the elevation of previously ignored crafts. The movements that most fascinated and enthralled me were Pop art and Photorealism. I have spent most of my career as a painter experimenting with different approaches to Realism, and have often turned to subject matter that would not have been considered suitable before Pop art changed the art world. The vintage comic books which are the subjects of my current *trompe l'oeil* series were also favorite subjects of mid-twentieth century Pop artists. While they were celebrating post-WWII American exuberance and optimism, I am looking at artifacts from the same period, now yellowed and worn, in a more reflective mood and with today's more measured attitude towards progress and modernity. I follow many of the traditions and conventions of historical *trompe l'oeil* painting techniques to create compositions that are filtered through more recent art history, with an awareness of social changes that were often noted in the comic books. The depiction of Wonder Woman, in particular, reflected changing attitudes about women over the decades. Comic books seem especially appropriate to me as subject matter for *trompe l'oeil* paintings because for centuries, printed paper objects have often featured in these spatially shallow compositions. Finally, they exemplify the artwork-within-an-artwork trope that has also often been seen in *trompe l'oeil* compositions.

What drives you to be an artist?

From childhood onwards, I've found making marks with whatever tool came to hand to be deeply satisfying. I don't know what causes that feeling, but it has been a constant in my life.

How would you describe the art that you create and what inspires you?

My work is illusionistic, so what the viewer perceives is not real. Even so I am a realist painter, and I am inspired and awed by the realist artists who came before me and the variety of ways artists have developed to convey their own perceptions of what is "real."

If you could overcome all of your fears, what would you do with your art?

Fears don't prevent me from doing what I wish as an artist.

When it comes to art making, how important is experimenting vs. sticking to a routine or set of rules?

An artist needs to find her own balance; that balance will change over time. Without experimenting, there is no discovery or growth; without a routine and steady work habits, there is no production. Both are important.

What are some of the challenges or experiences that have shaped your artistic journey so far?

First, the experience of gaining an education and training. Right now in this country, for the first time, it is probably easier for women than for men to gain an arts education (currently more women than men obtain post-secondary education, for a variety of societal reasons.) This is fortunate as historically women were denied art training. Next, the challenge for young artists is to develop her vision. The experiences that were helpful to me were simply seeing a great deal of art. Artists must go to the galleries, visit the great museums, read biographies of artists. The challenges also include finding a way to earn a living and possibly nurture a family, especially for women artists. Finally, it is important to find a way to shelter and protect one's studio time because of those conflicting needs.

"The depiction of Wonder Woman, in particular, reflected changing attitudes about women over the decades. "

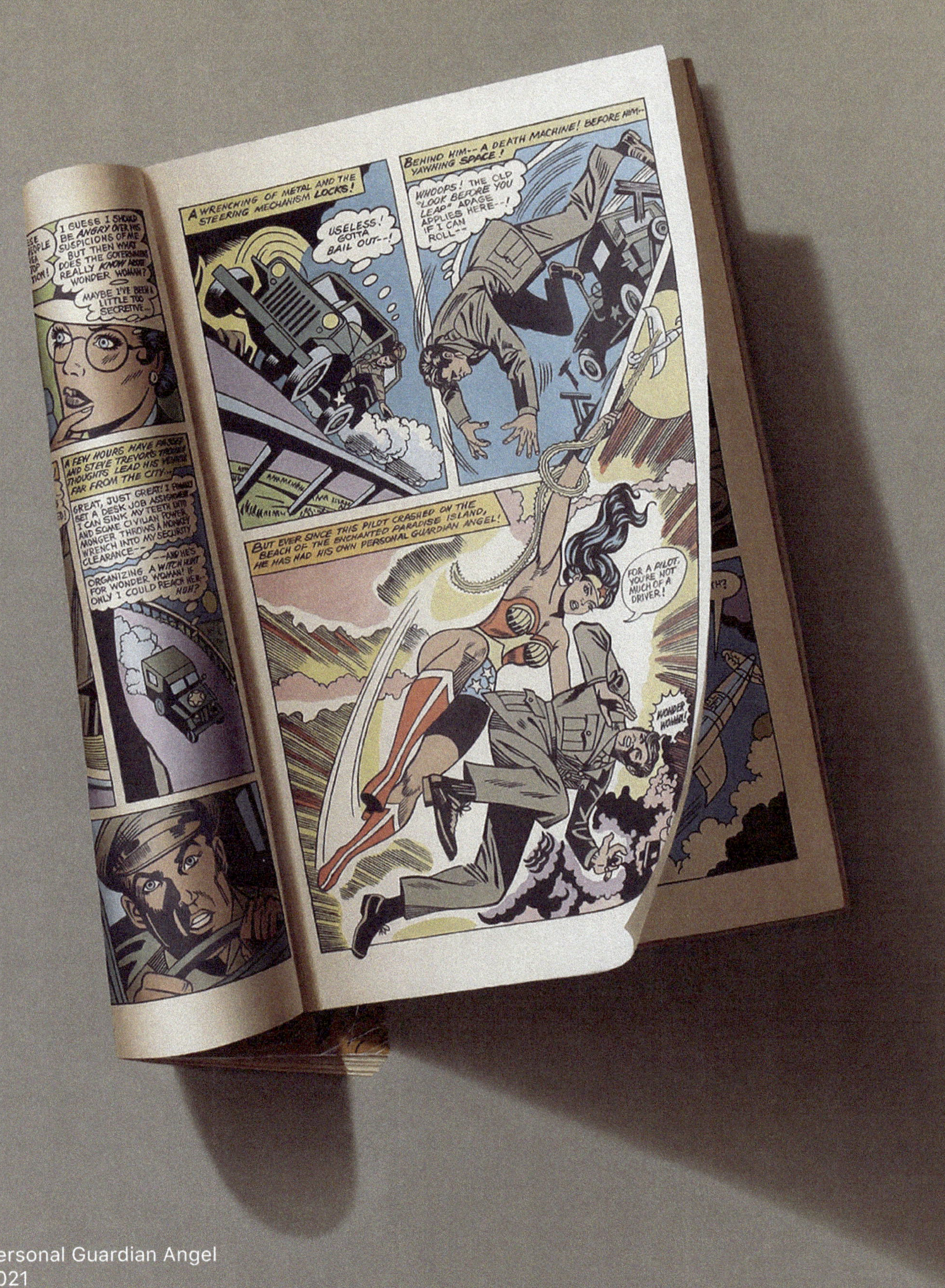

Personal Guardian Angel
2021
Oil on panel
20x16 inches

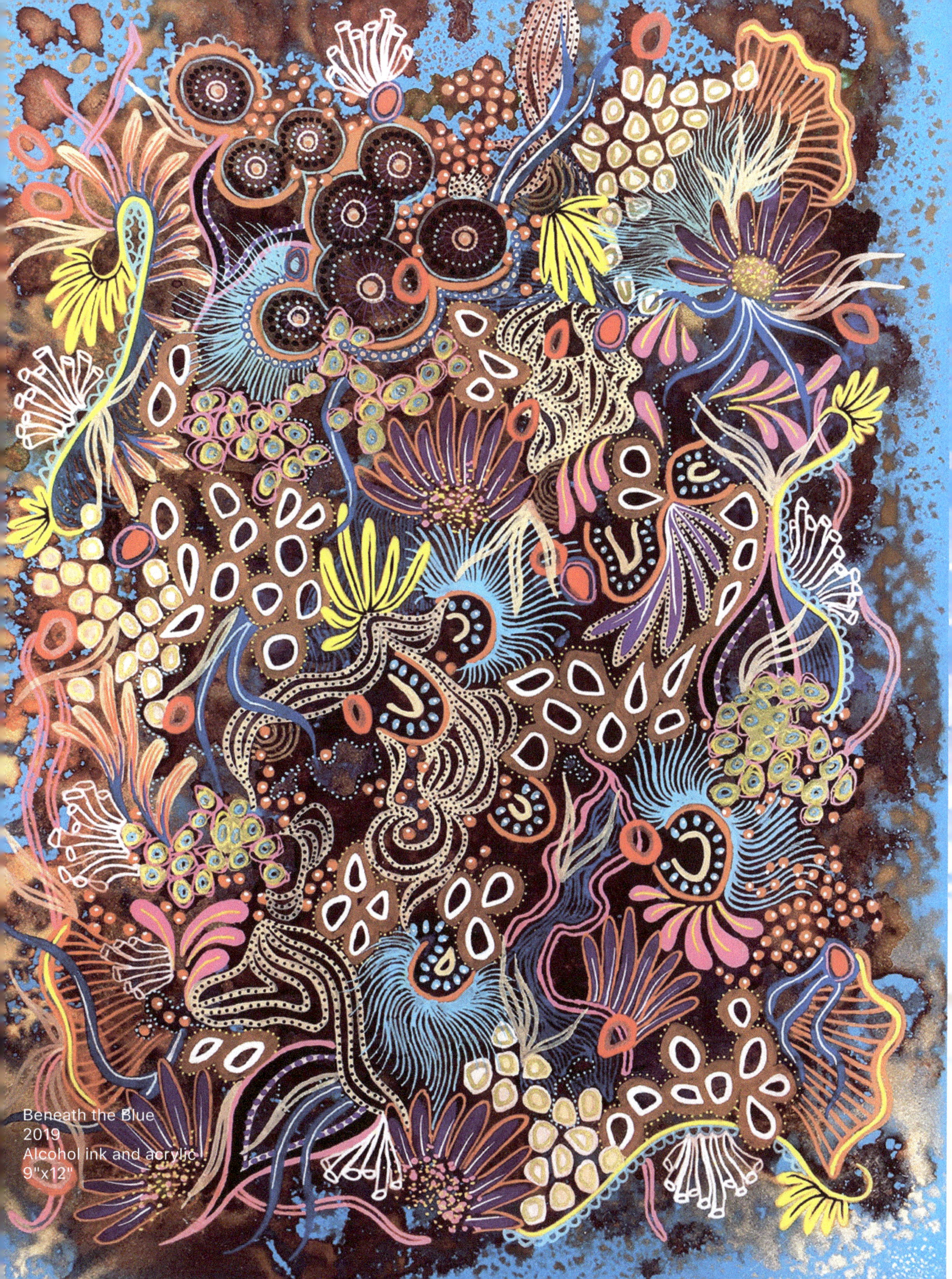

Beneath the Blue
2019
Alcohol ink and acrylic
9"x12"

Lauren Lewchuk

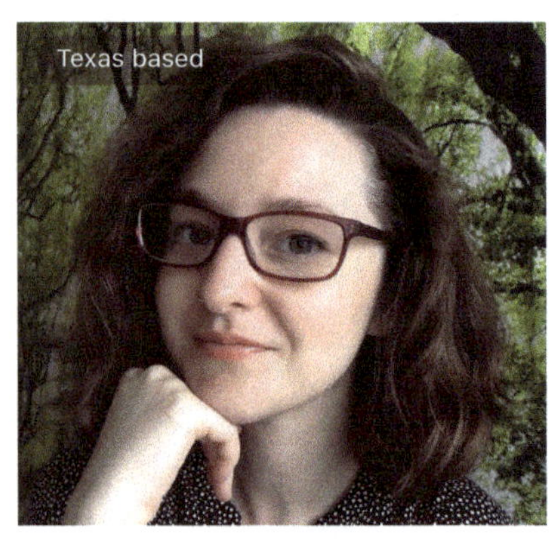

⚲ www.artbylewchuk.com
@ lauren@lewchuk.com
⧉ @art_by_lewchuk

> My art is a *meticulous arrangement* of all these components, like a *puzzle.*

Texas-based artist Lauren Lewchuk is a self-taught creative inspired by nature. She has 14 years of experience in various creative fields including graphic design, screen-printing, faux finishes, scenic art, prop fabrication, and mural painting.

Since her start as a fine artist, Lewchuk has been primarily working with acrylics, spray paint, and digital mediums. She creates detailed and elaborate compositions that are heavily inspired by nature, specifically micro-organisms and nature macro-photography. Use of color, movement, flow, patterns and repetition are important visual elements in her work that symbolize underlying themes having to do with mental states of being, identity, societal expectations, personal boundaries, spirituality, and existentialism. Mental health/illness is a major theme that directly relates to the use of these organic forms in her work. Spending time surrounded by nature has been shown to help reduce anxiety and depression. There is also a certain urgency to nature; a fleetingness and delicacy that creates a more visceral way to experience and appreciate the present moment, which many people with mental illness struggle with. Use of these visual elements are a way to contemplate meaning, purpose, and our limited time. The inviting and colorful compositions are both a form of escapism and meditation, but also symbolic of masking and concealing darker undertones.

Since her emergence as an artist in 2019, Lewchuk has been selected to participate in several exhibitions throughout Dallas/Fort Worth. Her hyper detailed space/seascape painting "Galaxsea" won First Place at the Precious Metals Exhibition with Texas Visual Arts Association in 2019; in 2020 "Oceanic" was selected as a gallery pick for the New Texas Talent Exhibition with Craighead Green Gallery, and Lewchuk entered the realm of large-scale murals by completing a 20'x50' mural for Inspiration Alley in the Foundry District of Fort Worth, and she also had the amazing opportunity to design an exclusive fabric collection for Joann Stores. Currently, Lewchuk continues to focus on larger scale fine art and murals as well as digital pattern design.

I have always been an admirer of the natural world. The shapes, colors, patterns, and textures. My art is a meticulous arrangement of all these components, like a puzzle. My process is unplanned yet logical and sophisticated, a natural flow of consciousness full of color, organic shapes, and movement inspired by nature. My hope is for the viewer to get lost in my dreamlike worlds; that they spark wonder, curiosity, and contemplation.

What drives you to be an artist?

I've honestly always been driven to do art. I can't imagine not being driven to be creative in some way. It's like it's in my DNA. Since I was a child, I was always drawing or painting or doing something crafty and my favorite things to paint and draw as a kid were animals and nature or landscapes. This of course has continued into my adulthood. I've always taken art classes in school and even though I didn't go to art school in college, I still majored in a different creative field which was graphic design. I've enjoyed many different types of art and creative work, which is probably why over the years I've developed a rather extensive set of creative skills from graphic design, screen printing, scenic art, murals, digital illustration, pattern design, and fine art. The drive is simply always present, and I am at my most content when I am being creative.

How would you describe the art that you create and what inspires you?

My primary inspirations have to do with nature. As I stated previously, I used to draw and paint lots of animals and landscapes as a child, so this all started a very long time ago. I grew up on the east coast in Maryland and my grandparents lived on a creek off of the Patapsco River, so I spent a lot of time outside and on the water, so I imagine this is partly why nature is such an important and recurring theme in my work.

A huge turning point in my artwork happened about 12 years ago however after purchasing a book on microorganisms and macro-photography. I really liked seeing different objects so close up that they became abstracted; just shapes, patterns, and colors. This is what led me to start creating very detailed and pattern-like work but work that was still very nature oriented and inspired. I like to think of my work as imaginary worlds or dreamlike landscapes. There is also something very therapeutic about creating such detailed and complex compositions. I typically work intuitively as well so most of my work isn't planned out beforehand in any way, save for maybe choosing a specific theme or color scheme.

If you could overcome all of your fears, what would you do with your art?

I have a lot of big ideas for my artwork. I would love to create large and elaborate installations or sculptural work, especially since I have experience in scenic art. I have ideas for fashion design as well. The main obstacles for any of my artistic ideas have to do with the financial aspect of creating the work, developing the skill to do different things I haven't tried yet, or simply having the space and means to do so. Fear isn't really the issue.

When it comes to art making, how important is experimenting vs. sticking to a routine or set of rules?

I would say that experimenting is very important. I think it's important to have a cohesive body of work, but you can do that and still experiment with different mediums and materials, and even subject matter. My work has definitely evolved over time. And through experimentation I've developed lots of different skills in which I can utilize my unique style.

It took a long time to get where I am currently and I will still try lots of different things throughout my career. It's interesting to look back however, even at the artwork I was creating while in college and seeing how much it has evolved since then. I've noticed that there are certain elements that have been recurring in my work for over a decade. It's almost subconscious and I don't even realize it. I think this is proof that there's no need to fear trying new things and experimenting because you won't lose what makes your work authentically "you". By contrast you're probably more likely to lose yourself by sticking to some routine and stifling your growth.

What are some of the challenges or experiences that have shaped your artistic journey so far?

One of my biggest challenges was just getting started quite honestly. It took a long time for me to actually take the first step and try to pursue a career in art after constantly being told that art isn't a viable career choice. But since taking that first step, there was a ripple effect and more and more great things started happening that encouraged me to keep going. I've been in lots of exhibitions, had lots of art sales and commissions, and I've expanded my work with large scale murals and even textile designs.

Also, as a self-employed artist/freelancer I think the biggest challenge is simply having a different set up than a 9-5 job with consistent income. It can be hard to not always know when the next job or art sale will be. But the important thing is to stay consistent, keep working and putting that work out there for people to see. I am always updating my portfolio, networking, and maintaining several websites where I can showcase my work. It might not sound like much but without all of those things, I definitely would not be where I am now.

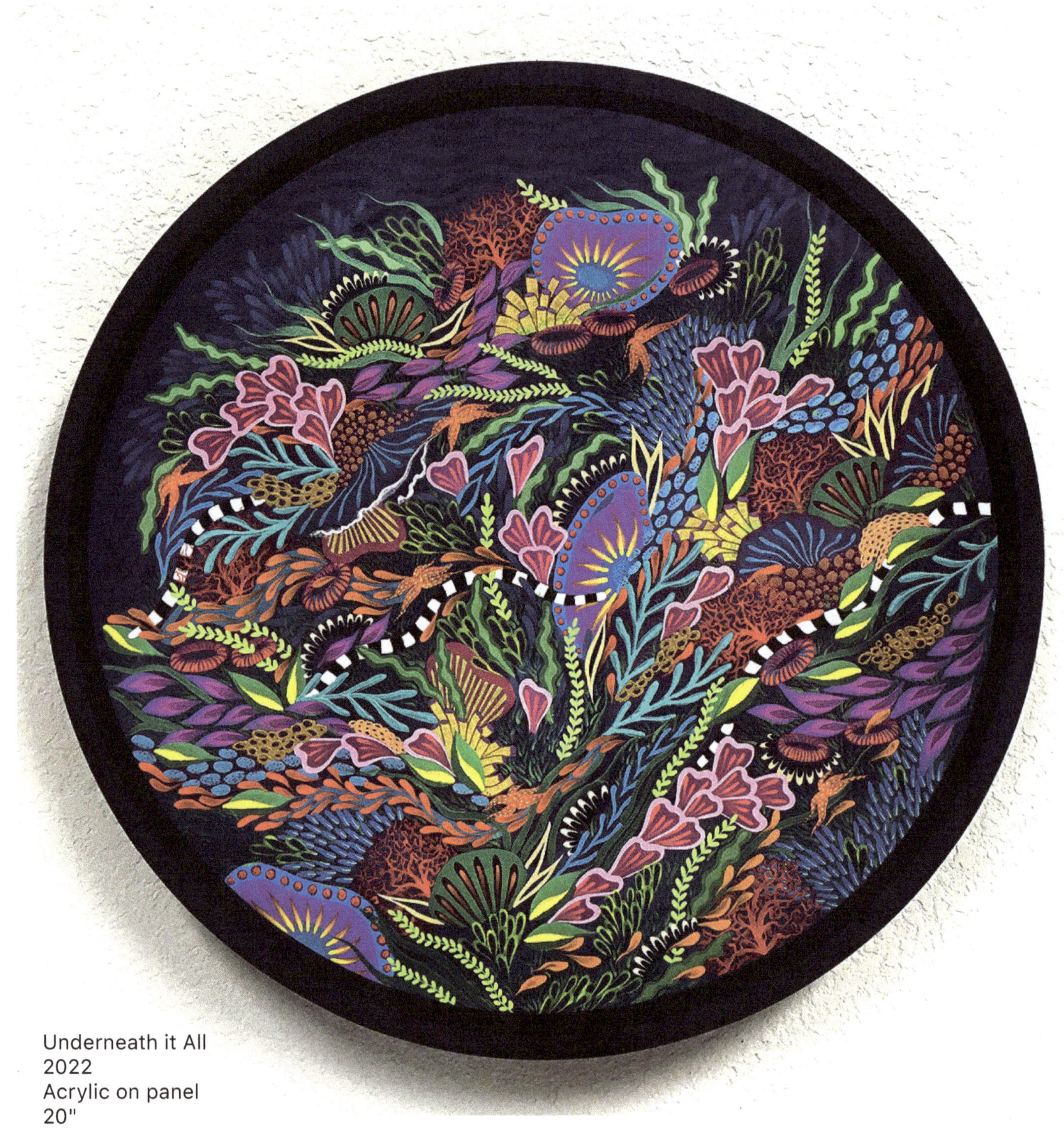

Underneath it All
2022
Acrylic on panel
20"

"A huge turning point in my artwork happened about 12 years ago however after purchasing a book on microorganisms and macro-photography."

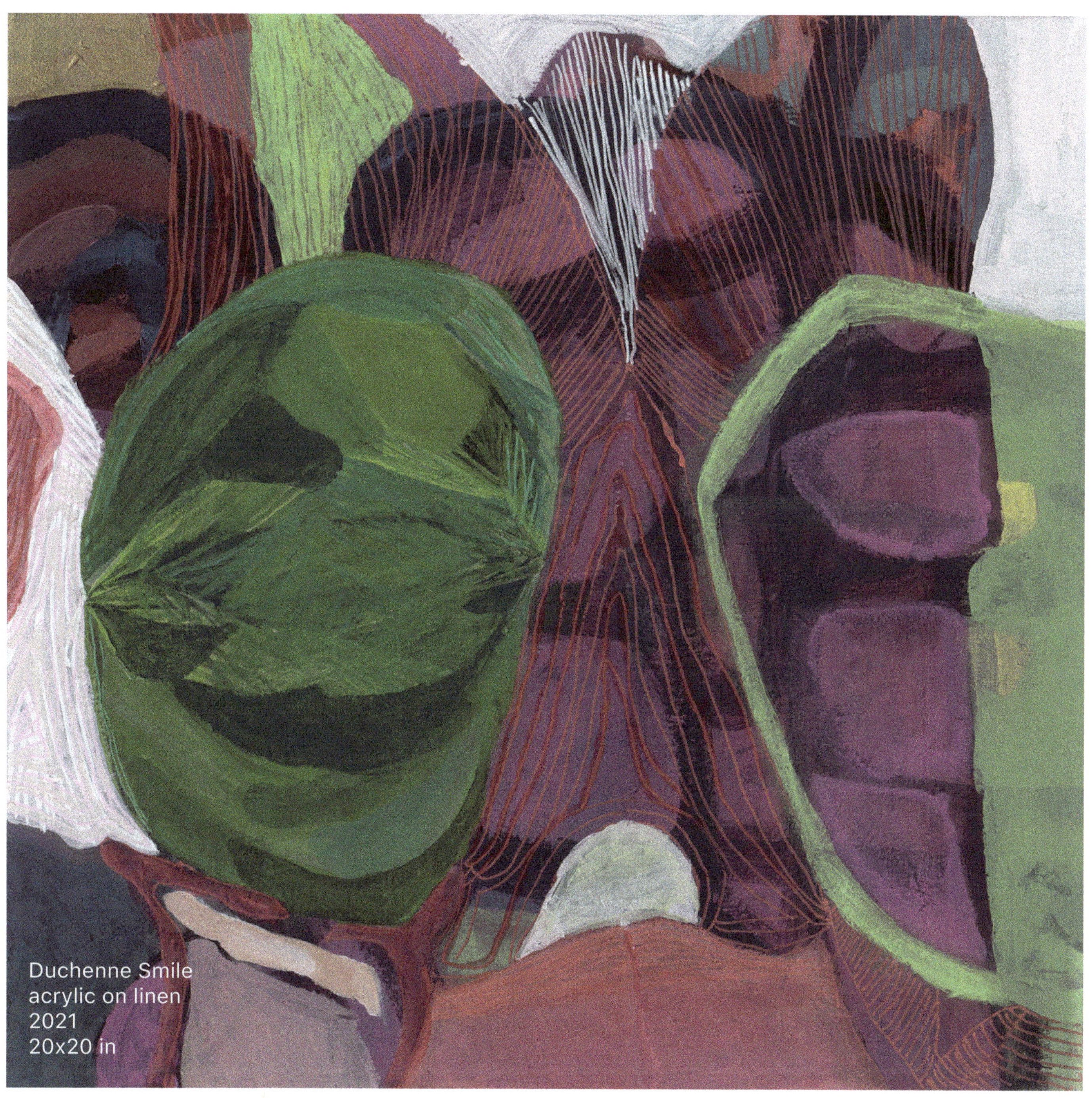
Duchenne Smile
acrylic on linen
2021
20x20 in

Ellen Burgin

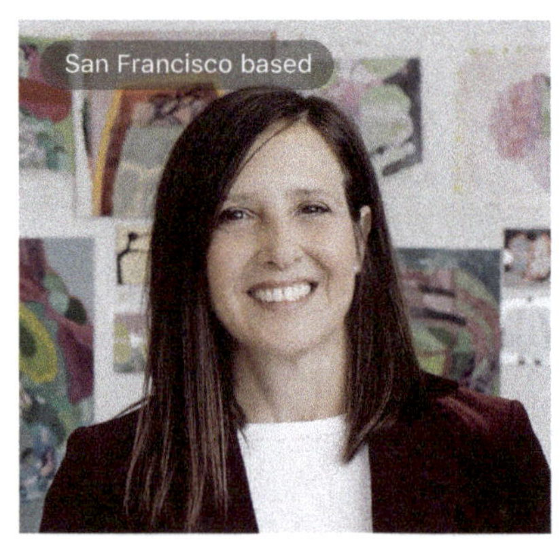

https://www.ellenburgin.com
ellen@ellenburgin.com
@ellenburgin

Art and *freedom* are *intertwined* and *experimentation* is essential, especially for a person like me who paints *abstractly.*

I am interested in re-evaluating stories that we have been told about femininity and womanhood. I grew up in a framework of femininity that prized agreeability in behavior and appearance above all which left me feeling silenced and unsure of myself. So I challenge and examine these proscribed notions in my work and create paintings that are large, expressive explorations of my voice.

Ellen Burgin received her BFA from the University of North Carolina at Chapel Hill and her MFA from Louisiana State University. Burgin's paintings have been exhibited nationwide and are included in the permanent collections of The Huntsville Museum of Art in Alabama and the Alexandria Museum of Art in Louisiana. Burgin is the recipient of several grants and awards for her work, including a Wake County Regional Artist grant and a Vermont Studio Center Artist Residency grant. Burgin was born and raised in Marion, North Carolina, a small town in the foothills of the Blue Ridge Mountains, and has called San Francisco home since 2006.

What drives you to be an artist?

I did not know how desperately I needed to be an artist when I was young. I needed an outlet for expression and a way to visualize my curiosity about the world around me. That desperation is what drove me to pick up a paintbrush in college, and I fell in love with the medium of paint. That is what propels me forward as an artist. For me, painting is about self-expression, experimentation, freedom from restriction and a personal rebellion from expectations.

How would you describe the art that you create and what inspires you?

I create paintings that are neither representational nor abstract – where shapes merge, couple and re-form and where lush, opulent colors assault each other in spaces that are intense with claustrophobia, tightness and sharpness. My paintings are characterized by a high frequency color palette where reds and their off-shoot hues of too-sweet pinks vibrate against complementary greens, colors that symbolize female lushness and nature's unstoppable force. I begin every painting with a loose direction knowing that it will undergo many mutations with the painting process informing the direction of the final image. The surfaces of the paintings develop thick, uneven textures full of lumps, bumps and drips from multiple revisions. I research subjects that interest me and am often drawn to scientific or medical topics relating to the human body such as the muscle mechanics of the face to create a "true smile", called a "Duchenne Smile" or migraines with auras.

If you could overcome all of your fears, what would you do with your art?

I would like to shift this question, "what would you do with your art" instead to ask, "what do I want my paintings to do"? The highest compliment someone could give me is that they can't quit thinking about a painting I made– that surprised, enchanted, bewildered, or challenged them in ways that they might not know how to explain.

If I could overcome all my fears, I would be much more extroverted about the business side of my art practice from pursuing galleries, applying to shows and networking. Exposure in publications like this one is a wonderful way to bring art to new audiences and I am grateful to be included.

"My only non-negotiable rule is that I go to my studio as much as possible and work."

When it comes to art making, how important is experimenting vs. sticking to a routine or set of rules?

Art and freedom are intertwined and experimentation is essential, especially for a person like me who paints abstractly. I always make a better painting when I let go of my agenda and experiment with new marks/palette/shapes. These experiments lead me to places where I would not go otherwise, and this is essential to creating a good painting. Freedom can also be found in setting rules. For example, I could say that my rule for the day is to only paint using my non-dominant hand and this structure will stimulate new discoveries. My only non-negotiable rule is that I go to my studio as much as possible and work.

What are some of the challenges or experiences that have shaped your artistic journey so far?

My biggest challenges came from decisions I made out of fear. I have gotten seriously sidetracked in my life by making decisions that were based on what other people thought and I wish I had learned to drown out the noise earlier in my life.

The pandemic was a turning point in my practice because the long pockets of time that were usually filled with driving children to school or afterschool activities were now filled with time in my studio. This was the only period of my life since graduate school where I had long stretches of time to work without other demands. I also used that time to think about how I wanted my art-life to look like post pandemic. I have been making good on these promises to myself and have been reaching out to artists I admire to trade studio visits, enjoying in-person gallery events, and volunteering in my art community.

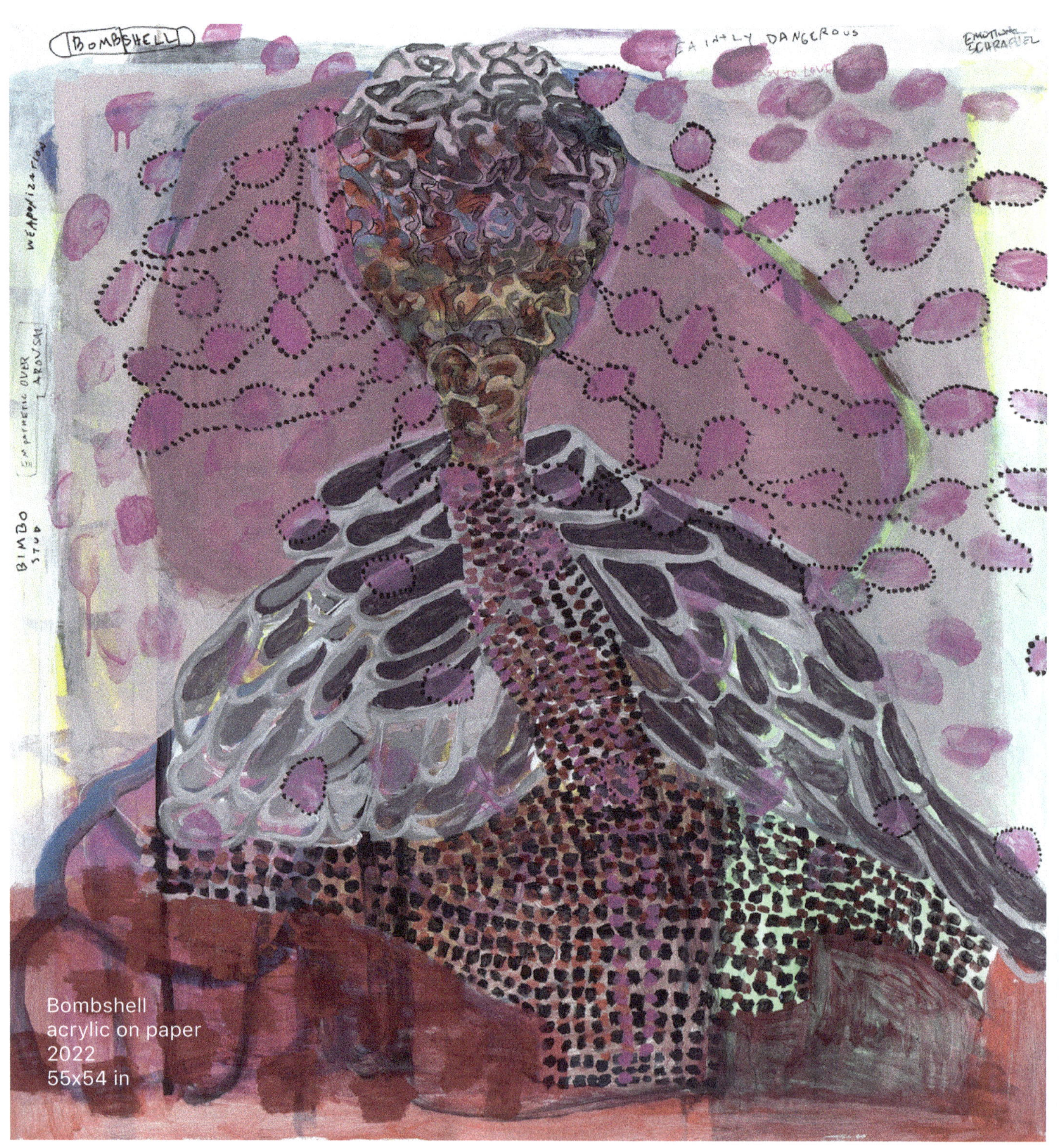

Bombshell
acrylic on paper
2022
55x54 in

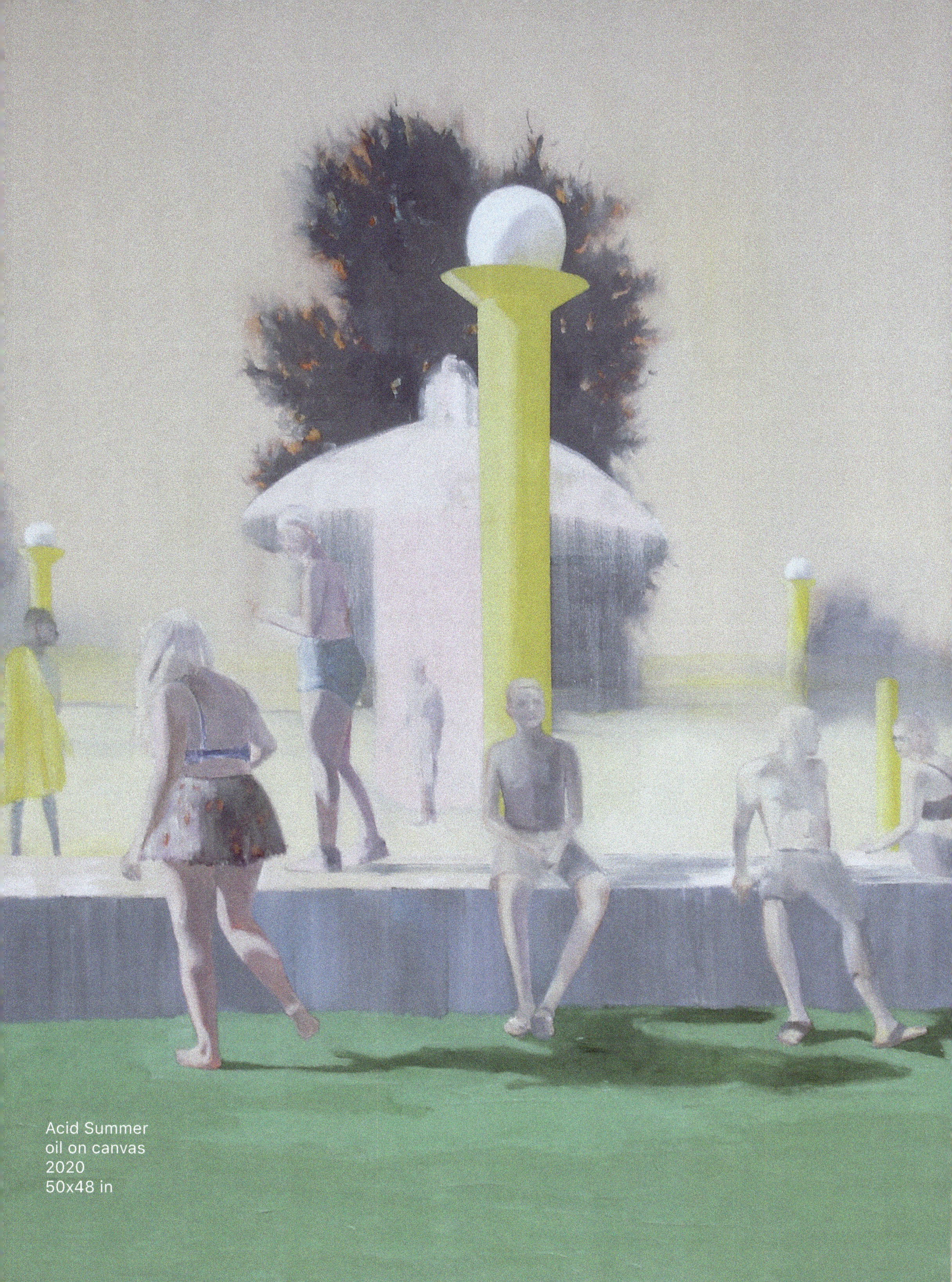
Acid Summer
oil on canvas
2020
50x48 in

Jena Thomas

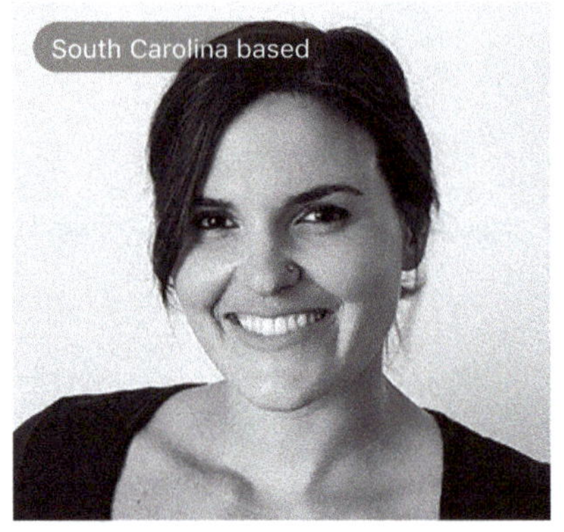

http://www.jenathomasart.com
@ jena.thomas@converse.edu
🄾 *jenathomasart*

There seems to be an *unnatural disconnect* between our *physical selves* and the *space* in front of us.

Jena Thomas's current work engages in a contemporary dialogue with concerns about land development. The artist assembles a perspective that concerns how human beings "idealize" what nature is and use this as a basis to create artificial environments for ourselves to exist within. However, at times, these perfectly fabricated environments can be deceiving. It is no longer just an issue of domesticating the land to make it livable. Instead, Thomas is concerned with the way we transform our world into a suburban theme park. Through the combination of synthetic colors and naturalistic landscape, she seeks to capture the unnatural oddities of spaces such as swimming pools, miniature golf courses and the medians used to decorate highways. In her recent series "Liminal Landscapes" Thomas examines how we as a contemporary society view landscape. Whether it is zooming by it in a car, out a glass window from thousands of miles above the ground, or from the comfort of our own homes through the magic of Google, there seems to be an unnatural disconnect between our physical selves and the space in front of us.

Born in South Florida, Jena Thomas is a South Carolina based artist. Thomas has exhibited extensively in Florida and the Northeast, with exhibitions at the Fernando Luis Alvarez Gallery, Boca Raton Museum of Art, The Momentary Museum, Context New York, and Art Palm Beach. With work featured in Studio Visit magazine and the art publication New American Painting, Thomas is a recipient of the Ruth Katzman Scholarship from the Art Students League of New York, winner of 701 Center for Contemporary Art Prize and a finalist for Miami University's, Young Painters Competition.Thomas received her Bachelor of Fine Arts from Massachusetts College of Art and Design in Boston, MA and her Masters of Fine Arts from the University of Miami in Coral Gables, FL. Jena Thomas's work is currently represented by the Fernando Luis Alvarez Gallery in Stamford, CT.

What drives you to be an artist?

I don't know that pursuing a career as a painter was the wisest as it is certainly a meandering path, but it is the only thing that ever really brings me satisfaction.

How would you describe the art that you create and what inspires you?

I paint fictional landscapes. I am interested in how human beings "idealize" what nature is and then use this as a basis to create artificial environments for ourselves to exist within. Constructs such as string lights, fountains and courtyards further highlight my interest in our urge to elevate the mundane as a means to make the world seem a little more spiritual and to find the connection and magic in everyday experiences.

Whether consciously or subconsciously, the innate drive to "make our mark" on the world motivates my work. Old found family photographs of people, usually young boys, are captured in moments of conquest and triumph while hunting, fishing and cliff diving, punctuate the presence of human nature and the need to assert our personhood- a natural and universal instinct as we set out to make a place for ourselves.
As I continue to work with this subject I strive to maintain a consistent vein between man-made objects, otherworldly colors, and a disorienting portrayal of sublime, in our quest to invent an artificial oasis, where the disparate images of nature and the man-made co-exist.

If you could overcome all of your fears, what would you do with your art?

I had never envisioned myself as a painter of landscapes... but I just keep coming back to trees. Someday I will pursue non-representational painting. For now I just lose myself in the corners of my work, those moments that could be painting within a painting.

When it comes to art making, how important is experimenting vs. sticking to a routine or set of rules?

I love starting a painting with a set of goals or challenges to achieve...but I almost always put those aside at some point and just build on each previous decision as I go. If I knew what a painting was going to look like when I started it then I would become bored very quickly. If I don't reach my goals then it is something to pursue in the next one.

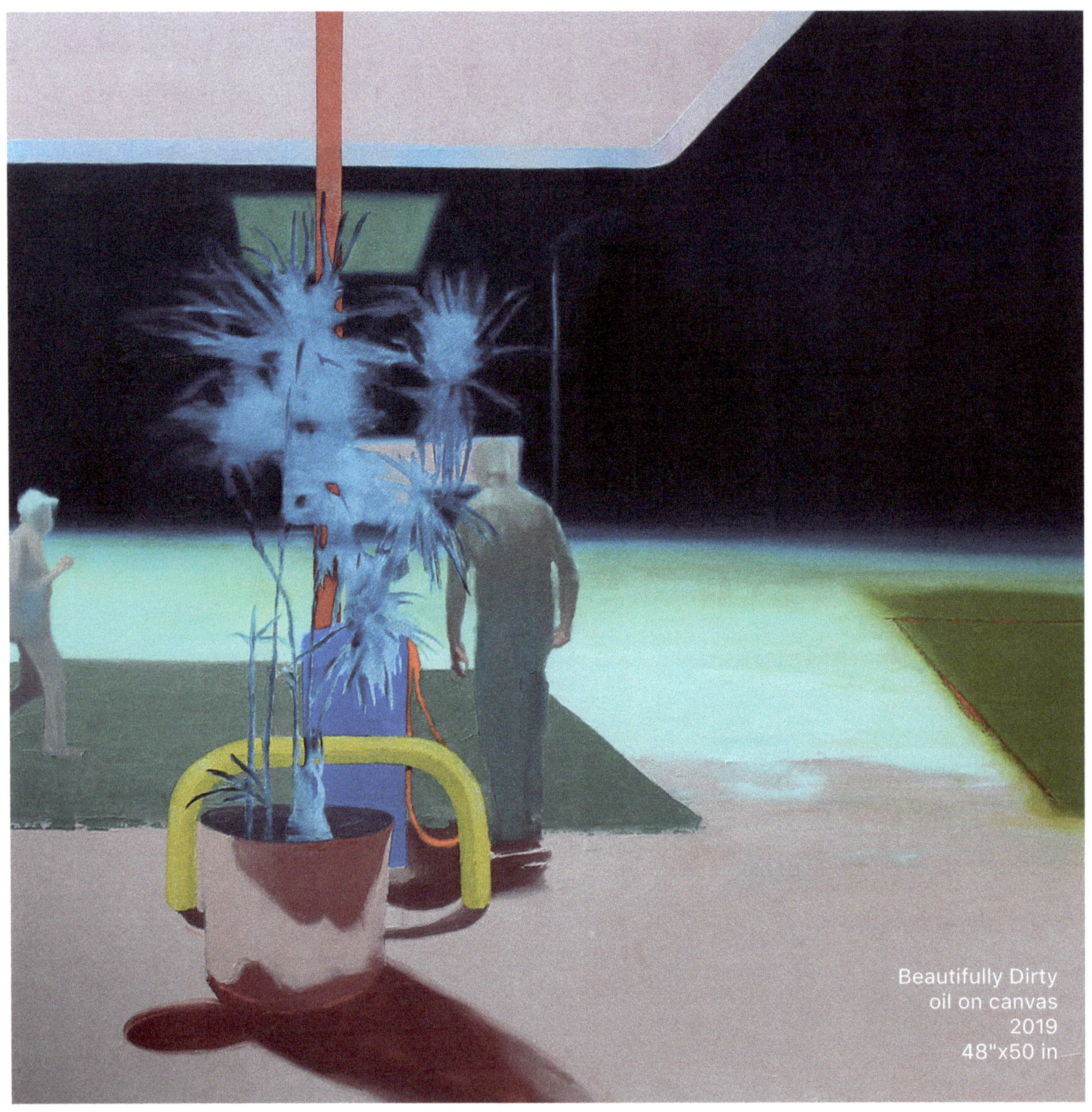

"I am interested in how human beings "idealize" what nature is and then use this as a basis to create artificial environments for ourselves to exist within."

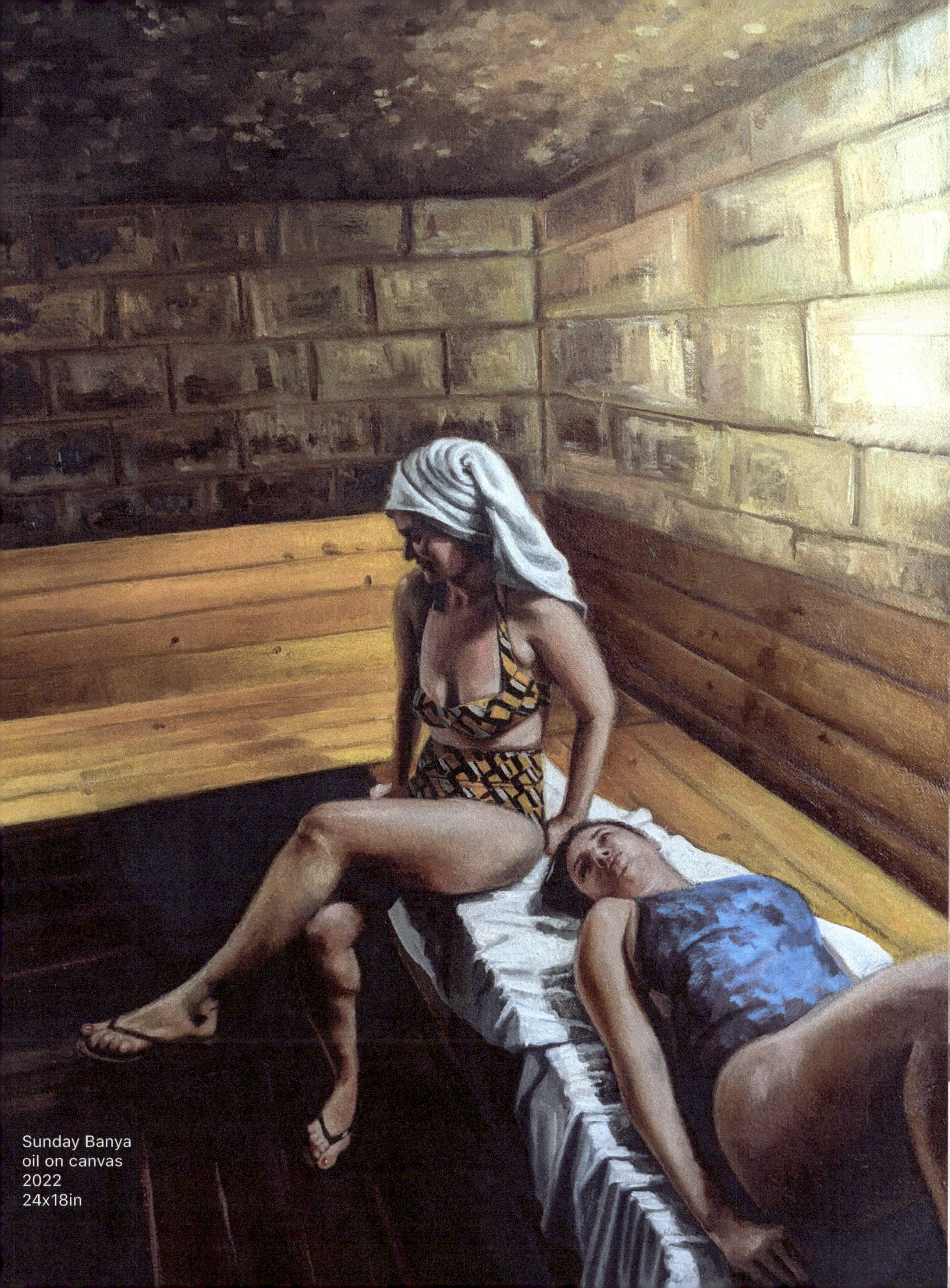

Sunday Banya
oil on canvas
2022
24x18in

Tanya Levina

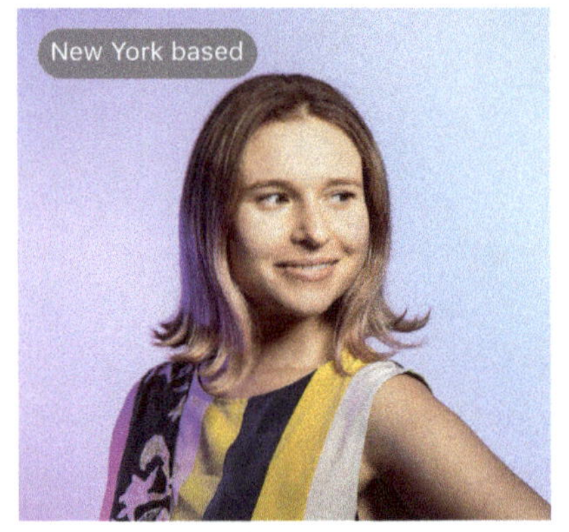

https://www.tanyalevina.com
@ tanyalevinaart@tanyalevina.com
@tanya.levina.art

My *subjects* are rooted in aspects of my *experiences* or *fantasies* derived from them.

Born in Minsk, Belarus, Tanya Levina moved to New York City in 1995. Levina studied painting at the Art Students League, Slade School of Fine Arts in London and The New York Academy of Art. Tanya Levina is a recipient of a COJECO Blueprint Fellowship award and has been featured in numerous exhibitions at venues including Trask Gallery at the National Arts Club, NYC, Annmarie Sculpture Garden and Arts Center in Solomons, MD and MoRA (Museum of Russian Art) in Jersey City, NJ. Her work can be found in private collections in London, New York, LA, Chicago and Boston.

My subjects are rooted in aspects of my experiences or fantasies derived from them. When I was 11, my family moved to Brooklyn, New York from Minsk, Belarus. As an immigrant, a refugee from the former USSR, I am fascinated by the Jewish immigrant community in Brooklyn hailing from former Soviet Union countries, and the absurdities and contradictions that abound in it. I paint the everyday moments which encapsulate that sometimes insular diaspora experience, where poverty and extravagance are inexplicably coupled, and where old-world values are constantly clashing with modern American culture. My series offers a small window into this world, from the eyes of an American who nevertheless has an intimate understanding of her subjects' habits and prejudices. Many of my portraits depict myself, family members, or friends, often placed in exaggerated, surreal, and colorful settings. Though I remain loyal to their physical features, I do not paint my subjects strictly "as they are," which gives me agency to re-evaluate both my perspective towards them, and theirs towards themselves. The results are potentially humorous, ironic, or even haunting and disturbing.

What drives you to be an artist?

As the world becomes more interconnected and people more often look for a better life in a new country, it's important to better understand what it means to be a transplant and how large groups of people try to make sense of their new home. My paintings offer a glimpse into an insular immigrant community that can often form in the new homeland.

How would you describe the art that you create and what inspires you?

I love genre paintings from centuries ago, where one can see a sliver of daily reality from a place and time very different from mine. I would classify my art as contemporary genre painting.

I am fascinated by the fact that many immigrant communities, if they are large and do not have close ties to their countries of origin, do not follow the political and cultural evolution in their home countries but instead create a completely new universe. The resulting subculture is based on memories of a place in time that no longer exists and is unlike their new home or the old one. I aim to document this way of life that is a fleeting cultural phenomenon. This Post-Soviet Brighton subculture will soon evolve into something completely different as older residents pass away, younger generations assimilate into more general American culture, and new waves of immigrants to the neighborhood will bring different views and ways of life.

If you could overcome all of your fears, what would you do with your art?

While I am interested in the intimacy small paintings can provide the viewer, I am hoping to expand my studio soon. I would like to paint larger because there's nothing like the impact a large painting can make.

When it comes to art making, how important is experimenting vs. sticking to a routine or set of rules?

It's incredibly important for me to paint everyday and have my studio space be readily accessible, in case I only have an hour or so for the process. This is why my studio space is located in my apartment, so that I can paint even for small stretches of time if there are a lot of other tasks that need to be done. Consistency for me is key.

What are some of the challenges or experiences that have shaped your artistic journey so far?

For the longest time I was stuck in a fixed mindset (brought on by Soviet Union style parenting). I believed that artists were allotted a certain amount of talent at birth and if they weren't amazing by the age of 20 - there was nothing to do about it. It was only years later, with the help of continuing education classes at The New York Academy of Art as well as Carol Dweck's book "Mindset" that I realized that there is no fixed talent ceiling. I can continue to learn and hone my painting technique year after year. I am now happy to see that each year my paintings improve, and the growth will continue until I can no longer hold a paint brush. I'm excited to see what the future me will be able to create!

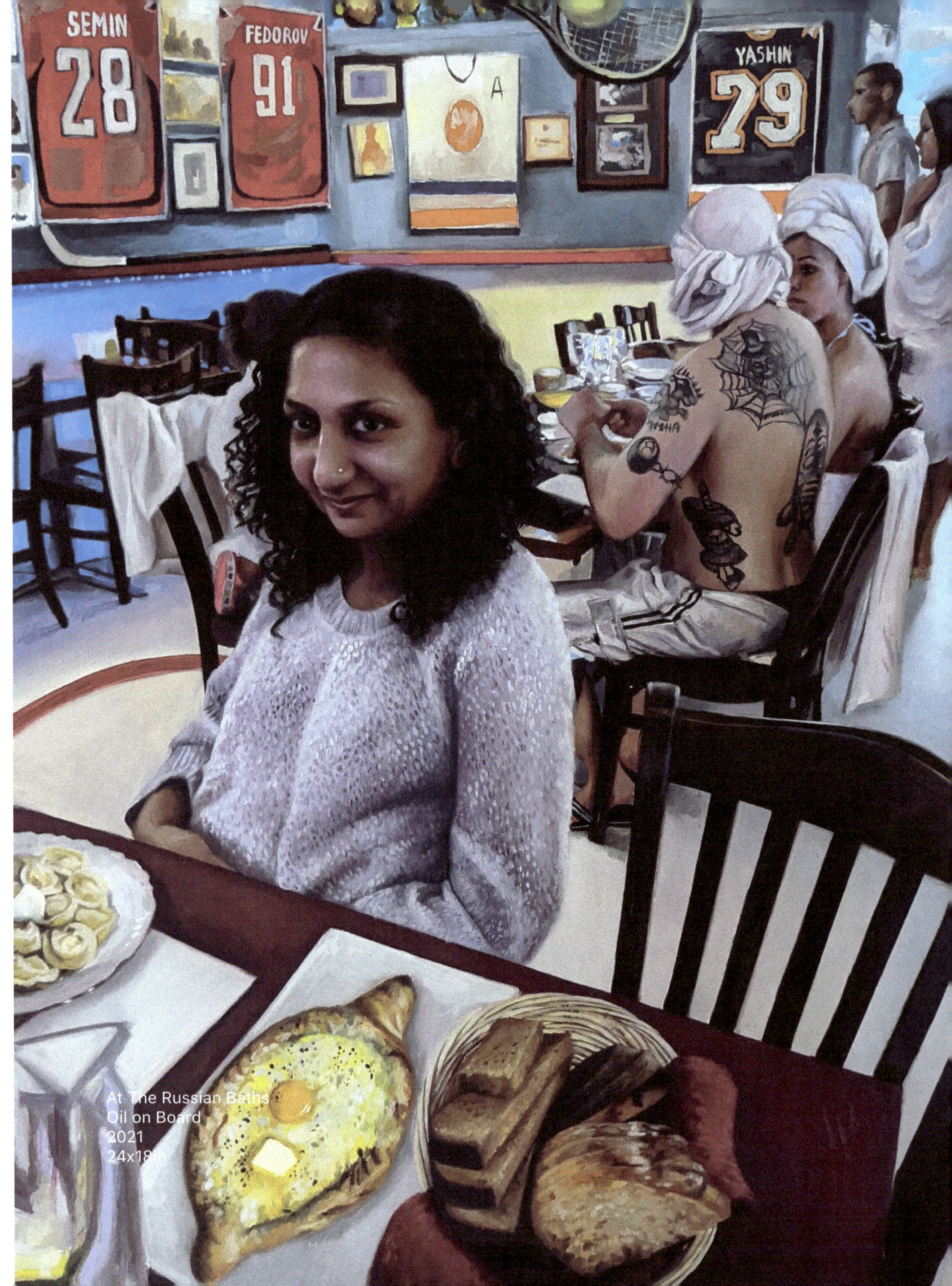

SEMIN
28
FEDOROV
91
YASHIN
79
At The Russian Baths
Oil on Board
2021
24x18in

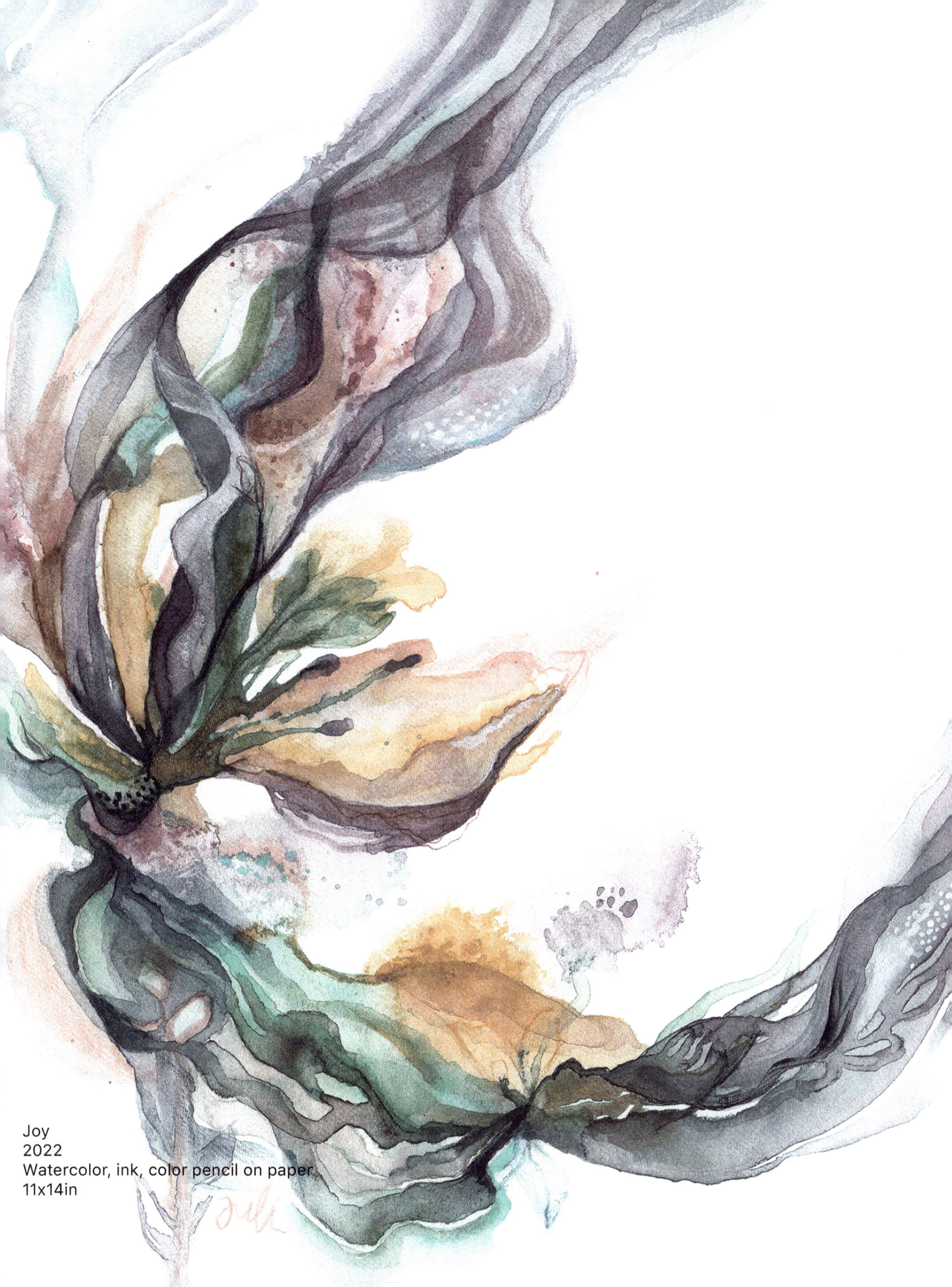

Joy
2022
Watercolor, ink, color pencil on paper
11x14in

Juliana Alonso Olarte

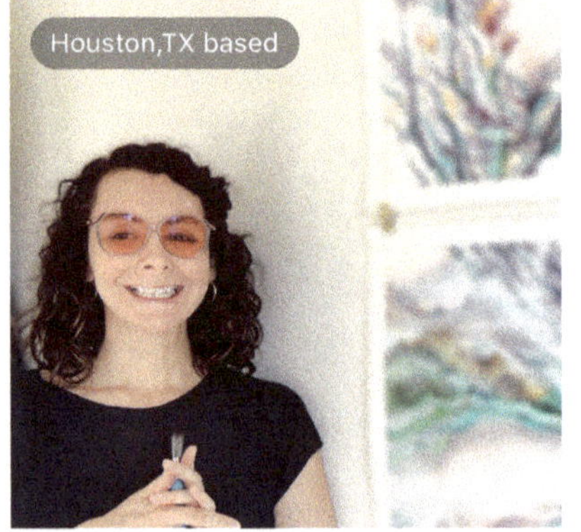

🐦 https://julianaalonso.com
@ hello@julianaalonso.com
⬡ *@juliana.alonso.art*

It is a space to *giggle,* to *struggle,* and to *resolve.*

Born and raised in Bogotá, Colombia, Juliana Alonso-Olarte, likes to say that she is composed of equal parts sentiment, compassion and goofiness. Influenced by her father's passion for nurturing appreciation of her native land and history through improvised bedtime stories and travel, she was often found painting and making.

While art remained at the roots, she studied Industrial Design and worked as a graphic designer until a strong desire to experience life outside the computer came calling a few years after moving to the U.S.A. This new perspective as an immigrant made her pursue painting to honor the most meaningful moments of her life and culture.

She now resides in Houston, TX with her husband Shawn and two old gatos, enjoying sunlight and bird songs from her studio windows. Exploring nature and abstraction through playful watercolors to create paintings and surface design collections is how she celebrates life after experiencing a neurological event that affected her motor ability, changing her life forever.

Through her healing and creative journey, Juliana thrives to bring moments of connection with our strength and imagination to recharge with hope, courage, and transformation, especially through adverse seasons. Her hope is to spark a light that shines on our worthiness to create more space for people with different abilities, and to honor the half-empties of our lives.

On my watercolor paper, I find my new voice emerging within the constraints of my limitations after having lost my motor ability, one day at a time. Each art piece feels like a timestamp that reflects my ever-healing path combined with childhood memories of a horizon drawn in the high altitudes of my Andes mountains. My process honors my worthiness beyond my ability and connects me to my homeland and family; It is an exploration of curiosity and play through uncertainty, expressed by way of abstract mark making mixed with a child-like practice filled with freedom. Much like in a sudden event, the first painting brush strokes are unplanned, bold, and impulsive. I then let each stride lead the next intuitively; pausing to look closer into the shapes to find feelings and life revealing before me, somewhat mirroring the unpredictable ways of life-changing experiences. Slowly, looking inward, each step becomes a possibility to find a sense of direction, a deep knowledge of where I have come from. Letting my imagination chase vibrant colors running through water, my hands move however they are able without a plan, and adapting my tools. This is how I experience transformation, work through the griefs of trauma, and find renewed belief; I exist in both the strength, and the innocence of my own spirit, I create for the joy of being.

What drives you to be an artist?

Believing I can create space for others to find their own joy for life and infinite hope to recharge, especially when in grief or adversity, gives me purpose to create! Creating has been the one consistent activity in my life I return to, while others have disappeared by way of grief or radical life changes. Art gives me space to be persistent, to connect with my imagination and to transform and become in hope, where everything is possible. It is a space to giggle, to struggle, and to resolve. A drive that comes from who I am in my essence; something I confirmed even further when I restarted painting however I could, as soon as I could do more than basic caring for myself.

How would you describe the art that you create and what inspires you?

I often refer to my work as a spell of colors and organic, uncoordinated marks coming together to conjure playful surprises, imaginary horizons, joy, and possibility within limitation. Other times, it feels like detangling knots made by life-imposed arbitrary circumstances, catharsis and transformation to find flow and blooming. I am inspired by my favorite memories in connection with nature and innocent times; the Colombian Andes mountains, and the freedom of chasing them with a child-like wonder through uncertainty, similarly to making up stories while looking into clouds, feeling limitless. I am also inspired by the painting process: Ethereal movements of water and colors blending in the company of simplified botanical elements and beautiful sounds, especially of birds.

If you could overcome all of your fears, what would you do with your art?

I would collaborate with entertainment, wellness organizations, and other artists with disabilities to create an immersive experience where our art and process is projected following themes like imagination and imperfection. The audience would create tales about what they see, feeling boundless, curious, and joyful. The artists would have a transformative story to share and together we would celebrate our unique perspectives and life experience beyond ability. My art would also hold space for people to share both grief and joy and to process how they feel, especially children facing extended periods of distress. My art would offer a key to open their own inner garden where infinite recharging energy grows in connection to their imagination and most uplifting moments to distill joy and hope from them so that they continue navigating their experiences in as much wellness as possible. This could be through original art, experiences or art products and hospitality and entertainment environments. I've sometimes dreamed my art is in a Cirque du Soleil show, as part of their costumes or scenery and whimsical themes.

When it comes to art making, how important is experimenting vs. sticking to a routine or set of rules?

Experimenting has been the only way to crack open to rebuild from what is possible to me, in full acceptance of who and how I am in the present moment. Having come from leaning on rules and techniques that became unreachable, relearning to create has only been possible in willingness to explore without attachment to the outcome; this is where intuition and resolution one step at a time come from, as well as letting the process guide me into discovery. Adventures with blowing on paint, tying up brushes or unconventional mark-making, and scribbling my shaky lines freely are essential to discovering my voice, followed by integrating them into techniques, limited routines, or "rules" that support my practice, my health, and my purpose.

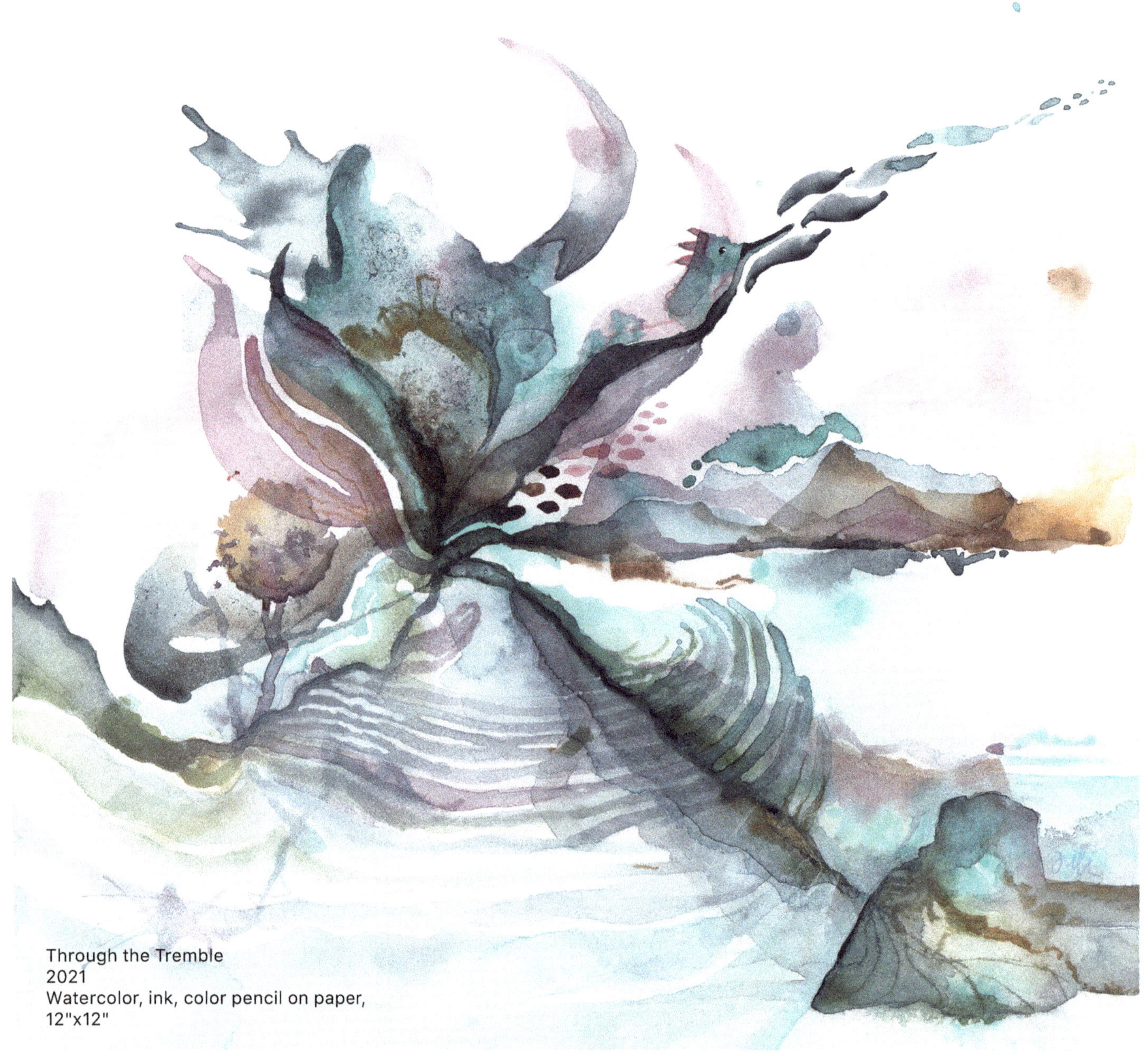

Through the Tremble
2021
Watercolor, ink, color pencil on paper,
12"x12"

What are some of the challenges or experiences that have shaped your artistic journey so far?

My loss of motor ability has influenced me most. Having to find my new voice and new adaptive ways to use tools, plus completely changing my creative rhythm to fit my physical needs sent me on a path of discovery, experimentation, and more focus on the process of creating for the joy of being. Extended periods of time in isolation and recovery along with being an immigrant living away from my entire family, have forced me to use my imagination as my main resource. I started focusing on expressing how I remember the way innocence, treasured love for nature and bedtime stories shared with my parents and sister felt, more than what they look like in reality. I am often looking for those connections with my roots and core memories of moments shared with people and places I love.

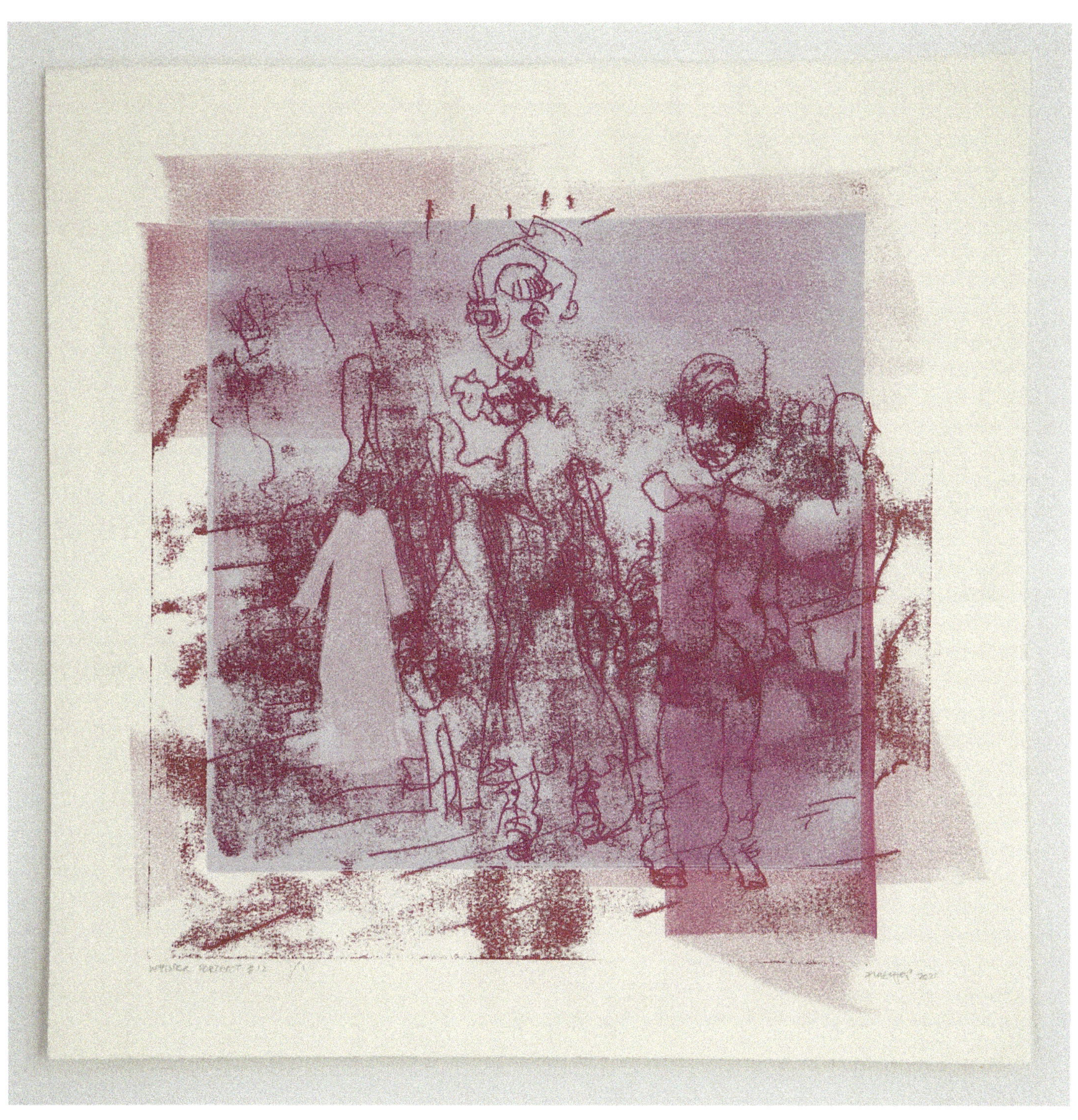

Whisper Portrait #12
2021
Monotype
18"x18"

Frances Melhop

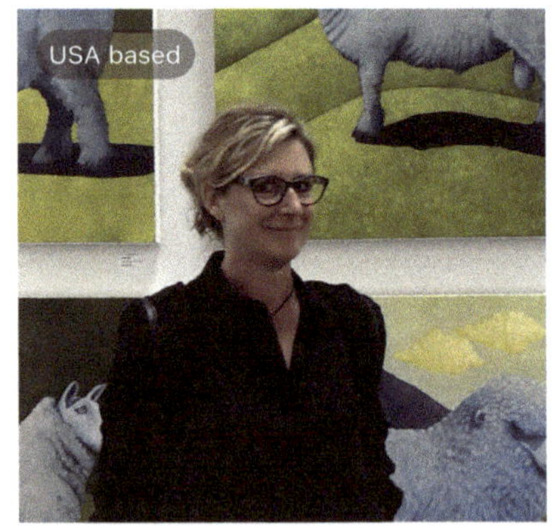

🖎 https://www.frances-melhop.art
@ studio@frances-melhop.art
◎ *@frances_melhop*

All the elements of the whisper game exist in these pieces - *transformation, surprise, amusement,* and *wonder.*

Frances Melhop works in tactile mediums, exploring the tensions between the virtual and physical ways we experience the world. Her current focus is impermanence, evidence of the hand, imperfection, and human presence and absence in our screen and material lives.

Frances Melhop, born in Christchurch, New Zealand, currently lives and works in Lake Tahoe, Nevada. She holds an MFA and BFA from the University of Reno (Nevada). Melhop's work has been exhibited in solo and group exhibitions worldwide at notable institutions such as Autry Museum (Los Angeles, CA), Brownsville Museum (Brownsville,TX), Cincinnati Art Museum, (Cincinnati, OH), Murray State University, (Murray, KY), Gertrude Herbert Institute, (Augusta, GA), and Arizona State University, (Phoenix, AZ). She has exhibited collaborative works with Susan Norrie at Nancy Hoffman Gallery (New York, NY) and the NSW Museum of Art, (Sydney, Australia). Melhop was awarded the Outstanding Artist Award in 2019 from the University of Reno, NNDA Innovator of the Year in 2014, and Luerzer's Archive World's Best Photographers in 2009/2010.

In 2020 she opened Melhop Gallery °7077, at Lake Tahoe, Nevada, representing 12 national and international artists. She also curates themed group shows with invited exceptional artists. For the last 5 years she taught in the art departments of University of Nevada, Reno, Western Nevada College, Truckee Meadows Community College and Lake Tahoe Community College.

Melhop's early career was spent as an acclaimed editorial fashion photographer based out of Sydney, Australia, London, UK, and Milan, Italy. She made narrative fairytale photographic stories of women for women. Her work appeared in Vogue Australia, Vogue Italia editions, Pelle and Gioielli, Elle Portugal, Gioia Italy, and Marie Claire Italy.

In 2020 she opened the contemporary art gallery, Melhop Gallery °7077, and initiated Melhop Projects, at Lake Tahoe, Nevada.

As children we would sit in a circle and start the whisper game. Each child would whisper what they heard to the next child, by the time it reached the end of the circle the whisper had changed beyond recognition. These works are the visual equivalent. The image of each girl transitions through various processes, to become another translation of a portrait. The pathway goes from living person, to a photographic fragment, a record of their existence, to a scanned file, to a computer screen, to a blind contour drawing in ink, with oil paint intervention, to a monotype print. In ways related to surrealist strategies, I reach for the essence of the subject or idea through deep observation, releasing visual control and allowing the unexpected to unfold.

All the elements of the whisper game exist in these pieces - transformation, surprise, amusement, and wonder. An entirely new image appears in the form of a monotype drawing.

Each evolves like a whisper across time....

What drives you to be an artist?

I think it is the complete physical, mental, and emotional discomfort that I feel when I try and do other types of work...and I have tried! The only time I feel like I am real, and growing and flourishing is when I am making my own artwork and looking after other artists.

How would you describe the art that you create and what inspires you?

I guess my work now explores the tensions between the virtual and physical ways we experience the world. I just get really excited about wonkiness, imperfection and the sense or evidence of the human hand in art. As a multidisciplinary artist, mediums such as drawing, stitching, wet plate collodion photography, oil paint, cast sculptural installation pieces and printmaking are what I have been working in to try and slow down, you know... to try and reverse out, extricate myself from texture-less screens.

If you could overcome all of your fears, what would you do with your art?

That is a good question....
I would persist and continue making things that are relevant, which make sense to me. Obviously, I would like to see my work in beautiful galleries and art museums around the world. My main shortage is time.... I would like to be able to focus more on my own work and not spread myself so thin with so many things pulling at my time....my art practice, the nomadic gallery, teaching etc....

When it comes to art making, how important is experimenting vs. sticking to a routine or set of rules?

Both are important. For instance, I teach the rules to my art students, but then also show them experimental work in that medium. I allow them to interpret projects as they will.... It is a freedom - a way of making decisions, and solving the strange sets of problems that appear when you get to work. You have to follow your own logic to find your voice. BUT sticking with a routine or set of rules can really help you maintain your art practice when you have those "meh" days. Throwing the rules to the wall and trying new, half-baked or even unformed ideas, mixing processes or just inventing a solution for yourself is extremely important to me. You can have some horrible mess ups...but then a magic wonderful image will suddenly emerge from the chaos. A work that makes your heart and mind sing, and all you want to do is more of that! It's the same with surfing and other sports...you are always hunting that feeling when you catch the perfect wave. Something very human, when everything is completely in synchronicity in mind, movement and action.

What are some of the challenges or experiences that have shaped your artistic journey so far?

I was an editorial fashion photographer for around 25 years, basically living my life through a lens. After a hot air balloon trip over the African savannah filming giraffe and elephants running beneath me, I felt like I was watching a National Geographic documentary on TV and not actually experiencing the moment. In the mid 90's this ongoing sense of distance began to really bother me. Now it seems to be happening to everyone, we all seem to be living a major amount of time through our screens. This on-going disquiet causes me to explore human presence and absence through my art work.

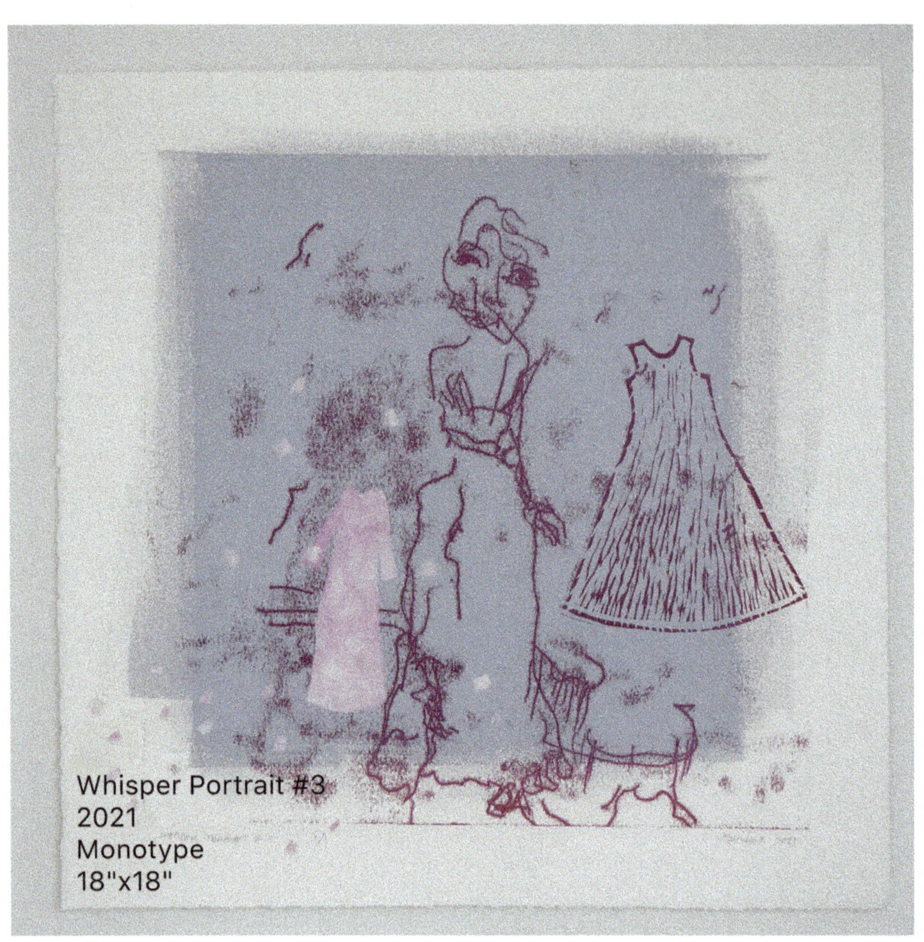

Whisper Portrait #3
2021
Monotype
18"x18"

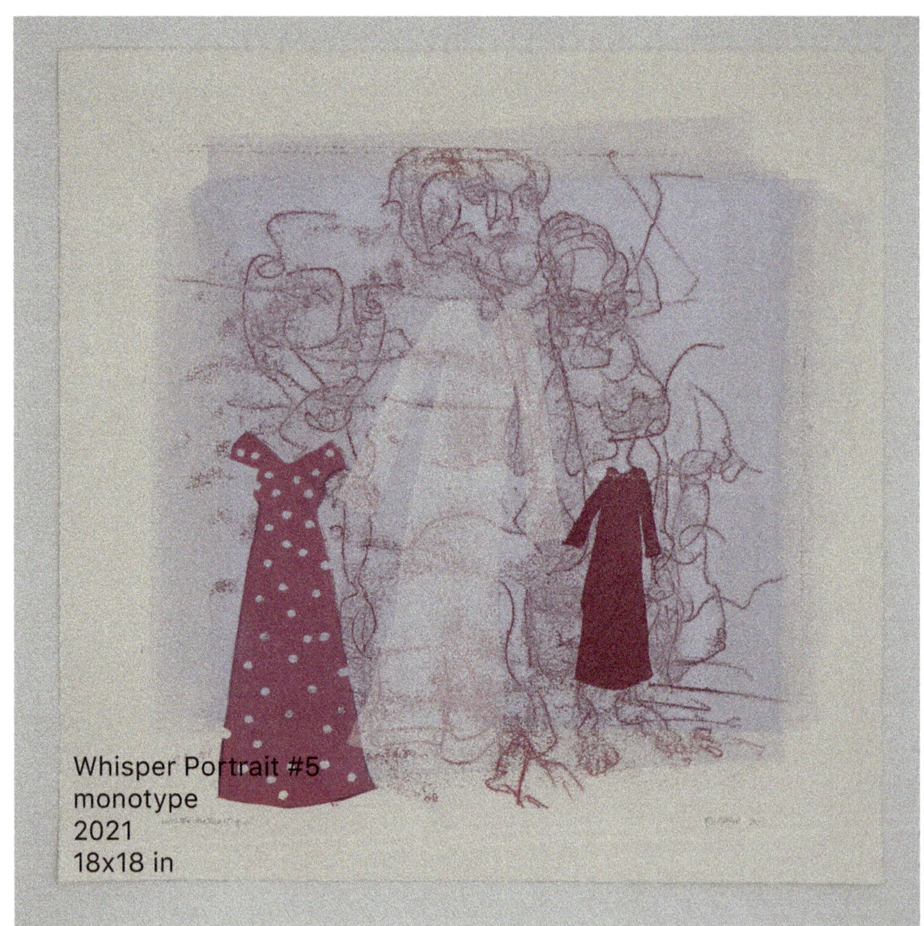

Whisper Portrait #5
monotype
2021
18x18 in

"Each evolves like a whisper across time."

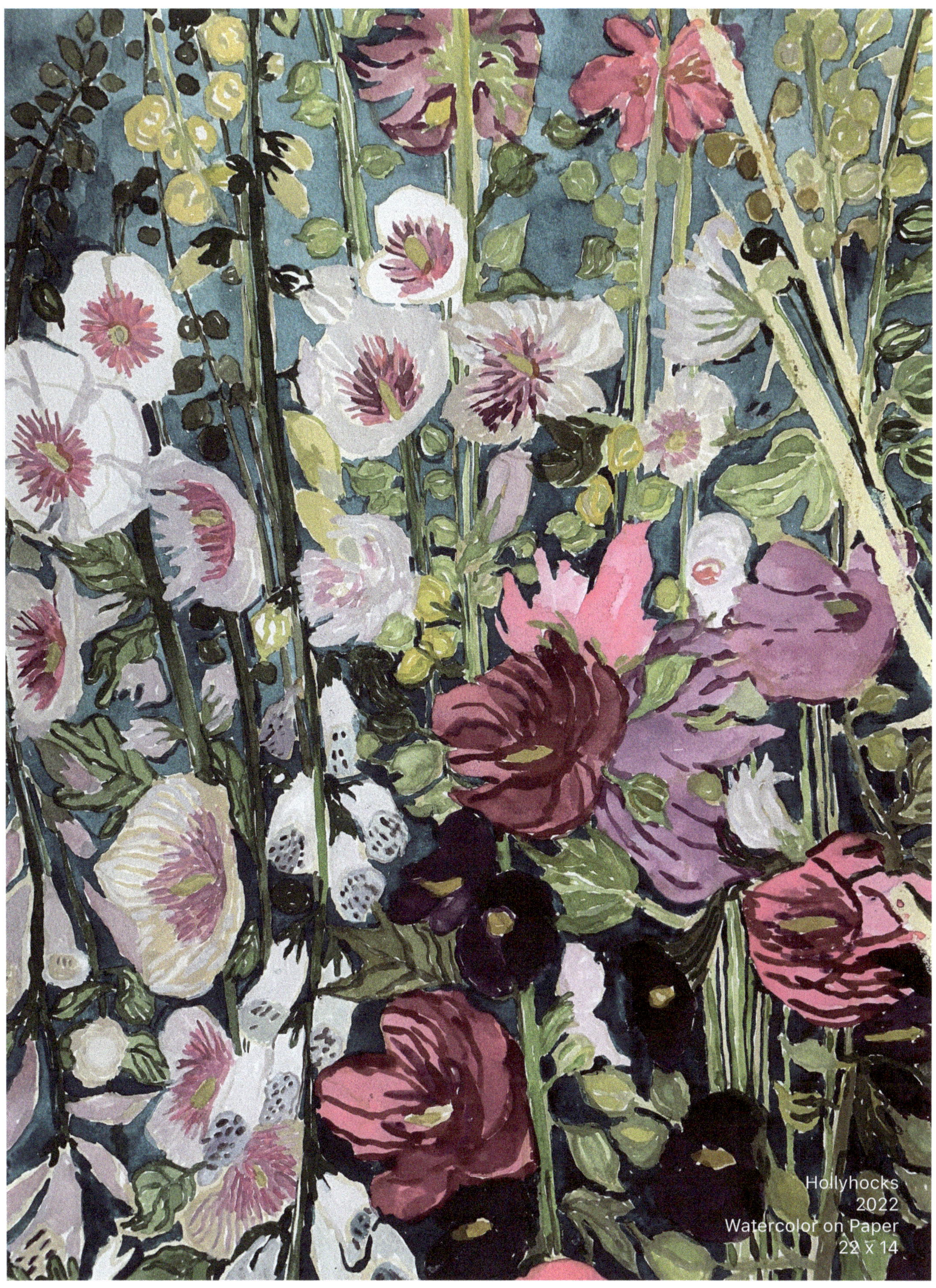
Hollyhocks
2022
Watercolor on Paper
22 x 14

Nancy Andruk Olson

I paint broad sweeping landscapes that use bright color to an imagined space.

Nancy Andruk Olson focuses on our human relation to nature while using improvisational painting techniques coupled with a high chroma palette. The high chroma signifies an imagined landscape that describes both the practice of painting itself and the experience of being in a landscape. Andruk Olson's work uses nature as a starting point to explore how paint can interpret our experience with the land and the experiences we have on the land. Natural objects are also used as a metaphor for human connection and a description of the feelings that arise as a result of human interactions.

Andruk Olson has been a lifetime painter. Andruk Olson started painting as a child with her mother, who is an art teacher, and never really stopped. Raised in Los Angeles, she attended Art Center College of Design as a high school student. Andruk Olson has a BFA in painting from BYU, where she spent most of her time working with Bruce Hixson Smith. Andruk Olson also has a Post-Baccalaureate certificate from The School of the Museum of Fine Arts, Boston. Her painting approach is direct, using a lot of impressionist techniques. The improvisation, the interaction of the paint, the interplay of the materials and the intensity of the color are part of the language for her. Andruk Olson makes a lot of her own paint to ensure the intensity of the pigment is as high as possible. Other artists who focus on color to capture memories such as Pierre Bonnard, Wolf Kahn, Inka Essenhigh and John McCallister are a major source of inspiration for Andruk Olson. Andruk Olson recently completed the A-I-R Residency at the Bountiful Davis Art Center.

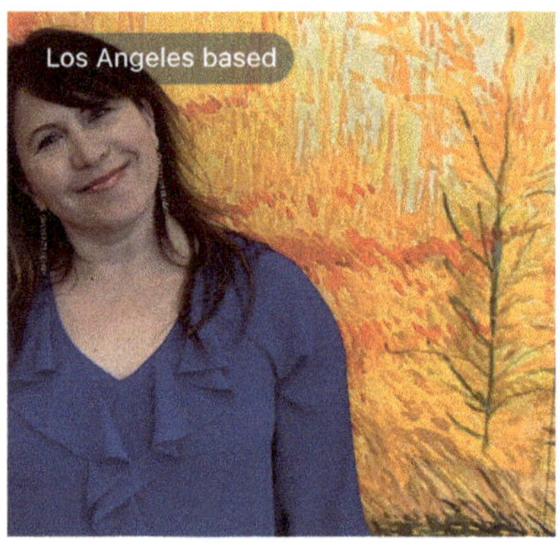

https://www.nancyandrukolson.com
nancyandrukolson@gmail.com
@nancyandrukolsonartist

What drives you to be an artist?

This is something that I think about all of the time! For me art is communication. What makes a writer write a book? That same desire to communicate is what drives me. Except I speak in images, which can sometimes be cryptic and easy to disguise the meaning, or have multiple meanings. Painting to me is like writing in my journal about my life. I do it ritualistically everyday and I regurgitate what I am thinking about in my life that day.

How would you describe the art that you create and what inspires you?

I paint broad sweeping landscapes that use bright color to an imagined space. I use landscape as a stage for human interaction and an escape from reality of life. The art that I create definitely has roots in my childhood experiences of looking at art. My mother is an artist so we were constantly going to museums and looking at all types of art. We looked at lots of impressionism and that direct approach to painting is deeply embedded in my mind. I use quick direct techniques that focus on feeling and emotion. I use very bright colors as a way to take my pieces out of a naturalistic space and more into a fictional one. I am definitely inspired by many contemporary artists who are very successful at creating imagined landscapes. Several favorites I have right now are John McAllister, Inka Essenhigh and Haley Barker.

When it comes to art making, how important is experimenting vs. sticking to a routine or set of rules?

Experimentation is very important to me. Maybe I even do it too much. It is a part of my regular practice. I think it is important because that is how you get better and how your work stays fresh and relevant. Experimenting is a way to keep from copying yourself which so many artists do. I make a lot of work that doesn't fit into a coherent body of work or look like existing work that I regularly show. Because of this I only show less than fifty percent of what I actually make. It is hard to tolerate experimentation because it means that you fail a lot. This year I have probably failed more than I have succeded! Hopefully it will be to my benefit in the long run and it will make me a better artist.

What are some of the challenges or experiences that have shaped your artistic journey so far?

The journey of an artist is full of challenges. I have experienced so many, but there are a few that really stand out to me that have really pushed me in my practice. When I was an art student I had a series of teachers who were very discouraging to me in my work. They really did not like the direction that I was working on at the time. One of my advisors told me, "Nancy, if you want to be successful you think that you would look around you and see what other people are doing and so something like that." At the time that really just ripped my heart out and basically made it very difficult to create. This advice was the antithesis of what I believed and continue to believe art should be. Really innovative artists that have made the most impact on the art world are the ones that are distinct and stay true to their own voice and experience. This experience pushed me into real soul searching and not really participating in the art world for about twelve years. During that time away I became a mother which I would say was another challenge which has shaped my journey. When you have children you have less time and focus on creating. This has forced me to become very concentrated and efficient in my art making. I have to plan very carefully so that everyone's needs are met and so I have time to create. While historically having children has been discouraged among artists because of the time it takes away from producing, I think that it has made me a better artist. Not only does having children give me rich life experience to draw from for my creative endeavors, it forces me to focus on what is really important in life and creative practice. Another way that I have adapted is incorporating my children into my studio time. I will often include them in my experimentation and teach them how to make art alongside me. A more recent discovery that has really shaped my journey and pushed my art forward has been making my own paint. I started doing this about 5 years ago and it is amazing what a difference it has made to my entire process. Because I make the paint myself, I am able to decide what is in it and I am able to control the results much easier than with store bought paint. This has been one of the benefits of constant experimentation. I have been able to develop something that has been successful in pushing my practice forward.

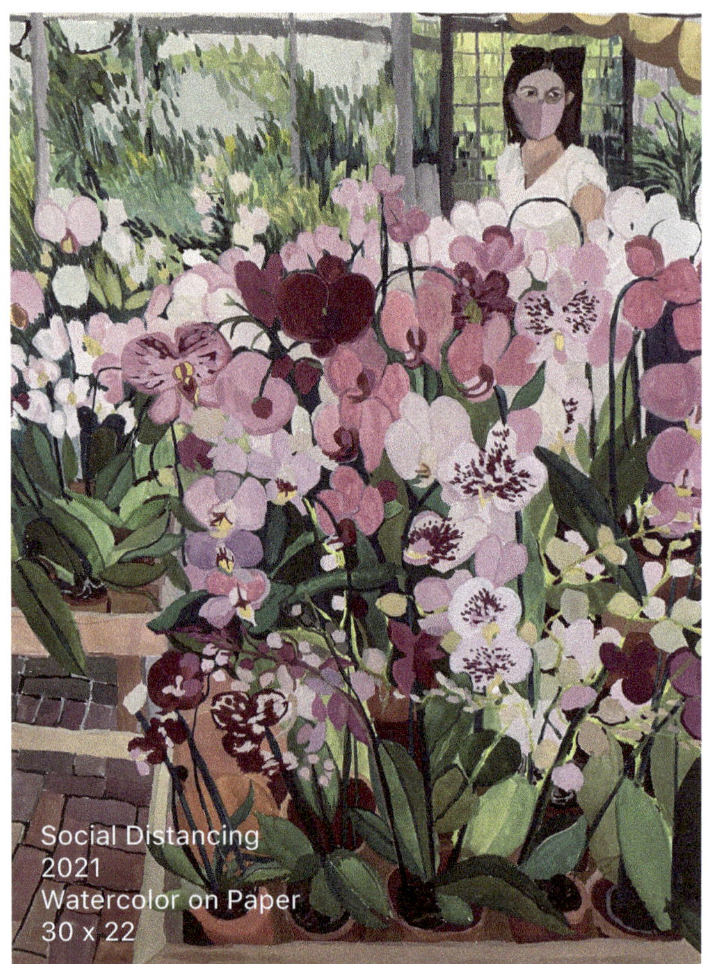

Social Distancing
2021
Watercolor on Paper
30 x 22

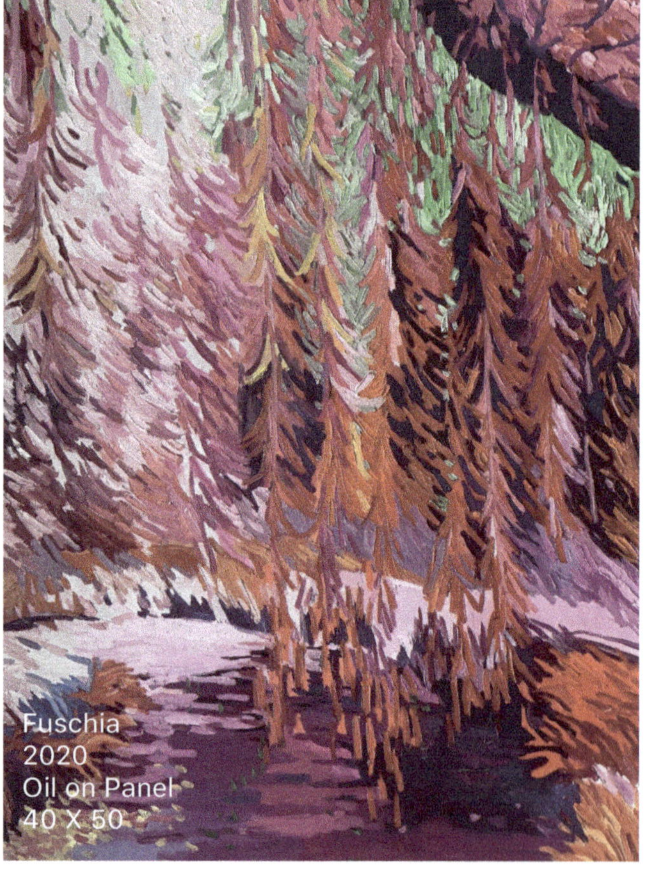

Fuschia
2020
Oil on Panel
40 x 50

"We looked at lots of impressionism and that direct approach to painting is deeply embedded in my mind."

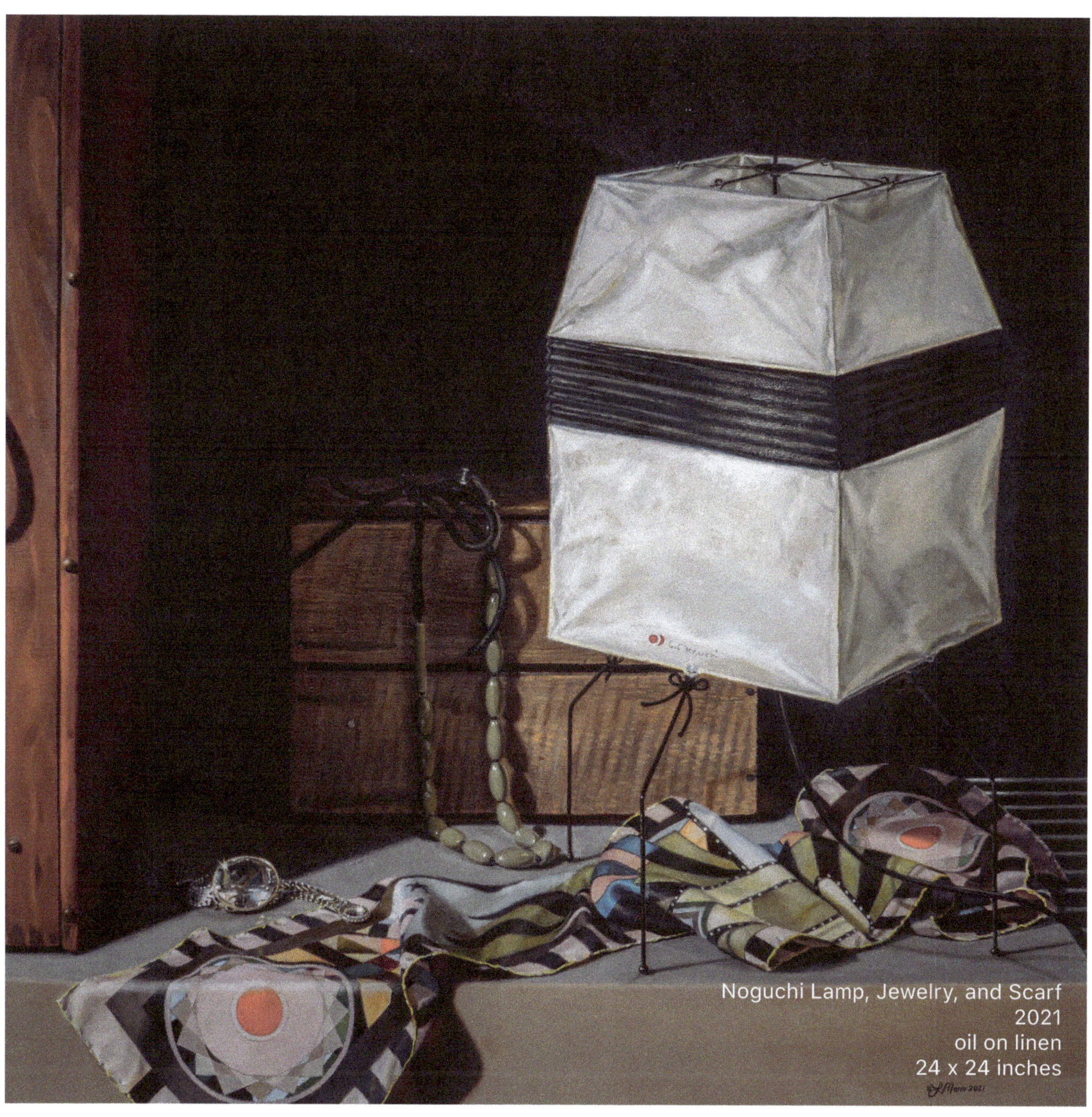

Noguchi Lamp, Jewelry, and Scarf
2021
oil on linen
24 x 24 inches

Linda Mann

I aim to *capture* the way that light describes *form, texture,* and *subtleties of color* to the *human eye.*

Linda Mann lives and works in Bellevue, WA. Mann studied at the Gage Academy of Art (Seattle, WA) and The Academy of Art College (San Francisco, CA). She has had solo exhibitions at the Hyatt Regency (Bellevue, WA) and Quent Cordair Fine Art (Burlingame, CA). Mann has been selected Associate Living Master by the Artist Renewal Center as well as a Finalist in their 2020, 2021, and 2022 International Salons.

In unstable times, it is valuable to step back and be reminded that despite chaos, the world is still understandable and beautiful. My still life paintings evoke this ordered, stylized reality. I paint with an understanding of how people see and understand, not by recording every detail, as a camera or computer would, but rather by observing the essential, and editing out the unimportant and distracting. Working exclusively from life with no reference to photographs, I observe the ephemeral effects of light and how they appear to the human eye, re-creating the experience in oil paint. Through my selective and heightened focus and dramatic lighting, everyday objects are imbued with weight and meaning.

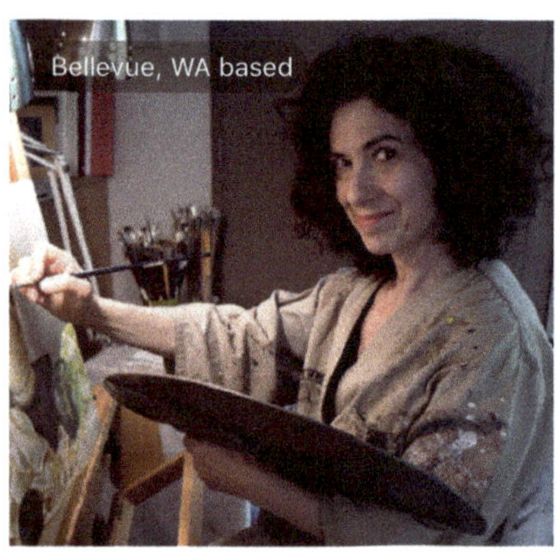

https://lindamann.com
@ linda@lindamann.com
@lindamannartist

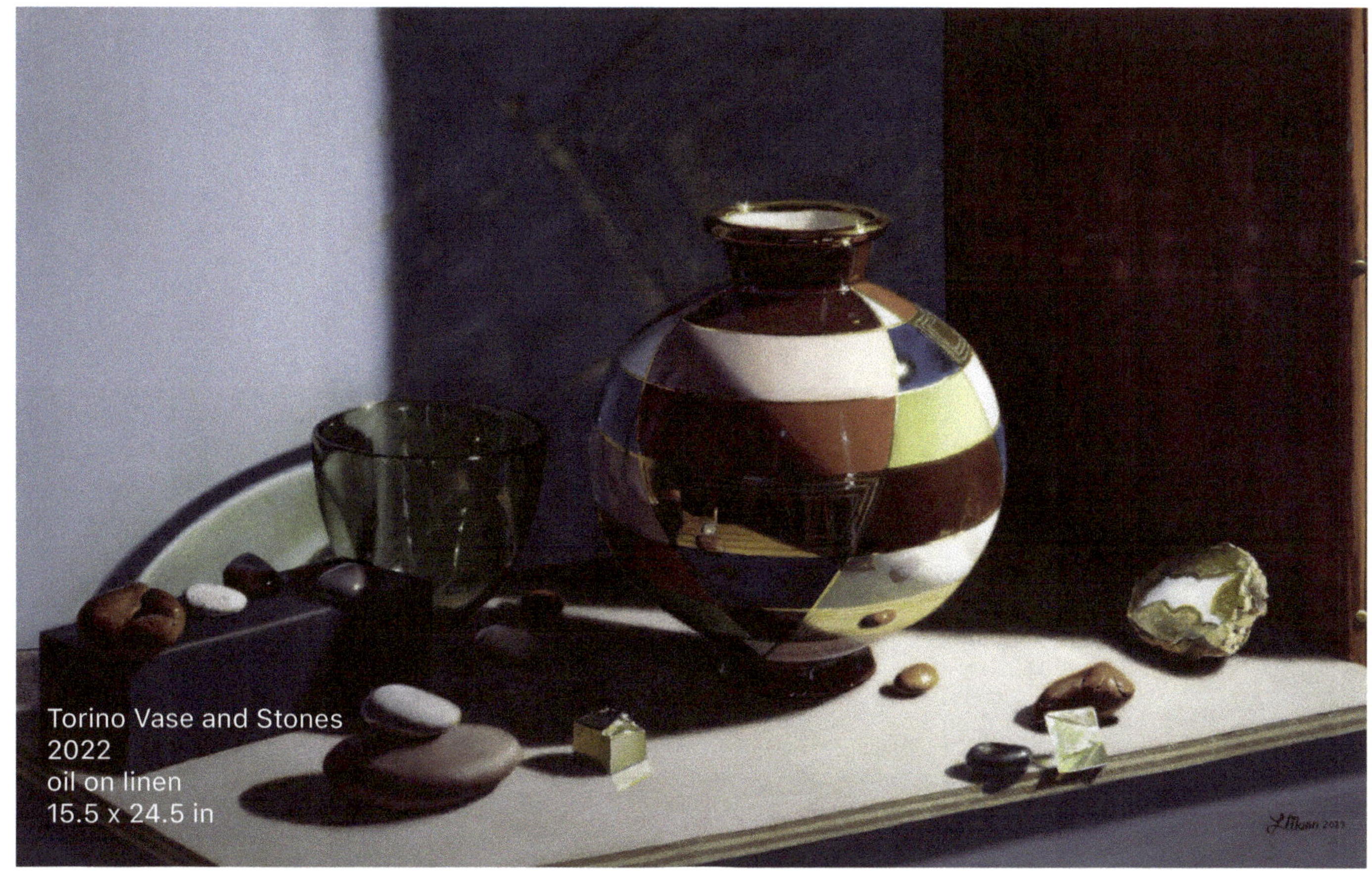

Torino Vase and Stones
2022
oil on linen
15.5 x 24.5 in

What drives you to be an artist?

I've always been fascinated by how to capture 3-D reality on a 2-D surface, at first, by drawing and learning perspective, and later, by painting the nuances of color and light. This fascination continues. Also, I find it so satisfying to select objects that I love and mold them into an ordered and compelling composition that reflects my view of the order and beauty of this world.

How would you describe the art that you create and what inspires you?

I paint realist still lifes in oil. I aim to capture the way that light describes form, texture, and subtleties of color to the human eye. By using dramatic contrasts of dark and light, and rich colors, I create little worlds to contemplate. I'm inspired by the Spanish still lifes of the 17th century, Velasquez, and Vermeer. I'm also inspired by my mid-century house and all the beautiful objects it contains, and the way the light flows through it.

If you could overcome all of your fears, what would you do with your art?

I might try to figure out NFTs!

When it comes to art making, how important is experimenting vs. sticking to a routine or set of rules?

After painting for 30 years, I've internalized and automatized much knowledge. I draw upon that every time I paint, allowing me to be quicker and more intuitive. Experimenting with new techniques necessarily comes with the cost of slowing me down. However, if I never experiment, I can get stale. The trick is to keep an open mind to try new things, but not to let go of all the stored experience.

What are some of the challenges or experiences that have shaped your artistic journey so far?

When I started to paint professionally, realist art wasn't very popular. I had a hard time finding instruction in the classical techniques that I wanted to learn, so I turned to hunting down and studying art technique books from the turn of the last century. Of course, many of the techniques and materials were out of date, so I had to interpret them in my own way using modern materials and my own sensibilities.

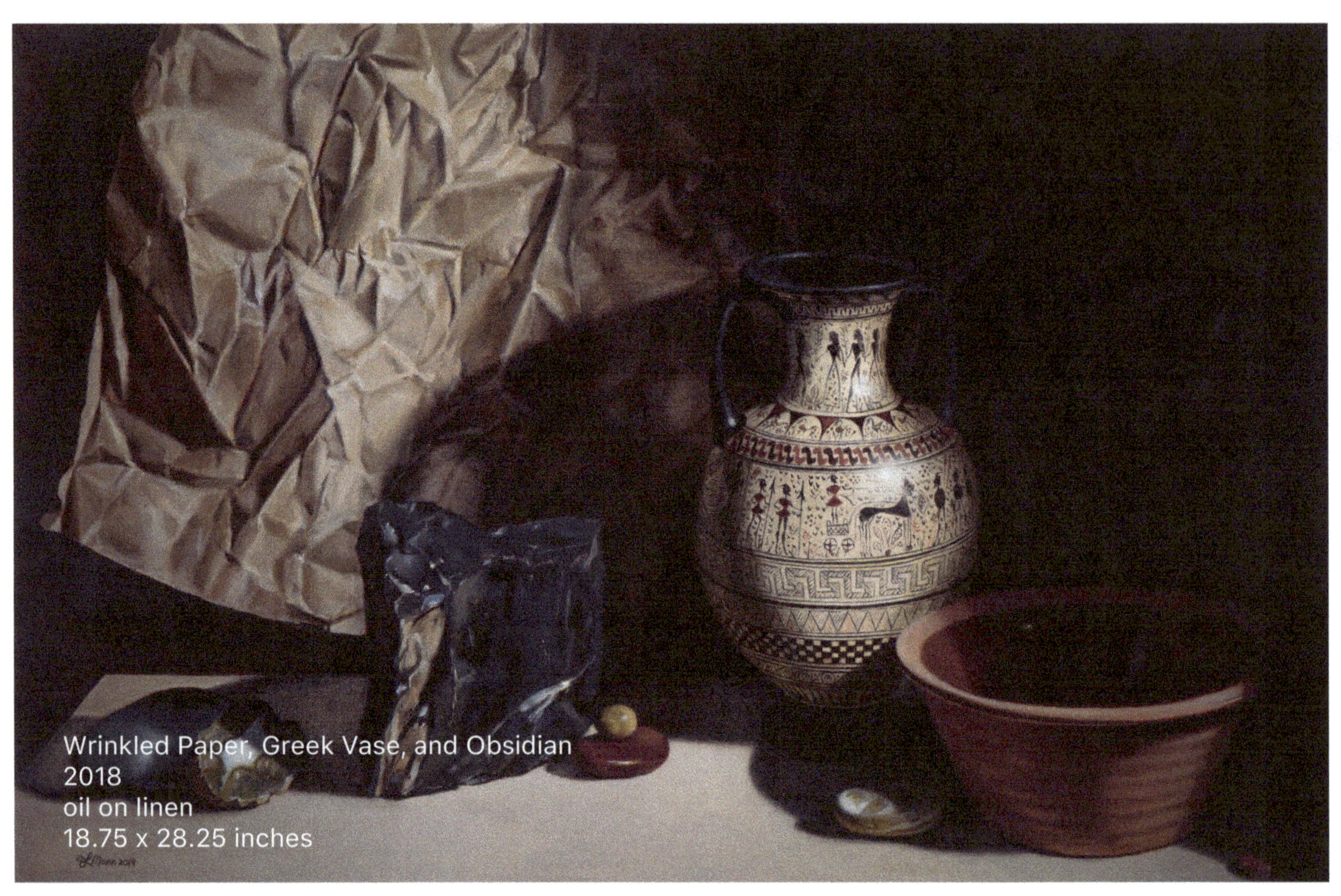

"If I never experiment, I can get stale."

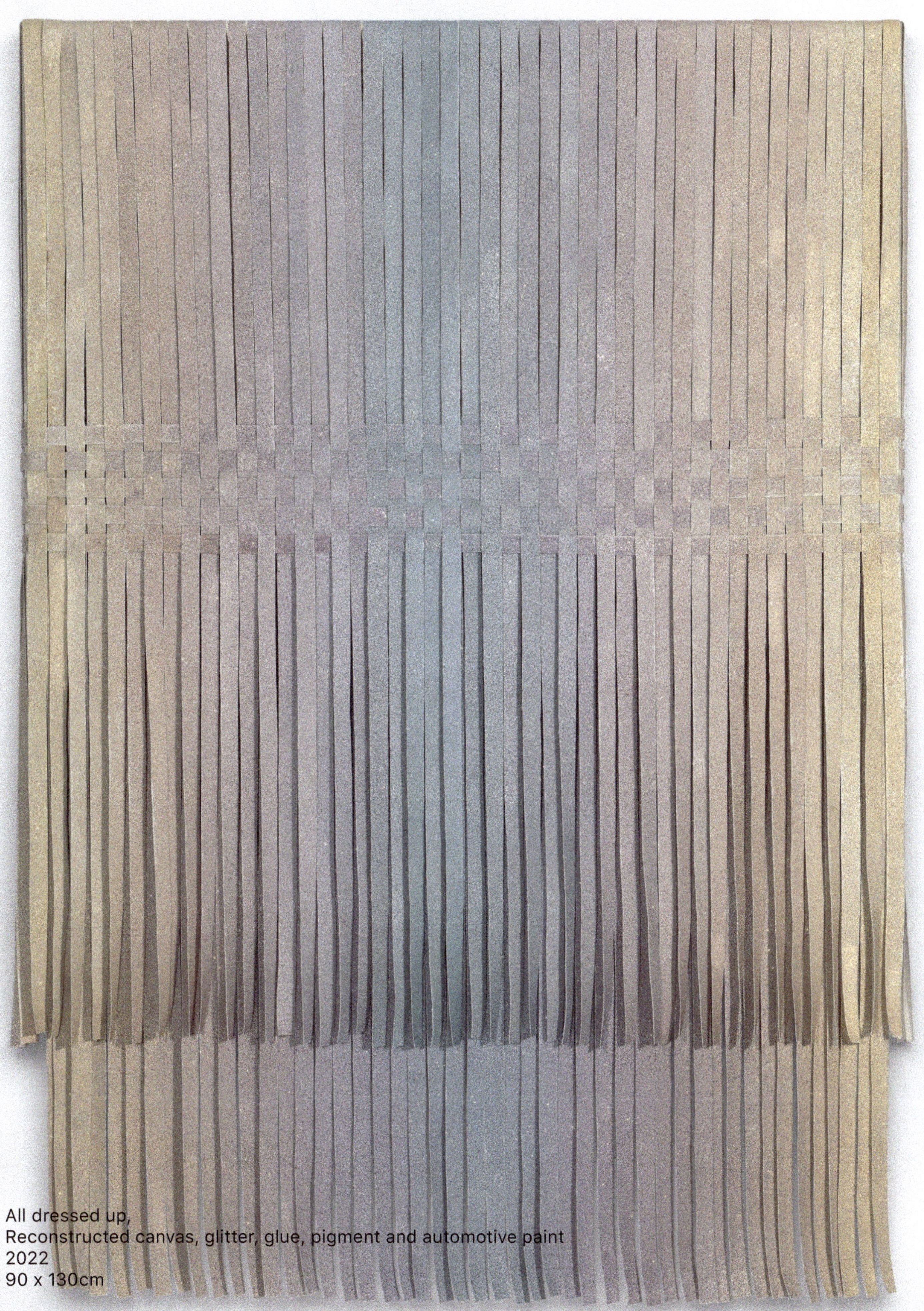

All dressed up,
Reconstructed canvas, glitter, glue, pigment and automotive paint
2022
90 x 130cm

Shelly Pamensky

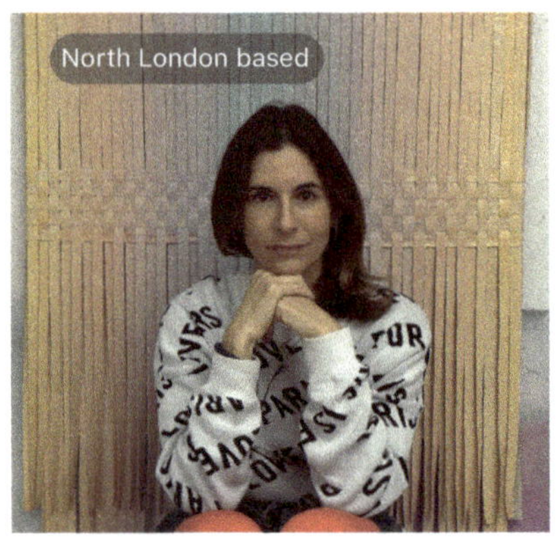

https://shellypamensky.com
shelly.pamensky@gmail.com
@shellypamensky

I do believe in the *power of routine* to establish a solid foundation for my *artistic practice.*

Shelly is a visual artist, raised in South Africa, of Israeli origin and now working from her studio in North London. She completed a Law degree in South Africa and is a self taught artist who turned her attention to painting, after a career in the City of London.

Her shimmering paired back colour field paintings explore a process of mixing unconventional materials together to create a surface where glitter, paint and pigment particles coalesce to incantatory effect. Her process-intensive paintings are reductive in nature, exploring elements of colour, materiality and intimacy and are a response to processes of internal enquiry and external visual influences derived from the world of fashion and social media.

Shelly's work has sold internationally to private collectors. She has produced numerous commission pieces and has collaborated with curators and interior designers such as Kelly Hoppen. She has exhibited in group shows as well as in Art Fairs such as The Affordable Art Fair, Roys Art Fair and The Other Art Fair. Her work has been been featured in numerous publications and online exhibition.

The two main elements of Shelly's work are colour and materiality. The artist believes in the emotive qualities of colour, it's ability to make one feel before you can process what you see. She works with colour intuitively and mixes it expressively. Her inner feelings, current environment and fashion influence her colour choices, but she also responds to the needs of the painting as it evolves. Her chosen paint medium is sprayed automotive paint, a source of highly pigmented and translucent, uninterrupted colour. Materiality is created through applying successive layers of glitter, glue and pigment to the canvas. As paint and glitter particles fuse a bed of shimmering colour is created and this forms the subject matter of the work. There is a delicate balance between colour and shine, too much colour and the luminosity is lost. This palpable surface tension imbues the paintings with a delicate nature which Pamensky believes establishes a sense of intimacy with the viewer as the dazzling surface draws one's gaze in.

To these shimmering gradients, she may add words based on her thoughts, memories and feelings. She also cuts these paintings into strips which are then reconstructed into fringed and woven versions, sometimes combining 2 or more paintings. The whole process is manual and laborious, a complete antithesis to the increasing digitisation of the art world. The paintings appear three-dimensional as they extend beyond the frame of the canvas and wrap around its sides. The surface created whether woven or not is immersive as is the creative process. which instills in her a deep sense of purpose. There is a feeling of slowing down in the manual processes which pervade the visual aesthetic of the paintings imbuing them with a sense of calm in antithesis to the frenzy of the outside world.

What drives you to be an artist?

I am driven to be an artist by my innate need to create. As an introvert, making art is where I feel most aligned with myself and expressive. It challenges me creatively, emotionally, intellectually and physically. I am at once shut off to the outside world, but focused in the present moment. The peace and deep sense of purpose which the creative process instils in me is reflected in the visually calming aesthetic of my paintings and is the reason I make art. Although my work is influenced by the outside world, it should serve as an antithesis to it's frenzy and is about finding inner peace both for me in its making and the calming effect it can have on the viewer in its perception.

How would you describe the art that you create and what inspires you?

My art has evolved out of my deep love for colour. I also love glitter for its ability to mesmerise. In combining the two I can make captive surfaces which I then often reconstruct. The work may appear sparkly, with soft pastel colours and the feminine shapes of weaves, but the underlying process is manually intensive and makes use of tools and materials from the male dominated automotive industry. I am inspired to make art I feel connected to that embody contrasting aspects of myself, whilst combining unconventional materials not usually associated with one another or the art world, such as glitter and automotive paint.

If you could overcome all of your fears, what would you do with your art?

I would experiment even more, not be afraid to fail, care less about what others would think of my work. Have more courage to talk about my work and get my work "out there"... I imagine my work would appear more freed up, bold, less restrained and scaled up.

When it comes to art making, how important is experimenting vs. sticking to a routine or set of rules?

I am very inclined to experiment. I am self taught so everything I have learned along the way has been through experience and experimentation. My process of combining spray gun with glitter, is uncommon. There are no set rules to follow. I learn mostly from the errors I make along the way. Mistakes are opportunities for evolving my work and I apply insights gained to the next piece. I always seek to push boundaries and think of what comes next with my work. I do believe in the power of routine to establish a solid foundation for my artistic practice. I always carve out time to be purely creative and for the making of art away from the administrative and business side of my practice.

What are some of the challenges or experiences that have shaped your artistic journey so far?

I think as an artist, there is much struggle involved in feeling worthy as an artist and staying true to yourself. You want some recognition for your work but you also want to make work that you feel connected to which gives you meaning.

*"I learn mostly from the errors
I make along the way."*

Sometimes you can be influenced by what other people you admire are making, or what you believe an audience would like to see and buy. These things can be distracting and I think staying true to myself has shaped my artistic journey and my work. More and more the true sense of achievement is in the process of making the work and in fact I feel I want to linger more on each piece. The process of applying glitter to linen and spraying it over with automotive paint has proven to be challenging and prone to failure, which is why I developed the weave and fringe as segway's to my work. I see that challenges can be rewarding as they necessitate new ways of thinking about doing things. As long as I am being authentic to myself I feel my work will be unique and have a natural evolution.

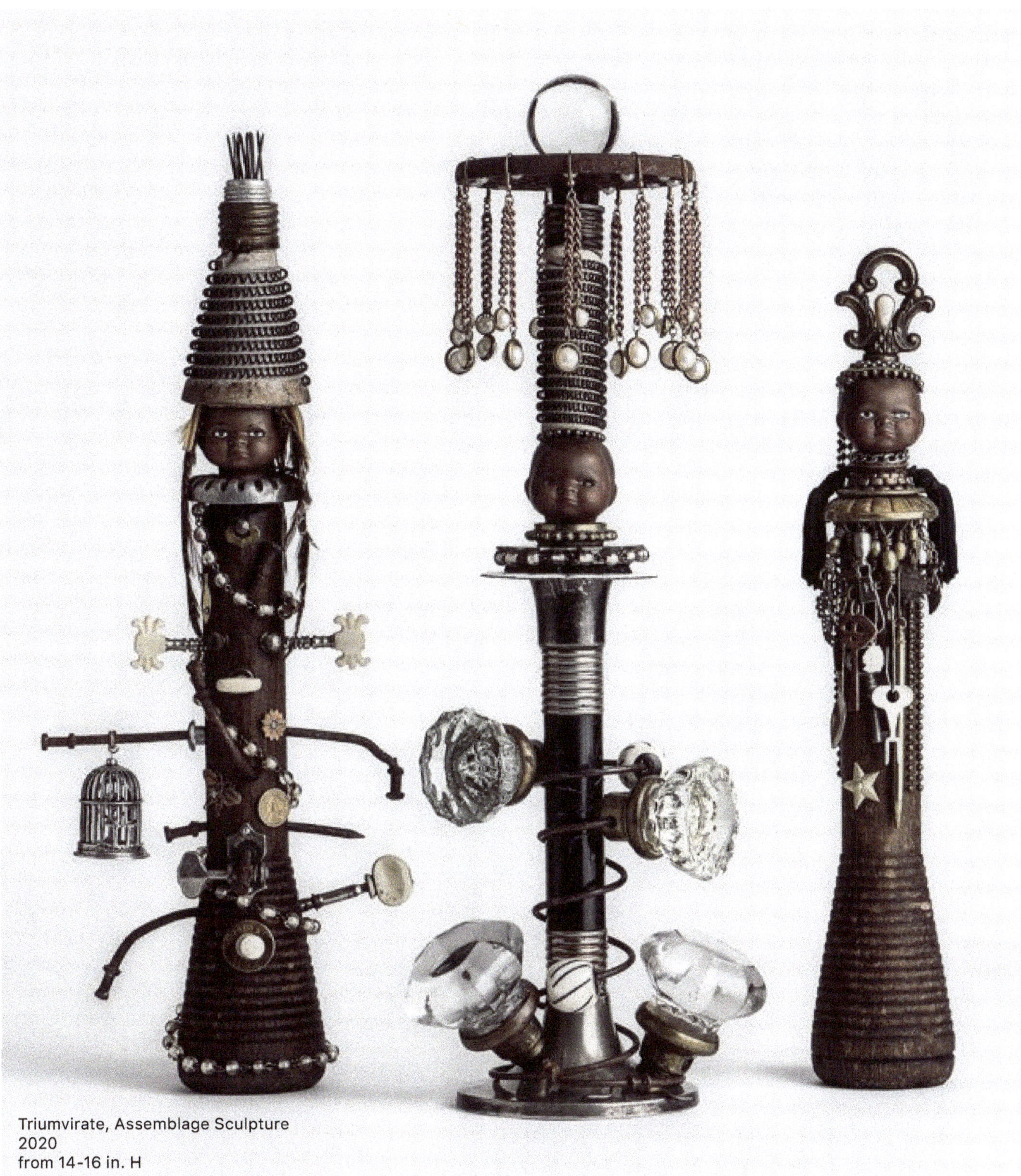

Triumvirate, Assemblage Sculpture
2020
from 14-16 in. H

Gale Rothstein

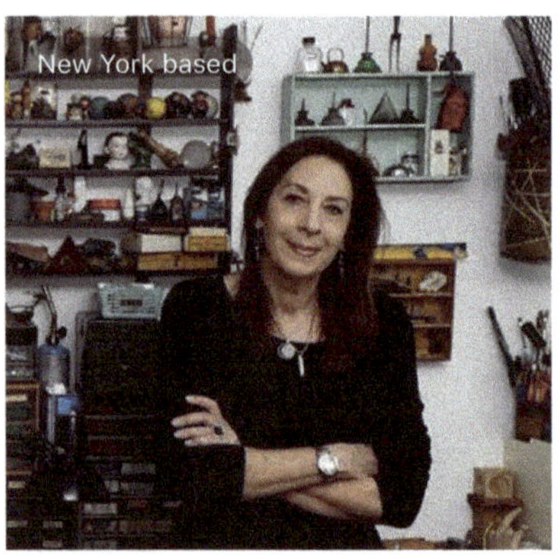

🔗 https://www.galerothsteindesigns.com
@ galerothstein@gmail.com
📷 @galerothsteindesigns

I am inspired by my various interests and fascinations, including *archaeology, time travel, the cosmos, nature, history, surrealism...*

Gale Rothstein's art practice has always been about putting together the pieces. Currently, Rothstein makes assemblage sculptures in which assembled boxes and environments (Inter-Exteriors) emerge from a strong narrative and historical framework. Referenced through reuse, the work is informed by her former career as a jewelry designer and life-long pursuit of collecting antiques, collectibles, found objects, harvested broken appliances, and other used items. Rothstein's work is influenced by her father's memory, who was a jack of all trades and one of the original recyclers and re-purposers decades before it was commonplace. She inherited his collection of parts and incorporates many of his objects into her assemblages, further supporting the work's historical and personal foundation.

Gale Rothstein lives and works in the Greenwich Village neighborhood of New York City. Rothstein's work has been included in three consecutive biennial group exhibitions of assemblage sculpture entitled Eye of the Beholder at the Maryland Federation of Art's Circle Gallery (Annapolis, MD). Rothstein recently had a solo exhibition entitled She Dreams at FX Collaborative, a New York City architectural firm, inclusion in Women Celebrate Women at El BarrioArtspace NYC, and Renanscence at Limner Gallery in Hudson, NY. She has received awards from the National Collage Society, Manhattan Arts, Artsy Shark, Fusion Art, and Light Space Time. Her work has been the subject of a feature article and on the cover of Broad Street Literary and Art Magazine. Rothstein's work has also been included in Feral Journal of Poetry and Art, Lumiere Review, and Artist Portfolio Magazine. In the 1980s and 1990s, when Rothstein was a jewelry designer, her work appeared in many fashion publications, including Vogue, Harper's Bazaar, Glamour, Women's Wear Daily, and several industry magazines.

Reimagined through re-use, my work is informed by my former career as a jewelry designer, my passion for foraging and collecting antiques, harvesting broken appliances and other damaged objects, and rescuing found objects from the street to recontextualize them in my assemblage sculptures. My goal is to go beyond obvious assumptions, prompting the viewer to wonder, "Where are we? Who is here with us? How big or small are we? Are we awake or dreaming?", continually challenging them to reevaluate one's sense of time, place, and orientation.

What drives you to be an artist?

The drive is innate–I was born an artist. It has always been instinctual to create, whether in illustration, painting, collage, crafts, and my first professional avocation, jewelry design.

How would you describe the art that you create and what inspires you?

My current work is the creation of assemblage sculptures, and it's a synthesis of all my prior artistic endeavors. I am inspired by my various interests and fascinations, including archaeology, time travel, the cosmos, nature, history, surrealism, and of course the objects I collect and incorporate into the work to tell my stories in these highly narrative pieces.

If you could overcome all of your fears, what would you do with your art?

I am not so much fearful as subject to some logistical limitations, like space in NYC.

When it comes to art making, how important is experimenting vs. sticking to a routine or set of rules?

I have been concentrating on this body of work for a decade now and feel no restrictions or rules to follow. My process is organic, and the work has grown and morphed along with the trajectory of my life and all its nuances.

What are some of the challenges or experiences that have shaped your artistic journey so far?

The moment I saw the potential in my vast collection of objects as materials to be reinvented into new artworks, my practice as an assemblage artist took off.

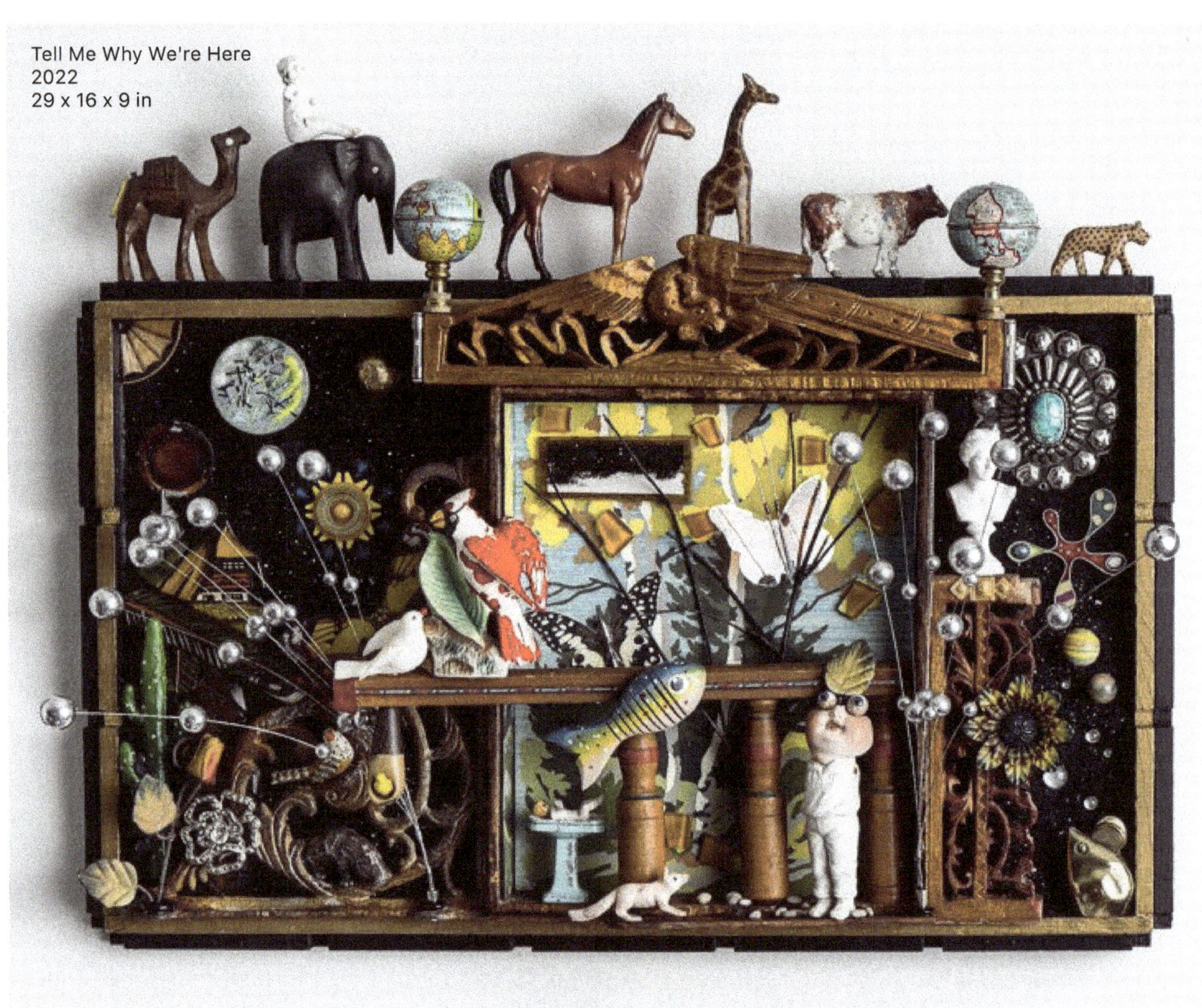

"The moment I saw the potential in my vast collection of objects as materials to be reinvented into new artworks, my practice as an assemblage artist took off"

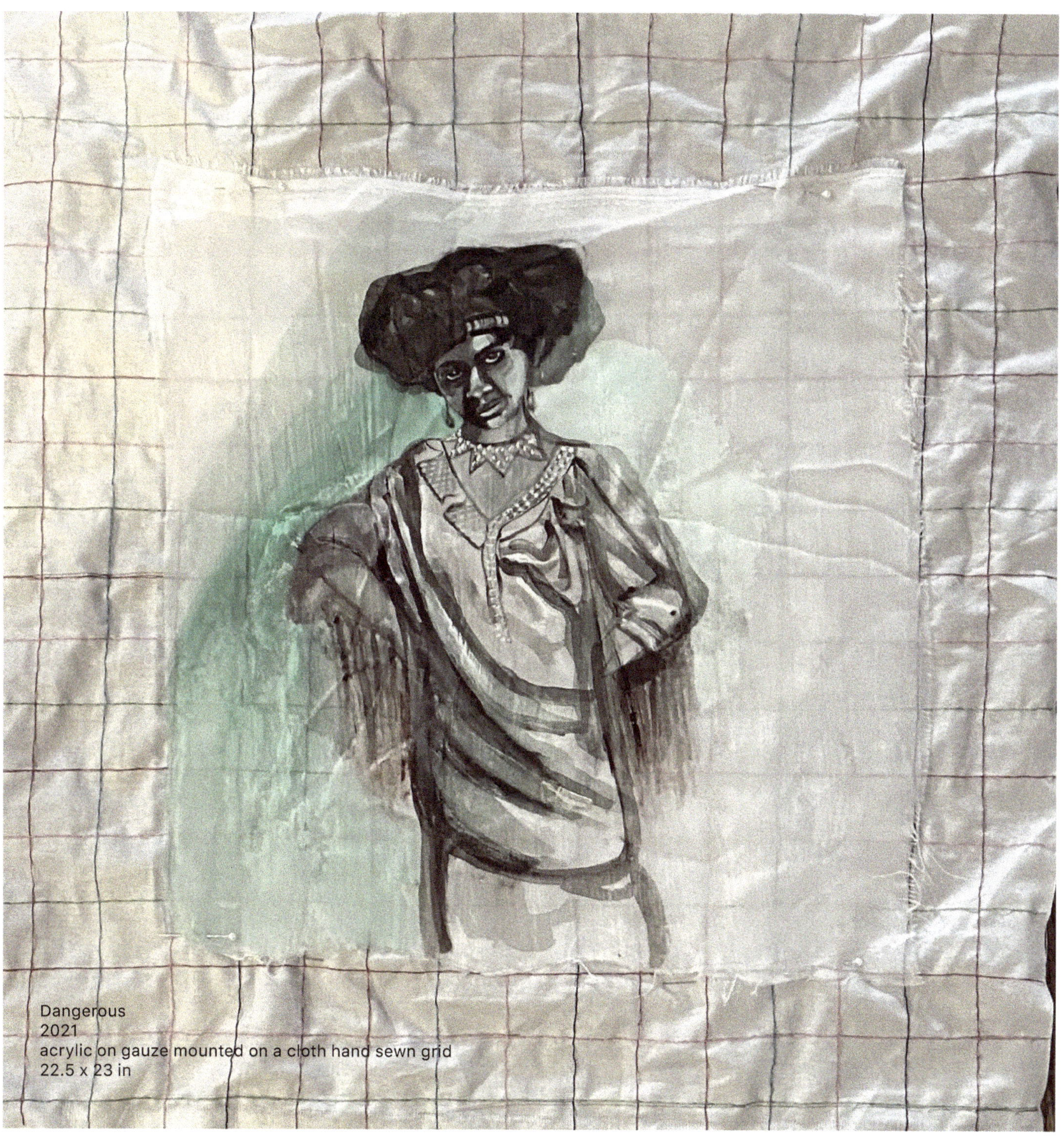

Dangerous
2021
acrylic on gauze mounted on a cloth hand sewn grid
22.5 x 23 in

Tricia Townes

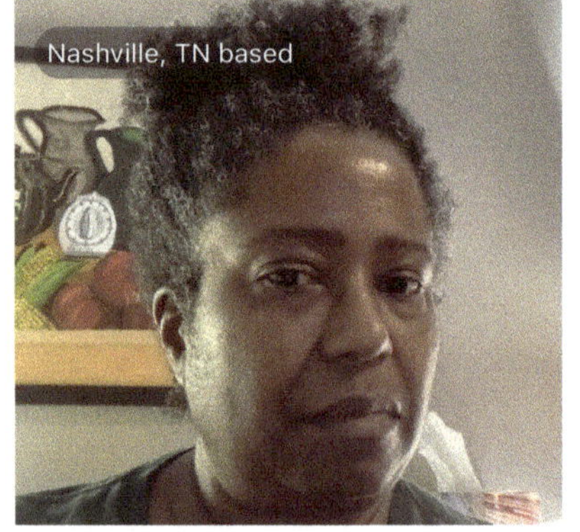

🖋 https://www.tricialynntownes.com
@ townestricia1@gmail.com
▢ *@tricial.townes*

I think *experimenting* and being *open to exploiting happy accidents* is *key* to moving *art making forward.*

Tricia Townes is a painter and educator from Nashville, TN. Townes' s practice consists of figurative, design-based, and social practice works focusing on healing communities of color and healing dysfunction across communities. Townes has attended several prestigious residencies, including those at Skowhegan, The Fine Arts Work Center, and MassMoCA.

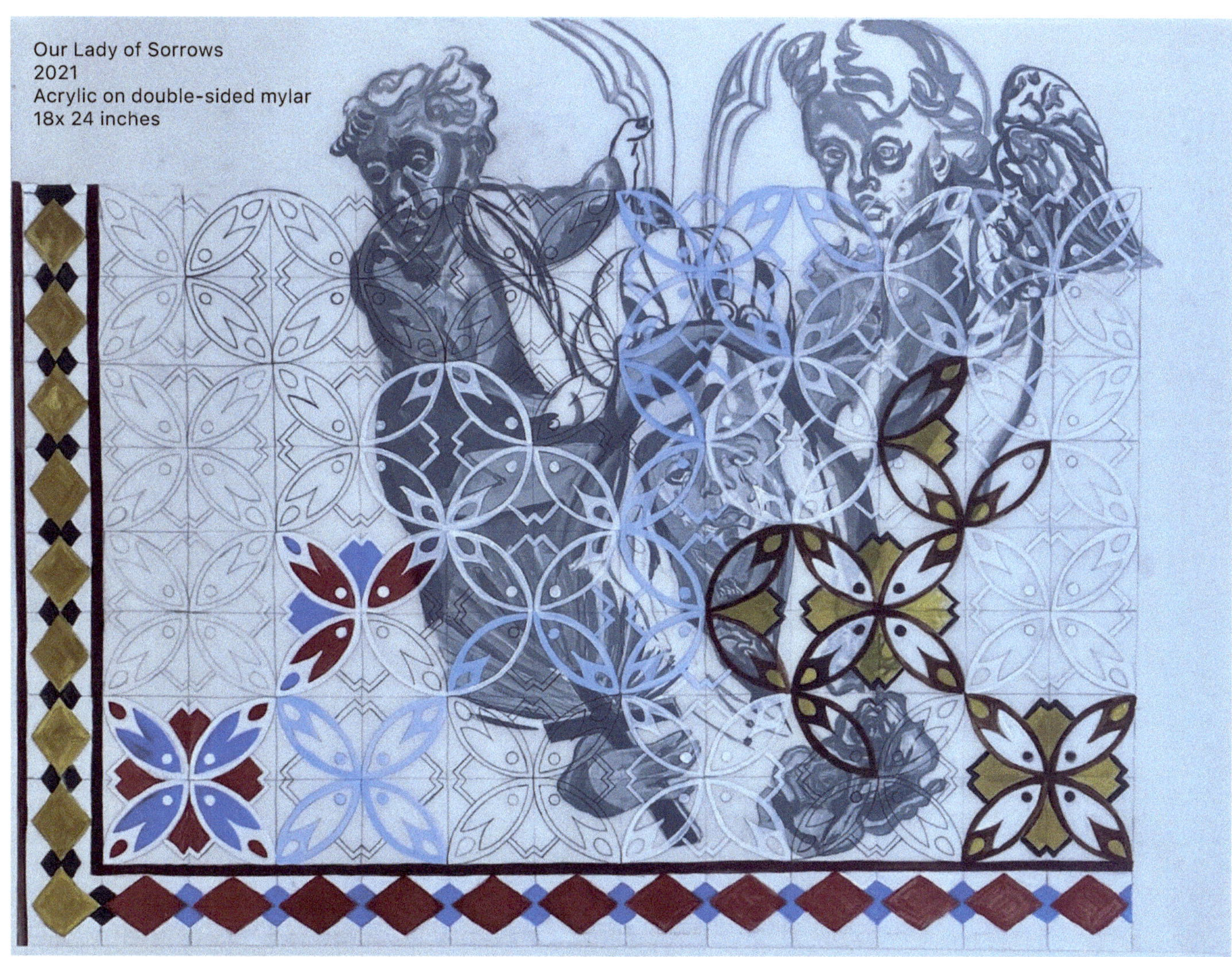

What drives you to be an artist?

I want to heal myself and others. Like many, I come from an "ordinary, dysfunctional" family. I try to understand some of those issues so that I can ameliorate them through art making. My desire to affect healing also extends beyond myself and my immediate family to other communities, especially those of people of color.

How would you describe the art that you create and what inspires you?

I make psychological portraits of friends and family, socially engaged artworks, and design-based works from marginalized cultures that position people from those cultures as first-class U.S. citizens.

If you could overcome all of your fears, what would you do with your art?

I definitely believe that I am already doing everything I can with my art at this stage, but my hope is to continually raise my upper limit.

When it comes to art making, how important is experimenting vs. sticking to a routine or set of rules?

I think experimenting and being open to exploiting happy accidents is key to moving art making forward. Otherwise you get stuck in a rut if you stick to old routines for too long.

What are some of the challenges or experiences that have shaped your artistic journey so far?

Some experiences that have shaped my artistic journey so far include the great teachers I've had over the years, taking classes at The Alternative Art School, and the residencies I've attended.

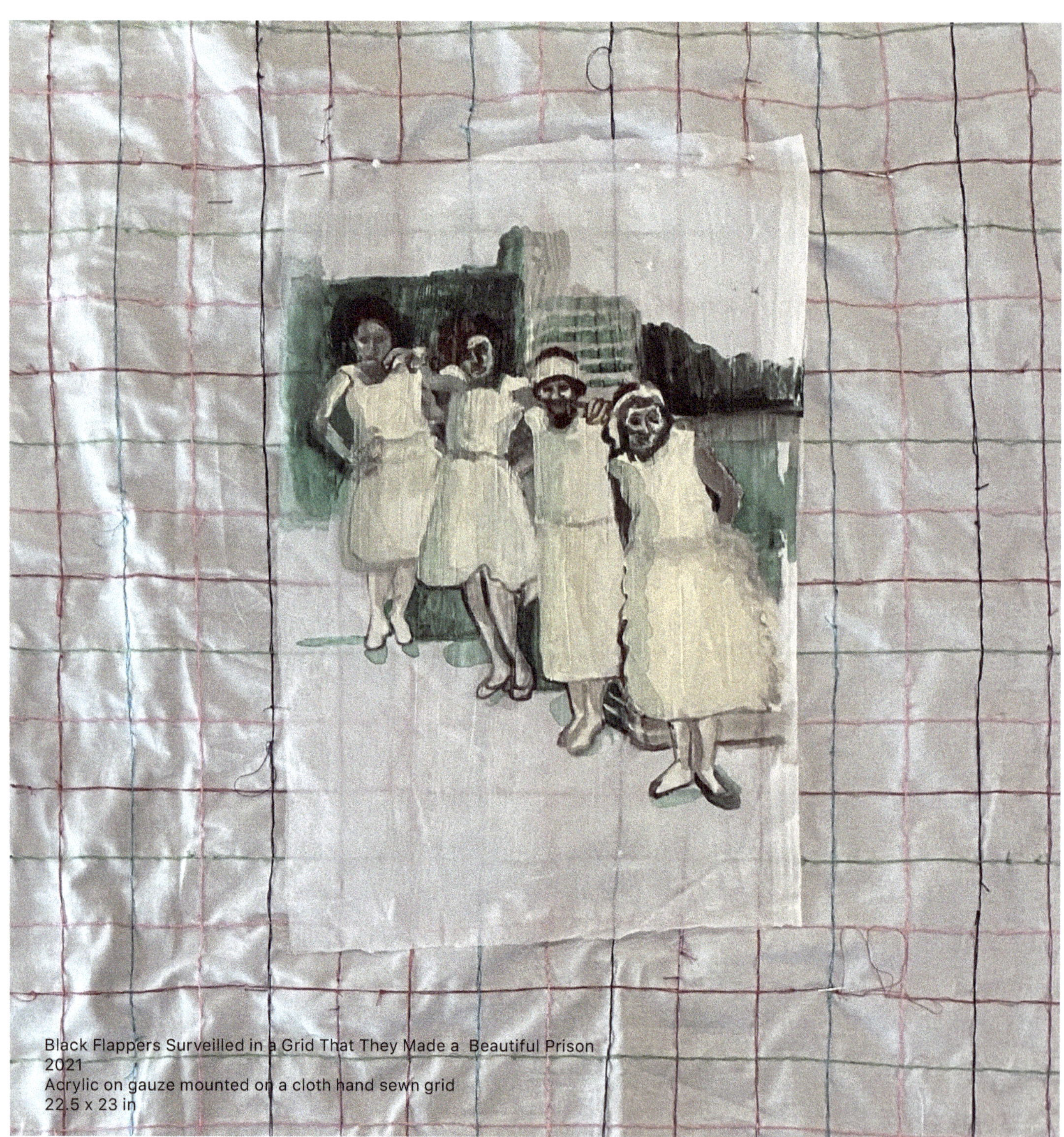

Black Flappers Surveilled in a Grid That They Made a Beautiful Prison
2021
Acrylic on gauze mounted on a cloth hand sewn grid
22.5 x 23 in

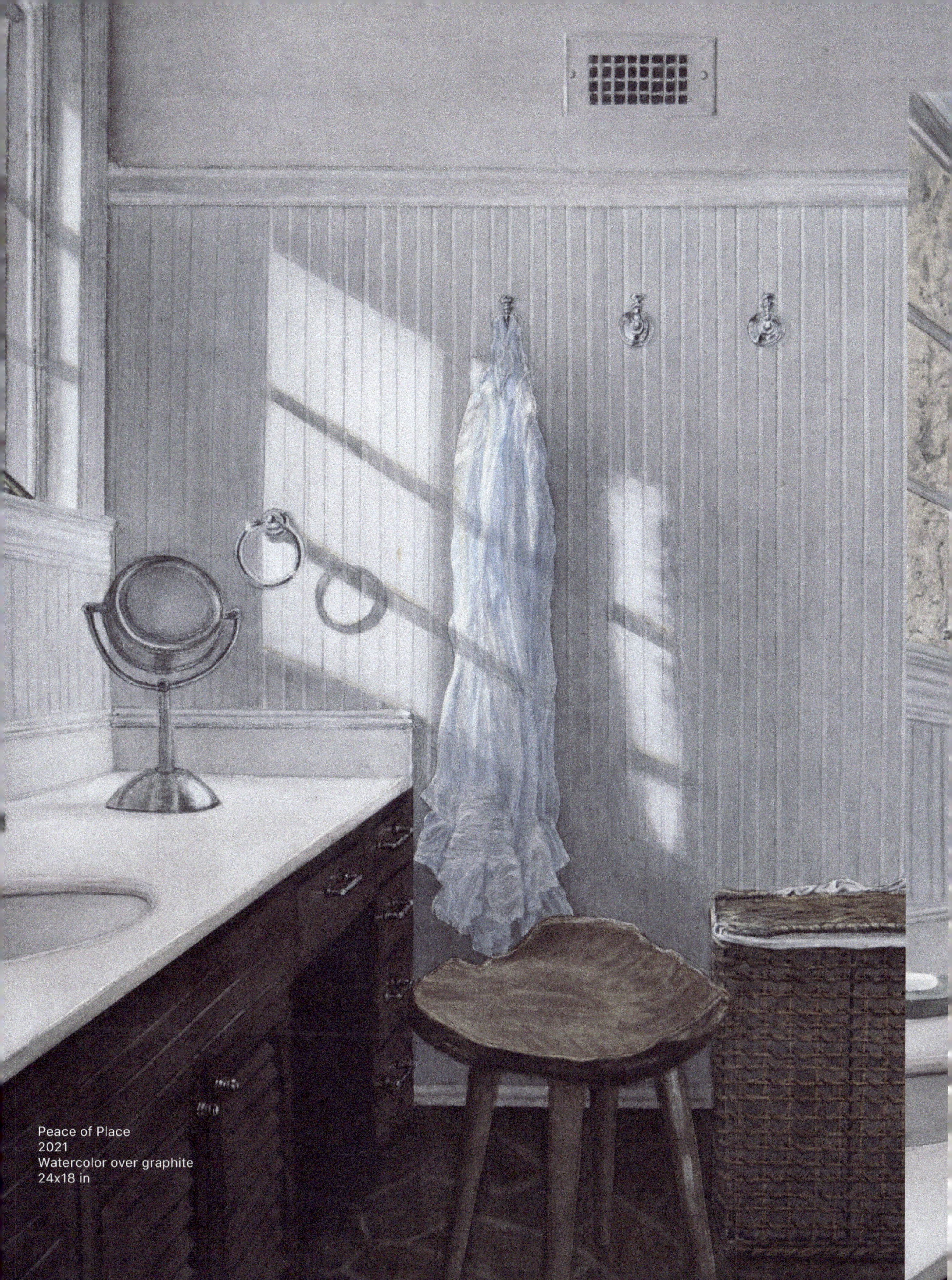

Peace of Place
2021
Watercolor over graphite
24x18 in

Arline Mann

I hope the art I make communicates some of that – *joy, clarity, calm, love of values.*

Arline Mann is a watercolor artist. Her watercolors contemplate light and shadow in personal spaces and on cherished objects. Building on the traditions of Nineteenth-Century Scandinavianp ainters such as Christen Kobke and Constantin Hansen, and on watercolorists such as Anders Zorn and John Stuart Ingle, her work seeks clarity, calm and joy, and projects a benevolent world. In Mann's watercolors, light often stresses the beauty and comfort of a distinctive room or familiar objects such as glass, books, and soap – always with a sense of human presence.

Mann lives and works both in New York City and in Chattanooga, Tennessee. Her work has been selected for some 35 notable competitive group exhibitions at the National Arts Club (New York, NY) and The Salmagundi Club (New York, NY), as well as for museum and New York City gallery invitationals. Mann had a solo exhibition at The Association for Visual Arts (Chattanooga, TN), and a solo show of her work will be sponsored by a major New York City corporation in 2023.

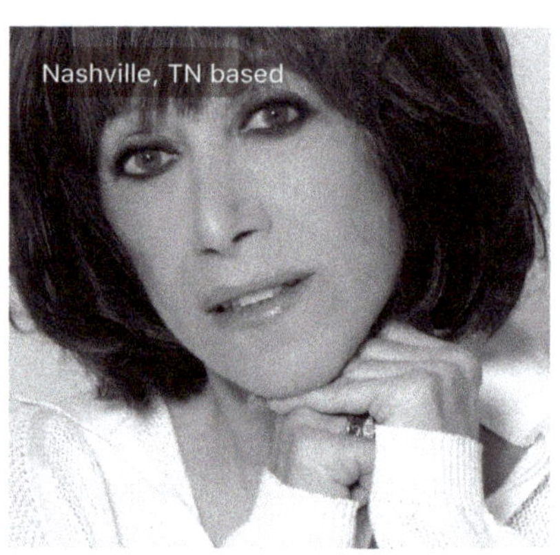

https://www.tricialynntownes.com
@ townestricia1@gmail.com
@ *tricial.townes*

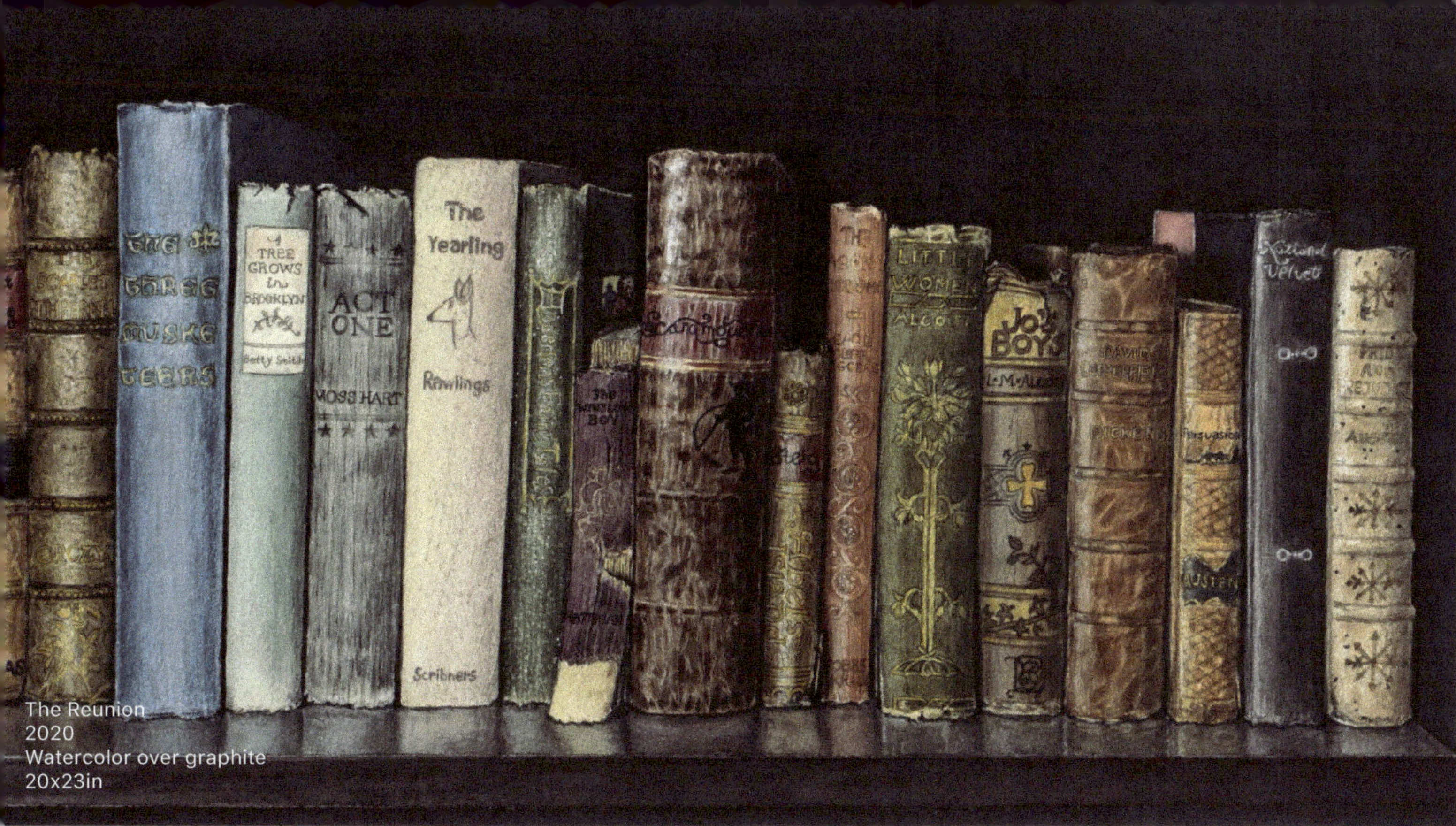

The Reunion
2020
Watercolor over graphite
20x23in

Among recent awards: first prize for Watermedia in he 2020 Catharine Lorillard Wolf Art Club annual exhibition and the Board of Directors Award in the 2021 annual exhibition of the American Artists Professional League. Her work is featured in the August 2022 issue of Fine Art Connoisseur Magazine and the 2022 issue of Studio Visit, and will be shown in Issue #33 of Create! Magazine.

What drives you to be an artist?

Two things: First, it is important to me to see my beloved values communicated in some concrete form. Second, I have always loved skills and accomplishment (could be knitting, could be swimming, could be singing). I crave progression.

How would you describe the art that you create and what inspires you?

I am always inspired by the same thing: A very specific moment in my childhood when I felt life had glorious things in store. I hope the art I make communicates some of that -- joy, clarity, calm, love of values.

If you could overcome all of your fears, what would you do with your art?

In my case, it's more doubt than fear. If I could overcome the doubt, I expect I would feel more free and more worthy of going after the right gallery rpresentation for me.

When it comes to art making, how important is experimenting vs. sticking to a routine or set of rules?

It is hugely important to be open. Every painting mark is an experiment (especially with watercolor), and I love "happy accidents." Equally, openness to the lessons to be learned from others' art and from speaking with other artists is critical.

What are some of the challenges or experiences that have shaped your artistic journey so far?

Since I began drawing and painting at a much later age than most, I have had to be quite creative about skill acquisition and career planning. I'm making it up as I go along!

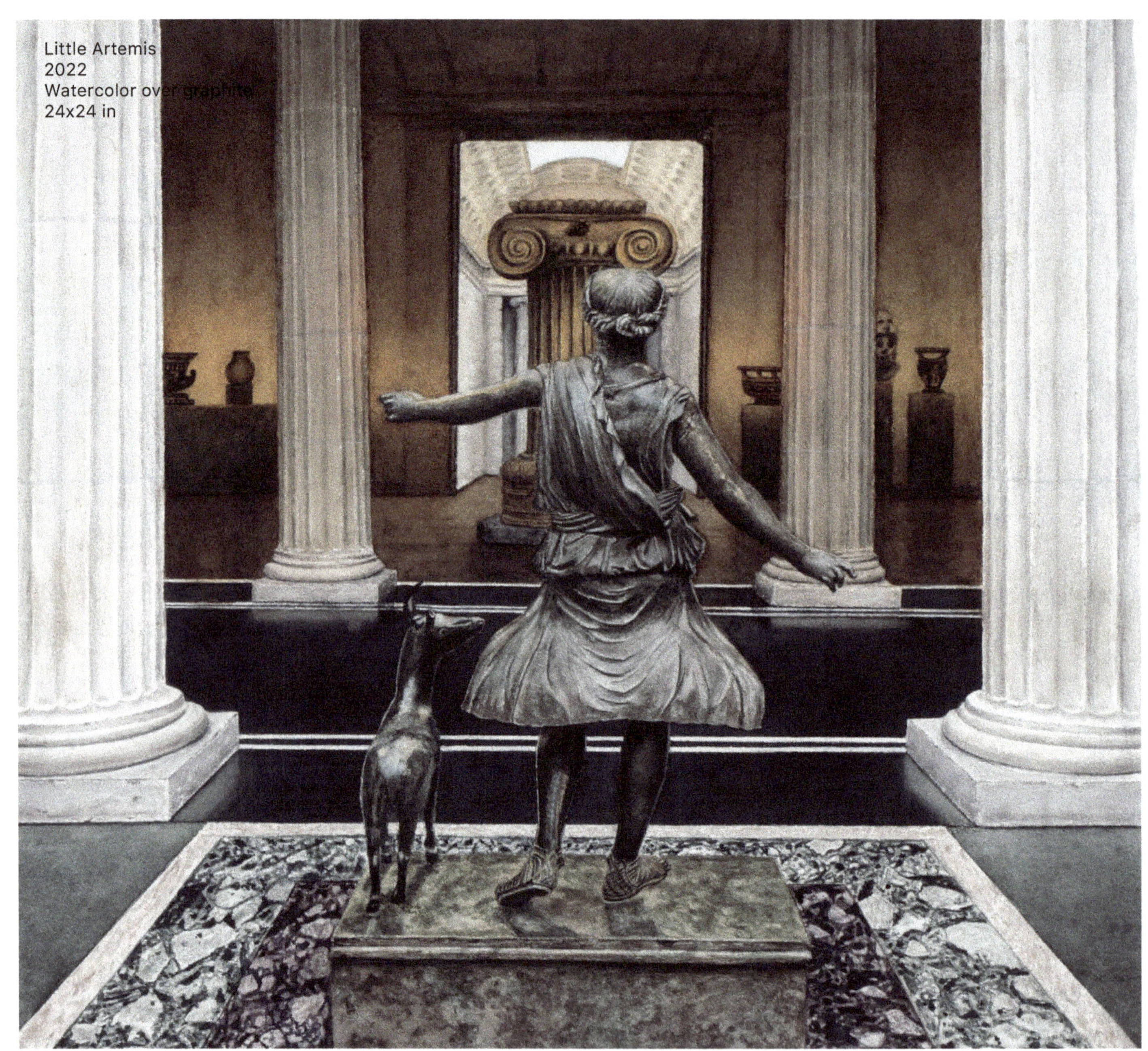

"Every painting mark is an experiment (especially with watercolor), and I love "happy accidents."

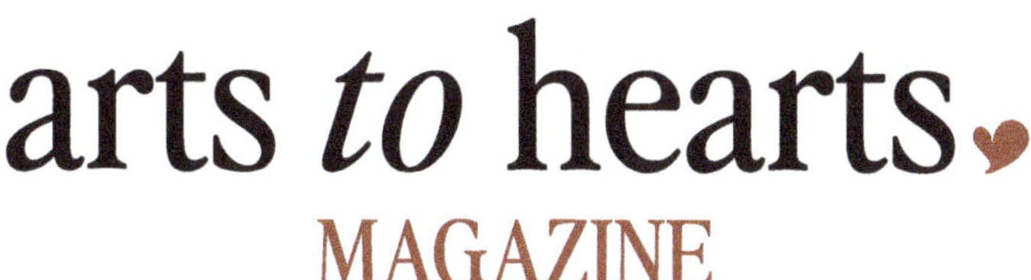

Arts to Hearts Magazine is a contemporary art publication with a mission to discover, connect, and engage with contemporary & emerging women artists from around the world.

A Product of

ARTS TO HEARTS PROJECT

We are a global creative community uniting contemporary & emerging women Artists to build successful, fulfilling, and money-making careers via collaboration, learning, community, networking, and peer-to-peer learning.

SUBMIT YOUR WORK

We have several opportunities throughout the year for people interested in the global arts. From open calls to grants to exhibits, you can stay on top of all our upcoming and ongoing opportunities by subscribing to our newsletter on our website.

COVER ART- BACK

Rebecca Brodskis | SIMONE | 2021
61x50cm
Oil on linen

JOIN ARTS TO HEARTS CLUB

http://www.artstoheartsproject.com/athclub/

VISIT OUR WEBSITE

www.artstoheartsproject.com

FOLLOW US ON INSTAGRAM

@artstoheartsproject

EMAIL

info@artstoheartsproject.com